Are You Still The Future?

How learning to be flexible and read the signals in the system kept me relevant and prepared for every step on my leadership journey

PIERS FALLOWFIELD-COOPER

First published in 2023 by Intellectual Perspective Press

To find out more about our authors and books visit:
www.intellectualperspective.com

Are You Still The Future?

Ultimately, this book is dedicated to Michael Anthony Knowles, OBE (received in 1997 for services to the Finance Industry), one of the best bosses I ever had. A man who saw real potential in this slightly wayward dreamer.

Contents

Praise for "Are You Still The Future?"

"An engrossing account of leadership learnt and lived. Packed full of advice and thoughtful reflection. A chuckle filled winner." – Andy Homer, Chair, Global Risk Partners

"Immensely readable and packed full of nuggets of wisdom. I read it cover to cover and I know I will find myself dipping back in frequently." – Barry O'Dwyer, Group CEO, Royal London

"It is wonderfully quite unlike any other book I have read on leadership." – Gavin Dalgleish, CEO, Illovo Sugar

"Piers is an outstanding mentor and I am deeply grateful for his support. A true Obi-Wan Kenobi. Anyone who is too busy to read this book, needs to read this book. Piers gives excellent and practical advice on how to lead by being worth following." – Caspar de Bono, MD, Edward de Bono Ltd

"Reading this book is like having a mentor in your pocket. Piers has worked with so many different people, in such a range of businesses and predicaments, that he has accumulated enormous wisdom and insight. Best of all, he shares this with warmth and humanity – not the cold abstractions of business strategy but the gritty reality of being in charge. I can't think of anyone who wouldn't find pearls of wisdom in this treasure trove." – Margaret Heffernan, Professor of Practice at The University of Bath, and author of *Uncharted: How to Map the Future*

"Piers has condensed a wealth of experience and knowledge into an informative and entertaining read. The advice is general enough to be enjoyed by most, backed up by examples from his own life and also his 20 years of coaching. There will be something insightful that applies to most life situations and any stage of life and career.

Whether you are looking for a biography of a successful, jet-setting executive or to further your own career and set your life goal, this is a book for you." – Dr Christopher Hong, Area Manager GB & Benelux, WingFan

"Do not read this book if you are just a PILP – a person in a leadership position – without the risky aspiration to become a true leader. You will – at best – not understand the multifaceted picture of leadership Piers is laying out, or – at worst – get deeply frustrated in view of the opportunities you are missing. Do read this book if you are a leader on a journey and feel unfinished (as we all sometimes do). You will re-discover the lost art of true leadership. How to be a signpost not a weathervane. Leadership as a mindset and culture, not as a position of power or a bigger office. Piers, with decades of experience in business and coaching – with this book does the 'magic trick': he compresses volumes of leadership literature into an almost transcendental experience. The book is like its author: informative but light, transformative but full of humor, direct but elegant, and full of deep wisdom. It is a work of coaching in itself." – Dr. Michael Kock, Senior Vice President, Innovation Catalyst at Inari

"This is not a cookbook on leadership wherein you can look up a recipe for any occasion (decision, situation, challenge, etc.). It is a lifetime's collection of anecdotes and insights that you will return to as you negotiate your career path and leadership journey. It will broaden your view of the world and of yourself." – John C Nelson, Founder, The Applied Research Company

"Piers has poured his years of experience of motivation and leadership into this book. A must read!" – Sahil Verma, CEO, The Cookaway.

"This book was the fizz in my glass of champagne and such was the perfect antidote to our collective post-pandemic fatigue. It's quite unlike anything you will have read before. Through an interweaving of personal experience, academic study and more than a sprinkling of magic Piers will take you through the really big questions on your leadership journey and provide you with the confidence to become

your authentic self. More than that though it will help you understand things about yourself in a profound and useful way and as such, it really is a book for life." – Rachel Grant, Executive Director of Communications and Advocacy at CEPI

"I started to read your beautiful book on Sunday evening and couldn't move for 175 pages. By then it was very late and I finally went to bed. I was incredibly moved by your writing; I didn't just read it, I heard your familiar voice guide me through each paragraph, retelling some familiar stories and then drawing back a curtain almost like a magician, revealing themes and stories from another life. It was authentic, well researched and familiar all at the same time. It wasn't at all what I had expected. It was personal, the language was digestible, understandable and sneakily rich. I have found other books in this genre a little preachy or maybe even pious. I think the heart of its success goes to the absence of judgement. The stories are thoughtfully laid out and there is room to breathe. It's a great book, Piers, you have nailed it!" – Robbie McDonnell, Director, Eventus

"Quintessentially, Piers is a natural mentor for leaders. He is always understated, a quality much to be admired in a sage advisor. His insights into leadership and its challenges are profound and wide-ranging, covering global themes, human behaviour and organisational culture. His own not insubstantial corporate experiences provides nuance within a clearly business-savvy approach. Piers is rarely dogmatic but seeks to mentor and advise through more subtle approaches, tailored to his clients, who he understands deeply. In his new book, Piers provides thought provoking explanations and examples of how his philosophy and practices developed over time. He has remained a trusted confidant over the last 15 years of my professional journey." – Allen Blewitt, Former Global CEO, ACCA

"Invaluable insights, an absolute must read no matter where you are on the career ladder!" – Lyndsey Clay, Founder, Connected Brighton, RWC Entrepreneur of the Year 2022

"It is said that you don't really understand something until you have experienced it for yourself but the humorous way in which Piers shares his stories offers a way of getting so very close to the ability to learn through his self-reflection. This book is a lesson in life-long learning, staying relevant and remaining authentic." – Jacqueline de Rojas, CBE

"If you're looking for a fresh take on the entrepreneur and leadership journey, this book is a must. It's a friendly and compelling read that will have you approach challenges in a whole new light. The book offers plenty of non-traditional insights that are sure to get you thinking and reflecting on your own experiences. Whether you're an entrepreneur or just curious about the path, this book has something for everyone." – Lee McCormack, CEO, MyGlobalHome

Acknowledgements

Saying thank you is a wonderful thing to do, especially to all the great people that have helped me with this book. It's also a very scary moment in case I forget anyone from the list. If I have, my apologies.

Firstly, I must thank the wonderful Debbie Jenkins, my book coach. Without her this would have remained as it has for many years just an idea. She has guided me wisely through the process, including at the very beginning, telling me to stop writing until I knew who I was writing for and what I wanted to say. She's been a delicious blend of keen supporter and at times finger-wagger. Debs – thank you.

I'd also like to thank the many people who have seen the manuscript at different times and made valuable and useful comments. They include Peter Hutchinson, Rudi Kindts, Alan Blewitt, Rachel Grant, Constantine Goulimis, Dani Harmer, Tim St George, John Nelson, Craig Berggren, Alastair Sharp, Christopher Hong, Michael Kock, and Gavin Dalgleish.

Chapter 0: One last trade

"It was the best of times, it was the worst of times"
– A Tale of Two Cities, Charles Dickens

The spring of 2020 was a spring like no other. Happiness seemed to be divided into those who had gardens and those who didn't. The very earth itself was quiet.[1] In a few short months the world had gone from "business as usual" with a bubbling stock market, an ebullient Boris Johnson with plans for "levelling up the economy" and an expectation of continued world growth – to a strange and new (but in some ways old) world where supermarket shopping became a blood sport – a cross between *Mad Max* and *The Hunger Games*. Shoppers created shortages by fighting over toilet rolls and disinfectant wipes. Shelves of fruit, vegetables and anything that had once lived were cleared by human locusts temporarily forgetting that fruit and vegetables are perishable and need to be eaten rather than stored. It was of course the year of COVID-19.

For me, it was an interesting time. I was celebrating nineteen years of my "new" career as a coach and mentor to C-suite executives and wondering if I should begin that gentle glide path that is known as "slowing down". On one hand that was an appealing proposition – to be able to spend some more time travelling, avoiding the British winter and learning new things. On the other, I had an itch. It's the itch that I knew from my days in financial markets and is known as "one last trade". It's that yearning, that desire, that need to have one final Peacock-like showy exit from a career. I suspect all professions are guilty

---

1. "A wave of silence" spread around world during coronavirus pandemic Seismologists said high frequency noise fell as much as 50% as planes were grounded and roads emptied. Ian Sample. The Guardian 23rd July 2020 https://www.the-guardian.com/science/2020/jul/23/wave-of-silence-spread-around-world-during-coronavirus-pandemic?CMP=Share_iOSApp_Other

of it – football managers who want one last season, property developers who want one last building, politicians who want one last election. For people in financial markets, it's "one last trade". I had that "one last trade itch", which for me, produced this book.

I'm entering my twentieth year of coaching and mentoring. I'm on client number 122. So this is a view into how over 120 senior executives operate, and it gives me some authority to write this book. About ten years ago, I discovered through working with my clients that, maybe like you, I'd been very effective as a CEO, but whoa, at what price, at what effort, at what cost. I've left that behind me now – not only out of choice but also out of need, a need for autonomy – I'm also probably now unemployable as I'm rather unmanageable. If I were to do it all again, I would do it slightly differently. I'd just do two or three things really well. I would spend lots of time hiring really good people. I would continue to hire people who had integrity and ambition, but maybe I'd hire more people I didn't particularly warm to but who were clever and effective. I would double-down on understanding who my most important stakeholders were and spend lots of time with them. Classic 80/20 leverage. Where can I put minimum effort in to get the maximum output?

In the same way as parents deny they have favourite children, people in my line of work don't often confess to having favourite clients but I'm writing this for Greg when he was young – a favourite client. I'm writing it for the leaders of tomorrow. I'm writing it so they can put it under their pillow and sleep easy in their bed because I want them to understand all of this is a journey full of challenges, successes, failures, busy times and quiet times.

Greg said years ago, "What we need is Piers in your pocket." So here is my attempt at Piers in your pocket. My life has been extremely enjoyable. I just wonder if it would have been easier to follow my original plan, rather than to have been seduced by the system. I distinctly remember standing there as a seventeen-year-old saying firmly, I didn't want a career. I want to go and do lots of interesting things. The terrible (?) thing that happened to me was I was lucky and landed a good, very well-paid job at the beginning of my career.

I remember, as a sixth former[2], waiting outside the chemistry lab (no Health & Safety then – a Bunsen burner and matches for everyone to play with!) and my classmates were clutching their Simon and Garfunkel LPs – "Vinyl" for my younger readers – and their copies of Mao's *Little Red Book*, preaching revolution – I admonished them for their foolhardiness explaining that the secret was to get inside the castle and dismantle it from inside rather than throw bricks at the battlements. Strategically I was correct but alas neither revolution nor subversion of the system really excited me at that time – even today I'm slightly conflicted; a good friend of mine who is very connected said, "It's curious, you're a sort of 'anti-establishment' establishment coach".

So as a teenager, I never really had a clear idea of what I wanted to do as a "grown-up". I was seventeen and had just started driving my first car, a pale blue Ford Anglia which had an unfortunate "wheel wobble" at 38mph. All my career conversations at school revolved around what I didn't want to do. I was very clear what I didn't want to do; and that was I didn't want to work in an office – or commute on a daily basis.

I thought having to work in an office would be horrible, so all my half ideas and imaginings were careers that didn't involve working in an office. I also had a lovely fantasy idea of having a career where I did lots of different things. For example, I quite fancied being a butler or a chauffeur.

I flirted with university, I looked through the University Clearing House Guide and found a course that was only being taught in one place so I thought "that could be interesting, something different" – the course I found was a degree in cybernetics at the University of Bath. I was, at first, excited about this as I felt it was part of the emergent future of our world and went for my interview. My expectations were that

2. 12th Grade for my North American readers

we would discuss the philosophical, psychological and moral implications of the coming technology. How man and machine would interact through what became known as GUIs (graphical user interfaces). I thought it would be interesting. I thought I would be at the frontier of the new. We were asked to do some mathematics, quite complicated mathematics and when I was given my results the adjudicator said, "I don't think your maths would be good enough when we get to year two onwards." He saved me – I was not interested in mathematics and programming – I was interested in Man's relationship with machine and some of the deeper philosophical questions about what happens when the machines want to take over. I suppose I should have done a philosophy or psychology course.

I also had always had a secret desire to run a hotel so, when the university opportunity disappeared into the sunset, I went and got myself a place at Westminster Tech (then the best place in the UK to study for the hotel industry). It probably has a smart new name now – *The University of Parliament Square* or something – with a plan to follow with a year at hotel school in Lucerne but, as the line of the John Lennon song goes (although it's actually taken from a 1950s article[3]): "Life is what happens when you're busy making other plans". My hotel manager career wasn't to be, though I did have a short stint at Pizzaland as an assistant manager. For those who are interested, my favourite pizza was green pepper and onion. I still have the recipe: take a 28lb sack of flour...

The purpose of this book is to encourage you to think about things. Life is a journey – for all of us it's a journey – this book is a bit of my journey, my clients' journeys and a broader general leadership journey. I interviewed and chatted with dozens of clients and colleagues to get their insight into their leadership journeys. Their thoughts and wisdom are

---

3. The general words can be traced back more than two decades before the time John Lennon used it in 'Beautiful Boy'. The first known appearance was in an issue of Reader's Digest magazine dated January 1957. Following on from Proverbs "A man's heart deviseth his way: but the Lord directeth his steps".

liberally shared throughout – some as thoughts that emerged from stimulating conversations, some as interviews, some as anonymised comments. You can find out more about these wonderfully intelligent, gracious and generous people in the appendix.

This is a book in two halves, separated, appropriately by 'Chapter X', named 'The Pivot Point'.

The first half of the book is for the leaders of tomorrow. The ones who are hungry and thirsty for success in all its forms. The second half is more focused on those who have "arrived", for those who have some success and are wondering what to do with it. The two parts of the book are notionally aimed at different stages of a career, but the real "win" for you, wherever you are in your career, is to look forwards to future success, and backwards to gain hindsight in your decision-making. If you've "arrived" you can use part 1 to understand how you got there, what influenced you and what you learnt on the way. This may guide you further, sparking connections. For the younger audience you can read ahead, the second part will help plant the seeds of future success.

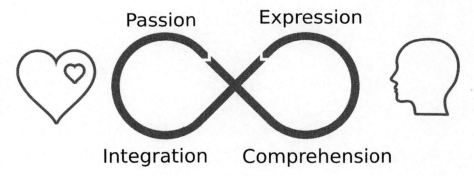

Wherever you are in your journey, be there. There is no wrong place. Just be truly present wherever you are.

Keep in mind the idea of integrating words, ideas, thoughts, plans and ambitions with both your head and your heart. Think about the over-arching idea of a journey from heart to head and back again. This may happen just the once, or several times. You might start with the over-arching idealism of youth, the practicality of the head in the early years as your career develops, and back to your full heart in a later career. Along the way there will be lovely moments of heart and head as they dance around. In my case the romanticism of the heart followed by the practicality of the head with a great career, took me back to the heart and my deeply fulfilling journey of mentoring. I've reinvented myself three times along the way.

I've written about what happens when you don't have big plans and you surrender to what unfolds and, although I'm not naturally very ambitious, it turned out all right. I hope I've written an interesting read with some good tips. I'd be interested to know what you think.

Chapter 1: Where is Tom Next?

*"It is the very nature of knowledge that it changes fast
and that today's certainties will be tomorrow's absurdities."*
– Peter F. Drucker, Post-Capitalist Society, 1993

When beginning our "career", our "work" or whatever we choose to call it, the world we are stepping into is going to be very different from the world we are leaving behind. Our challenge is this – how do we approach this new world? Are we shocked? Excited? Intrigued or perhaps even enchanted? How do we go forwards on this journey? Sometimes we'll feel a phenomenal, inevitable pull into the new world like being caught in a science fiction tractor beam. Other times we'll be catapulted into an unknown future, fearfully looking over our shoulder back towards the safety of the known we are leaving behind. Navigating this tension – seduced by the familiarity of the past, attracted to a new adventure – requires trust, confidence and optimism... and perhaps even, a dash of naiveté.

I arrived there by mistake: I left as a master of my craft

It was not a dark and stormy night but a bright and sunny morning when I found myself standing outside 52 Cannon Street, in the City of London, staring up at the offices of M.W. Marshall & Company, Foreign Exchange and Currency Deposit Brokers – its origins in smoky, industrious, mercantile Victorian London (it was founded in 1866 by the son of the Chief Cashier of The Bank of England as an East India Exchange and Discount Broker). The City, when I arrived, had elements of both its Dickensian past and its new emerging dynamic future. Beer was still brewed on Chiswell Street at Sam Whitbread's Brewery. Top-hatted Gilt Brokers could be seen walking, briefcase-less, between clients. Evenings in El Vino in Fleet Street witnessed the arrival of low-loaders with giant rolls of newsprint ready to feed the presses. But what was I doing here? My family, on my father's side, had been Raj – engineers, builders and military men in Lower Bengal and Upper Burma – so I suppose there was a tenuous connection there, separated by a century. One of those antecedents owned a circus. Well, maybe "circus" was a tad extravagant as a description; he had some dancing dogs, cats and horses and a rather tired lion that he trooped around the country. I think there was a general level of eccentricity in the family: one of the members (on their return to the UK) designed and built a model railway. A train set – but not as we know it. For his miniature world, he also invented a country in which it operated, wrote the timetables and designed the uniforms which, apparently, for the senior staff at least, would have made a Ruritanian General proud. My mother's family were herbalists and healers and had kept the ferry at Throstles Nest until the canal with its lock took their trade. Neither, I felt, would have particularly approved of this adventure. Now here I was ready to start my first career on the floor as a trainee broker.

It had all started at a sort of "one-man Brook Street Bureau" in a basement, with a recruiter who could get young men a great job. He was a very modern recruitment consultant using evaluation testing, so he put me though my paces with some joining the dots and mazes. Each maze got progressively more difficult. My intuition got the better of me on the fourth maze. I started at the entrance and, since it was so hard and I could see no way through, I jumped to the exit and worked my way backwards. The recruitment guy was astounded, he jack-in-the-boxed out of his chair, "You should be a broker, I'm sending you for interviews at the two best brokers in London!" And that was that.

I wasn't so sure, but my father encouraged me, "Just go to the interviews." So, I went for the first interview at R.P. Martin, nonchalant and just a little curious. The company brochure was shiny. The private brokers' glass lift was sparkling. The road to fortune was paved with overflowing tumblers of gin and tonic – at eleven thirty in the morning – tumblers so full it was only the strength of the meniscus that held the liquid in their glasses. Coming from a family of fallen Catholics and lapsed Quakers it felt I was in an alien world.

I was invited for the other interview at Marshall's with one of the partners who had led the management buyout. I wasn't so sure. My father encouraged me, "Just go to the interview then you have met them both."

So I went for the other interview. This was friendlier. My resistance was waning and it just about disappeared when the solidly built, Derek Scotchbrook, a double of my old headmaster called me, "Mr Fallowfield-Cooper". I narrowly avoided the urge to look over my shoulder for my father. Had he followed me to the interview to make sure I turned up? My identity had been unveiled: *I* was Mr Fallowfield-Cooper.

Scotchbrook, emphasising the importance of quick wit, sharpness of mind, agile thinking and numeracy threw some questions and simple mental arithmetic at me, "Can you take 158 from 183?"

I said, "Yes, of course." I paused, waiting for applause. "Oh, would you like me to do it now?"

The dark tufts of hair above his ears quivered and he raised a bushy eyebrow. "If I were to offer you a job what would you expect to be earning?"

I puffed out my chest, "Two and a half thousand pounds a year, Mr Scotchbrook."

The other eyebrow joined the first, "Are you sure you're not selling yourself a bit short?"

In glorious innocence and not recognising sarcasm, I leant forward across his desk, looked him in the eye and said, "I may be, but I want the job."

And that's how I found myself, a couple of weeks later, 8.00am on a sunny Monday morning, looking up at 52 Cannon Street. Twenty years old, a bashful trainee broker, sold slightly short.

The fifth floor of Marshalls was where all the action happened. The curious experience of stepping out of the lift and then stepping up onto the false floor marked my entry into the world of finance. I would step down a different man just eight years later.

The false floor hid miles of cables that electrified the trading floor, telephonically connected the brokers with their counterparts around the world and moved the dollars and pounds, yen and marks, around the globe. We walked and worked on giant metal tiles that constrained the expanding wires below so we could hit bids and take offers, construct broken dates – the cleverest of which was forward-forwards – and work the Clearing Funds – Fed Funds weekend arbitrage. Borrow Thursday / Friday money and keep it for the weekend using "price on book" to make a small risk-free profit each time. The testosterone rose even more thickly than the cigarette smoke, coating the flickering fluorescent overhead lights strobing the action.

I was tasked with learning my trade on short-date dollar deposits. I cautiously placed my jacket on the overflowing coat hooks, caught some tickets before they slid off the desk and nearly knocked the ripe ashtray onto the floor. I found my spot in the huddle of brokers barking into their Bakelite phones and sat down to my first task as a trainee broker – writing dealing tickets.

Perhaps I should have mentioned I was dyslexic at one of the interviews?

My first dealing ticket was one small part of a large order left overnight from Royal Bank of Canada, based in Montreal (before they moved to Toronto). It was a ticket for $25 million borrowed from Citibank London. Dollars to RBC New York, repaid to Citibank New York. The rhythm of the tickets became seductive. These multicoloured sheets, with eight rows, one each for the borrower, the lender, the amount, the interest rate, the start date, the end date, receiving bank and repayment bank were to be my life for the next few months. The background music of shouting trades, telephones flashing, telexes hammering, squawk boxes – well, squawking and chest thumping – was scored with undecipherable lyrics and the regular beat of: "Where's Tom Next?" The arias of the opera and beauty of the ballet were missing in action. This was not my idea of an interesting career.

During the day the cry of "Where's Tom Next?" interrupted my every thought. Why were they looking for him? Where had he been? Where had he gone? Surely they should know by now? That evening I told my father that I wasn't going back. The job was a disaster, the people were silly, they still hadn't found Tom. My father encouraged me, "Just go back for one more day – it will soon be the end of the week."

I went back. One more day. Maybe they'd find Tom. I wanted to be there to welcome him back. They didn't find him the next day, nor the next. By Friday my curiosity was piqued. Had Tom stepped through the wardrobe into this Narnia-esque world and got lost, like me?

One week completed, I told my father, "I'm not going back." He suggested I try for just one more week. I did. Two weeks completed, "Why don't you just work till the end of the month and collect your pay cheque?" So I did.

By the end of the week I had worked out the Tom Next mystery. Tom Next is short-hand for Tomorrow Next (which is where a short-term foreign exchange or deposit transaction is priced over two separate business days – being tomorrow (one business day) and the following day (two business days from today). Two business days from today is known as the Spot Date. An overnight transaction starting on the Spot Date was known as 'Spot Next'. I was getting the hang of this, so I decided to stay for a while longer.

My cursed dyslexia proved to be a gift as I was able to remember all the orders in my head. I got moved to the International Desk, where I was adopted by two great mentors, David Spillman and Mike Pyle. Spillman was a wiry, ex-Territorial Army pugilist, who always dressed in an immaculate pale grey three-piece suit. He was one of the few men I have met who was able to use a cigarette holder with style. He drove his Bristol[1] up to his farm in Leicestershire at the weekends, tapping his Dunhill ash out the window as he checked the time on his silver pocket watch. Pyle was a wiry runner, an Essex boy made good.

Under their tutelage I learnt the trade, bought my first flat, travelled first class from London to Paris and back again and found my voice.

Most of my earnings in the early days went to pay for my flat. To manage my outgoings and pay for both the flat and a trip to New York, I lived on black cherry yoghurt, Ryvita and Wensleydale cheese. It was thus a no-brainer to go for the early, paid for, lunch when I was at work. I would also frequently cover the desk at lunchtime, so they'd ship sandwiches in for me with "gannet bags" of extra chips, and tumblers of gin and tonic. Half of the brokers were the worse for wear in the afternoon, leading to frequent cries of "Bog roll!" to mop up the spilt coffee from the dealing boards.

I was quickly promoted and by then was running the European desk when my boss arrived with the head of a potential new correspondent from Amsterdam. He brought them onto the floor where I was trying to be invisible. It's quite difficult being invisible when you're running a desk, have a phone to each ear and two squawk boxes clicking and clacking. I decided in that moment that I would have to get over this learned shyness. If I wanted to have a career anywhere, I just had to get over myself. In that moment, I decided to change. I stood up tall, walked over, put my (slightly clammy) hand out, and introduced myself.

This was a seismic shift for a socially competent but very introverted boy who was also taught never to talk to strangers.

---

1. Mature readers and classic car enthusiasts will smile, once the name "Bristol" is mentioned, for the rest of you, Bristol Motor Cars was the 4 wheeled division of the Bristol Aeroplane Company.

My new-found "extroversion" was tested when I was invited to take one of our European clients to town and show him a good time. I was recommended The Stork Club in Soho and given £500 from petty cash. We sat with a couple of over-glamorous ladies, who really liked to drink and smoke. "Some cigarettes for the ladies?" "Er yes," I replied, not wishing to look cheap. Suddenly we had bought them cellophane wrapped packs of two hundred Benson & Hedges and plenty of Champagne-ish liquid. I was completely out of my depth. By midnight I had fled to my flat leaving him to his own devices.

The following morning, my boss asked, "How was the evening?" "Fine, we bought lots of overpriced fags and booze." I took the pitiful change back to petty cash. Like the rumble of an earthquake, my innocence and naiveté had been somewhat shaken.

This was a glorious time for me. I was on the up-and-coming list. In today's HR terms, "high performance, high potential". I was frequently invited to "lunch with the board" type meetings, where you think you're supposed to talk a lot and be clever. At that age I thought that the more I said, the more they'd notice me and being noticed was important for my career progression. Dribbling borscht down your shirt then trying to hide it with a starched white napkin which then had a spreading red blot wasn't a smart way to get noticed. I started to look like I'd been shot. The final ignominy being when Scotchbrook leant over and said, "I think you should go and get yourself sponged down."

I was also infamous for the unfortunate incident with the buffet table. I was invited to one of the boardroom lunches, where a Caravaggio-like white linen clothed table was groaning under the weight of cooked meats, smoked salmon, quiches, salads, cheeses and draped grapes. I was drooling nearby, waiting for the off, when I heard a creaking. The masterpiece slid to the floor, completely unaided by me. Despite my protestations of innocence, I wasn't invited back for a while.

Of course, success has many fathers while failure is an orphan. The sponsors who enjoyed wining and dining this up-and-coming young lad stopped showing up when I showed myself up. I hid for a while, then upped my game, became respectable enough to be invited out again to eat freshly-caught wild salmon spring lamb cutlets with fine white Burgundies and well-aged clarets at The Podium restaurant situated on the Barbican Highwalk.

This high life became my new normal. Working hard, dining well. A truly binary life of working or not working. Tearing off the sheet at the end of the day, wiping the slate clean. Today's "digital life" requires us to be always on. The boundaries are less clear. It's the antithesis of my binary life as a broker. I was phenomenally good at my job, I was excited in the environment, but it was a drain on my psyche and energy. Of course, the excellent pay packet helped keep me going. And soon, opportunity was to come knocking...

"It must be wonderful to be seventeen, and to know everything."
— Arthur C. Clarke, 2010: Odyssey Two

Be adaptable

You're here, it's new, what do you do? I was at the beginning of a journey, everything was unfamiliar. I was nervous, of course, but I showed up. I learned to love being exposed to different types of people. I was finally out of the closed circle of family and friends.

The masculine, competitive energy was endemic. It was a true meritocracy; we promoted the best, irrespective of background. We hired the first black broker in the City. You were on the floor because you were good, not because you knew somebody. Someone would call you a stupid idiot at 10am and buy you a drink at lunchtime. There was no malice and no grudges held. It was remarkably unpolitical.

I was also a bit of an outsider. I think I was pretty much the only person who regularly went to the theatre, listened to classical music and went to the ballet. I probably did more artistic things than all the rest of them put together.

The first thing is to decide if you really want to give it to go. If you decide yes, then do it with good heart, good mind, good intention. A client of mine from Dublin reminded me of something I forgot I had said to her: "If you're going to do it, do it with good grace." Grace is an underappreciated trait. If you are going to be there, be there with grace. Commit, adapt, make it work. Otherwise don't accept the role (or the invitation) in the first place.

An upside-down approach to leadership development is to focus on your weaknesses in an attempt to improve them. Sure, if there are any "fatal flaws", you must address them but in my coaching with clients my whole approach is strengths based: work with what's working. This is so important I'll say it again: work with what's working.

You need to adapt to survive in your new environment, without losing yourself. How do you balance the fitting in? You have to assimilate in some way. Korede Agiri works in sales for a large investment manager. He is a first-generation Brit raised by Nigerian parents. Growing up, he maintained a desire to build a career in financial services. At university, as he began to build close friendships with people, he found that many were from more privileged backgrounds and noticed some clear differences in their respective realities. This was even more so in the corporate environment. In 2019, Agiri wrote *You Missed A Spot: We're Diverse, I'm Inclusive* addressing the questions of having to fit in in some way, without giving up who you are. If you're too far out, the system will reject you. You don't find many bright red animals in nature. In the same way that during a heart transplant the body rejects the heart if it isn't a good fit, you need to adapt to fit in to your new environment or find a suitable coping mechanism.

In your new environment, if punctuality is highly regarded, then turn up on time. If the highest priority is that everyone is at their desk at eight, be at your desk at eight. If accuracy is the highest regarded thing, be accurate. It isn't rocket science.

I did some work with an investment bank; at the end of the assignment a senior HR leader was curious to find out what I thought about their organisation. I was honest: "I think you're great. You hire diversity and talent. You are gender, race and sexual orientation neutral. There's only one small thing. You only reward alpha male behaviour. If you don't nurture and reward diversity, you will waste that talent investment and, before you know it, create a lot of women pretending to be alpha males in Canary Wharf." Their diverse newly hired talent would adapt to the reward structure.

At this early level of your career it is unlikely that you are bringing a particular skill or talent, knowledge, experience, or expertise with you. For some reason you looked attractive, interesting, with high potential. You are bringing attitude and adaptability. The organisation is unlikely to go out of its way to accommodate you. When you're thirty-five and you're perhaps a bit eccentric, but you can do complex calculations in your head faster than a machine, they'll probably accommodate you. If you're thirty-five and you're the business's best salesman, but you don't know how to (or want to) fill out the forms properly, the company will find somebody to fill the forms in for you.

But at this early stage, you're the one who is going to have to adapt to the system rather than the system adapting to you. If you don't adapt, the body will reject you and spit you out.

Be adoptable

At this early stage being different is valuable, you need to make yourself more adoptable. I was competent, hardworking and likeable. I was willing to stand up and be counted. I wasn't looking for a fight, but I was willing to expose myself and take a risk. My adaptability in a meritocracy allowed me to be adopted into the inner circle.

It wasn't my first time to be "adopted". I've always been, as people always are, on a journey. I am aware of this idea of journey and introspection for a couple of reasons. As a young child, probably about four when I was at nursery but before school, for a whole combination of reasons, including several that were of my own making, I was packed off to Mid Wales.

Life as a child was strange. In London we lived in eccentricity in a sixteen room Victorian house in, what Thomas Love Peacock would have called "a picturesque state of semi-dilapidation". Faded Bokhara carpet covered the living room table as my mother attempted to recreate a Dutch masterpiece she had seen. My father had a collection of hats, kept in the front hall opposite the Zither where normal people hang coats: a bowler hat, a fez, his grandfather's top hat (the grandfather whose dad had a pianoforte made at the family factory and sent to Beethoven as a gift) and, the pièce de résistance, a Viking helmet!

We had a mad red setter called Toasty, because she was warm and brown, Fluff the cat and her daughter Kitty who was sleek and grey. Mother was the self-confessed "short order cook" but my dad was a good cook, who prepared all the main weekend meals. Sometimes we would have a curry which his paternal grandmother who had lived in India had taught him how to make. This included grinding all the spices to make his own curry powder and beginning a couple of days before the meal.

My first full sentence was "me write small cheque" learnt at my parents' knee. A small cheque for the milkman, a small cheque for the grocer, a small cheque for the newsagent. An early version of the cashless society. I suspect cheques were also good as they bought time while they cleared. I was a quick learner – after being slapped on the hand for throwing my bottle out of my pram. I learned to look up at my mother, smile, smack my hand – and then throw the bottle out of the pram.

I know I was too fussy and particular with child minders and nursery. I didn't like them. I frequently told Mother that I wasn't going back. So that didn't help. But I was surprised when my mother did a deal with her mother in mid Wales to remove me from her presence. I went to stay with my grandmother. At one level, that's perfectly reasonable, and it wasn't exactly abandonment. But for a four-year-old, it felt like abandonment.

It's had a lasting effect on me. In personal relationships, against my real nature, I have a fear of abandonment. By nature, I'm not clingy, it doesn't suit me. But I would find that we would get to a point in a relationship, where it was becoming important, and I would shift. Instead of continuing to be the perfect date, with fresh flowers on the table, beautiful music playing while I cooked a sumptuous meal, I turned clingy because I'd be scared of being abandoned. A quite paradoxical position. It's OK to intellectualise the fear of abandonment, I knew I was being triggered, but it's another thing to stop it. I've worked through it now.

Even as a trainee, I was willing to step up and be a leader. It came to me completely naturally to get stuff done. For many of the early years I didn't have a formal leadership role, but I was a person being a leader. You have to be seen. Even if you do not have the experience and the knowledge yet, demonstrate that you have the attitude and aptitude. Skills can generally be taught, so get hired for your attitude. I also believe when you're in a position to hire, hopefully you can find both great attitude and good skills; if you have to choose between experience or attitude, unless you have a time-based need for experience now – for example you are stepping up and this is your replacement. if you can, hire for attitude.

If you don't know what your bosses want, ask them. It's madness to sit there guessing what other people are thinking. If you want to know how you're doing, what you could do better and how you can progress, go and ask. I'm not sure why people don't ask, maybe they're afraid of hearing the answer, or they don't ask because they think they shouldn't.

Next, find out how your bosses want to be communicated with. Do they want the newspaper or novel version? There are two ways to give people information. The "dark and stormy night" way: "Dear Doctor, I had an itch on my leg, then two weeks later it was even more itchy, then yesterday it dropped off. I'm finding it quite difficult to walk, I keep going in circles. Do you think there might be a cure?" Or the headline way: "Doctor, my leg has dropped off. What are we going to do?" Make yourself adoptable by delivering it in the way they want it. Share information in the style that's most appreciated.

Alastair, a friend of mine had always worked in small and medium sized businesses. He went to work for a division of General Electric and couldn't believe what happened on his first day on the job. Firstly, which isn't always the case with a new job, they were expecting him. They took him to his desk. His business cards were in a box. There was a flashing light on his phone indicating a message. He picked it up: "Hi, this is Jack. I just want to say welcome to GE." My friend was hooked from day one. He had a personal message from Jack Welch. Alastair felt he had found "home" and been adopted.

To be adopted is all about match and fit. It's like when the cogs of a machine smoothly come together. You get adopted for your talent, enthusiasm, potential and behaviour. Every business is looking for high performing, high potential people. That's the box to be in. People who are highly adept at being FIFO – fixed on the inside, flexible on the outside – know what they're doing and know how to behave. Their moral compass is firm and strong. For me, this is an intuitive process. I never thought once about who I should be adopted by, I just turned up every single day and did my best.

Sahil Verma had a stellar career in risk and finance; working for IWG, the parent company of Regus, he was acutely attuned to – and understood – what was driving different stakeholders in the business and put that first before his agenda. Sahil: *"I was heading internal audit and risk management which was seen as a necessary evil. From day one I presented a profit and loss statement to the founder to show him that we were actually a profit centre, not a cost base for the business. My attitude was not to undermine nor dismiss the immense talent in the organisation. I showed respect, sought insight and honoured their experience, which allowed me to get much closer to some of the stakeholders than other people did."* You'll hear more about Sahil in the final chapter and his journey.

If you are adaptable and have decided you want to be there, then you can become more adoptable.

I was innocent then, but I learnt to recognise who had power and influence without actually consciously thinking about it. Being adaptable and adoptable are two easy and early ways to navigate the environment. I was drawn into their gravitational orbits. It's not as crass as taking up golf because your boss likes golf. Be smart about it. I think people recognised raw talent and were willing to support it. I blossomed. I was lucky.

Attention and initiative build sensory acuity

Looking back at that time I was frequently in the flow, intuitively using my skills of reading and decoding the signals in the system. I was curious. So, in many ways, it played to my absolute strengths.

I don't think I had many "conscious" thoughts about what I should be doing or how I should be doing it; I certainly didn't have a career plan.

Historically, and throughout storytelling, the innocent have always had an incredibly strong moral compass – think Harry Potter, Snow White, Cinderella, Forest Gump and Candide.

This can also be their downfall when their compass and their modus operandi leads them to believe everyone's good and nice in the world. That nothing bad will happen to them. To be in the moment you need to develop your sensory acuity.

I urge you to listen to the whispers in your own mind and body. The head, heart and gut. Neuroscience has demonstrated that they can put you on a CT scan, poke your left toe and your prefrontal cortex or some other excitingly named part of your brain lights up. Well, that's really good, but they tend to forget both the broader humanity and also the embodied experience. So, if you've got a little twitch in the gut, pay attention, it's sending you a message. Start to learn to pay attention to the signals. Signals, insights, knowledge, wisdom. This is how we shape who we are becoming.

I suspect, although I had no conscious understanding of it, I kept doing more of what worked. It seemed very natural to me.

So, what are the building block basics for being an adoptable and adaptable employee, who pays attention and takes initiative?

1. Be moderately competent. Remember, you've probably been taken on for attitude, but you do need to build competency. I am constantly surprised how many inept people manage to hold down good jobs. If you're moderately competent, with a good attitude, you're going to do just fine because you're going to be so much better than all the others.
2. Pay attention and follow up. If you're exposed to new knowledge, information, or possibilities, follow up.
3. Turn up! Aim for your Andy Warhol fifteen minutes of fame, or Woody Allen's 80% of success is showing up.
4. Do a little more than just the basics.

If you follow these building blocks you will start to pay attention, take initiative and to build your ability to read the signals in the system. Then there's no going back. Once you stimulate your receptors – eyes, ears, taste, smell, touch – they will be attuned to your environment.

Ask yourself, how do you want to be perceived? How do you want to be viewed? This is obviously your choice. I was enthusiastic, committed and good things happened. I noticed that the senior people were very happy to take the bright younger ones out for lunch. So I'd go and ask them if they had time for lunch with me. The environment was supportive of it, with a very flat management structure and strong meritocracy. So pay attention to the environment, it's all about the context.

It's interesting that, although my work now as an executive coach and mentor is completely different from my life as a young broker, this career also plays to my absolute strengths. These are the bookends of my business life, both grounded in reading the signals and using my intuition.

Piers in Your Pocket: Be committed or leave

"Parenting is the closest thing to leadership." – Simon Sinek

Give it all your energy. Once I decided I wanted to be there, then my question was, so what do I have to do to make this successful? Learning what works and doing more of it was the foundation of my life – although I didn't realise then that it was a process.

I gave my work a lot of energy and took it seriously, even before my feet had truly settled and because I did, I was very good at it. My dedication led to my success. I'm always quite disappointed when people aren't really committed to stuff.

The founders, my bosses, the board – all were willing to invest in me. They gave me a bit more soil, put some fertiliser on me, made sure I got some of the warmth of the sun. If you're young make sure to show your talents. Contribute and be seen for your contribution. Be part of it, make it work and get on with it. If you're a more experienced leader, ask yourself, are you tracking for talent? And if you are, make sure you support the talent you adopt!

There are only two ways to have a happy life: find a world in which you fit or create a world that suits you.

Are you in the right environment? Could you be in the right environment, but doing the wrong thing? Are you doing the right things, but in the wrong environment? Maybe different answers at different times. Current economic needs may force your hand.

As an artistic daydreamer by nature, the career seemed a slightly odd fit for me, but time proved it to be the right choice to have made. Although in some ways it was completely the wrong career for me, in other ways it was completely the right career for me. It sharpened me up. I was highly successful but not in the most fertile of soil.

Signals, insights, knowledge, wisdom – then application. This is how we shape who we are becoming.

I had developed confidence and trust in myself, I was optimistic about the future. I was ready for a new adventure. It was time to be brave again and do something new. It was time to leave the safety of the shore behind.

Chapter 2: In the desert with Stormin' Norman (again)

"To lack feeling is to be dead,
but to act on every feeling is to be a child."
– Brandon Sanderson, The Way of Kings

There are moments when we have to be brave as we're called to action. Where we must stand up, for example, to the bully and summon superhuman strength in the face of adversity. When we feel the weight of power and responsibility, and we're called to our primal leadership function. Will we be ready, prepared and capable? Smart, intelligent soldiers hate wars but prepare well for them. Have you summoned the discipline, courage and determination to lead? **The energy of the warrior leader must be used wisely.** *It is about stepping up and being willing to be brave and strong.*

The missing briefs

It had been "one of those trips". The Cathay Pacific flight to Bahrain was delayed, I had received a second phone call to update me on the delay to the delay. For those eagle-eyed readers who think they have spotted an error – not those known as "avgeeks" as they would know it wasn't a mistake – it was indeed Cathay Pacific who dropped me off in Bahrain, and my luggage in Hong Kong. Boeing 747-200s couldn't make London to Hong Kong non-stop – well, technically they could but without passengers, freight and luggage – which rather defeats the purpose of an airline. I wouldn't see my Calvin Kleins until it was time to return a week later. It was January 1991, a period of heightened concern because Saddam Hussein had invaded Kuwait. Would I need those extra briefs?

The car that took me from the airport to the hotel, one of a fleet my host seemed to have access to, appeared to have a very special number plate as I was picked up from virtually inside the airport terminal and I can't remember the car stopping for any traffic lights on the way to the hotel. On seeing I only had a briefcase the driver enquired how long I would be staying. "About a week," I replied. He looked at me quizzically but asked no further questions.

If you have ever wondered who actually buys anything from those strange hotel boutique shops full of overpriced, just out of fashion but not yet quite classic clothes, I can now tell you – people like me. People who need to speak to a group of about 100 people in an hour or so and who only have the clothes they travelled in.

So, here I was, short of sleep, dressed like a Riviera playboy being offered breakfast canapés when I was approached by a smiling man dressed in a white dishdasha with traditional keffiyeh headgear. "Hello Piers, how are you?" I looked blank ... who was this man who knew me? Suddenly, I realised who it was and said, "Oh, hello Khalid, sorry, I didn't recognise you in your costume." Not the best start to my visit. At our previous meetings in the UK, his "costume" was Savile Row's finest, not desert gear. Khalid showed me with pride his brand-new gas mask to protect against the threat of Saddam Hussein's sarin gas. Unfortunately, there weren't enough masks to go around, so, the visitors – like me! – would have to do without.

As any frequent international business traveller knows, what we would most like to do on about day three of the trip is go and hide quietly in our hotel room but no, our local hosts want to make sure we have a "good time" and take it in turn to look after us. Khalid's GM was assigned to provide some entertainment. "Would you like to see 'Phantom of The Opera'?" Before I knew it, "Yes, I would love to," came out of my mouth.

The event was not quite what I had expected. I had been told it was the original cast singing … indeed they were but I would have happily paid to use Khalid's mask to block out the surreal sights and sounds that we were being subjected to: the old Bahrain Fort had been turned into the subterranean labyrinth beneath the Paris Opéra House, as "actors" (and I use the word loosely) mimed to the original cast recording on scratched and clicking records played a little too loudly on an antiquated sound system. The GM was incredibly proud. Me, however, coming from the centre of the known world, where I could enjoy a dozen different musicals, varied concerts, plays and three world-class symphony orchestras on any given night, I was less so. Time to go back to my digs.

I'm a fan of Middle Eastern food and mild exotica: Pomegranate Molasses, Tahini, Rose Harissa and Preserved Lemons are often to be found in my fridge but, by now, the hummus, labneh and tabbouleh for breakfast – every day – was growing tiring. My mum called, increasingly concerned about my safety – had she heard about the appalling am-dram miming? My underpants still hadn't been returned.

The trip over, I was heading home. At night, Bahrain airport was a hub of activity – all the flights from Asia and Australasia would stop in the darkness of the early hours for refuelling on their way to European capitals. On my return to the airport, we were witness to a small squadron of fighter jets flying over, fast and low. For a brief moment I wondered: are they theirs or ours? Herbert Norman Schwarzkopf Jr. and his men were in town. It was time to leave. I boarded one of the last planes out of the Gulf before the battle started, before the valuable warrior energy was put to use.

It was a few years, and a completely different desert later, before my path would cross again with Stormin' Norman.

Brave by accident – courage

All journeys have a start, middle and end. Some begin when a grey wizard asks a hairy-toed hobbit from the Shire to carry a ring into the Cracks of Doom in Orodruin. Others begin a little more circumspectly. These are the liminal moments when you are called to action, to nobility and maybe even to fight for what's right. If you get caught in one of these moments will you have the bravery and the quiet personal courage, to act with the determination of a warrior as you meet the monsters, battle the demons and save the day? Will you be brave by accident?

Accidental bravery shouldn't be underestimated. It's a chance to learn, to test oneself against previous performance.

There's a subtlety in leadership that may be overlooked. You have to be willing to make decisions, take the role and run with it, and you have to create the right environment where you also get input from those who know better.

I had a mentoring client who was appointed to an interim position, where the incumbent, who was unwell, might not be returning. I spoke to him about the challenges of the "interim" or "acting" role. I told him the first thing to do was to find out if his brief was just to keep the seat warm or was he supposed to do something, now? He was very gung-ho, ignored my counsel, and within two days produced a video about all the changes he was going to make. He didn't bother understanding his brief. It ended badly. There is a danger, a creative tension, a burning desire to stamp your authority on any new role. You see it in many leaders, a kind of top dog energy. The Myers Briggs ENTJ, the charging Field Marshall. If ever I'm in a group with them, I always let them take over. They generally are very natural, willing leaders.

About six years into working at Marshalls I was selected to go to Chicago to learn about the futures markets. I was the unanimous choice of the ExCo because I was perceived to have the intellect to get the job done. It was completely out of the blue. I was running a desk all week, and on Friday, my boss asked me to read up about derivatives and the Chicago Futures Markets. I had only one thing on my mind: Saturday night. A friend who'd just bought one of the first Golf GTIs in the UK was having a Saturday Night Fever type party.

I never got to the party – I spent the weekend reading and on Monday, even though I didn't really understand what I'd read, I was given tickets to fly out to Chicago the following Saturday. I had to adapt. I didn't think about it for a moment – it was an opportunity. There was no rationality. I accepted the unexpected invitation to step up.

Domestic arrangements sorted and I could look forward to the adventure. I thought Chicago was going to be a land of stockyards, railroad tracks and gangsters (of gangsters – more later). On the four-times-weekly flight I remember I sat on the left-hand side of the plane and watched from 35,000 feet as we flew over the Isle of Man heading out over the Atlantic excited at the prospect of the long-haul adventure, delighted to see a different part of the United States – the curiously named "Midwest" that actually is located, map wise, more like the "Mideast" – appear below me.

We had bought a business and my job was to see how we could replicate it in the UK. They were unprepared for me. They put me in the turret of a dreadful, 1930s hotel, The Allerton, on Michigan Avenue. It had a tippety-tappety neon Fred Astaire style figure with a cane marking the time. It was like trying to sleep in a disco as the neon sign shone into my room. I understand it was very glamorous when it was built. It could all have been original for all I know. When my boss in London asked how things were going, I complained and as the impact of my conversation rippled through the system, I was advised by my Chicago hosts that I should take into account the "nuances" of reporting back to London about my experiences. I kept schtum going forward – it was the land of gangsters after all...

The lawyer who had done the deal was running the newly purchased business. He and his wife had a beautiful house, with a very formal dining room stuffed with fancy china, in a way only Americans are able to pull off. That evening, although early autumn, the food was being barbecued outside. He flew into the dining room, singed eyebrows and smoky hair: "The barbecue just blew up in my face." His wife, perfectly cool, said, "Can we sue?"

We went to see Macbeth, Kabuki-style. Kabuki is a style of traditional Japanese theatre that includes music, dance, drama with wooden blocks "clacking" to mark the movement of the story .... and an awful lot of makeup. The lawyer husband didn't particularly enjoy it, but I think he didn't want to leave a young man about town alone with his wife. I wasn't too fond of it either. My artistic curiosity had got the better of me.

It was early October when I arrived and it was impossible to dress correctly. The mornings and evenings would be six or seven degrees and at lunchtime twenty-two and sunny. Did you want to be hot at lunchtime? Or did you want to be comfortable at lunchtime but cold in the mornings and evenings? That was my warm welcome to America, Chicago style.

My chairman, Robert Renny St John Barkshire, a swashbuckler who straddled the old City and the new, was known to those in the know as John. He was also the first chairman of LIFFE, The London International Financial Futures Exchange – modelled after the Chicago Futures Exchanges. It was this very British Colonel in the Honourable Artillery Company who sent me off to Chicago. John was ice cool and could handle himself in the land of gangsters, which was fortunate because during the deal to buy the Chicago business, the seller got a little impatient with the progress and pulled out a revolver, aiming it squarely in John's face.[1]

I had seen the pictures, read the brochure and the briefing papers, but nothing really readied me for Chicago. New York I knew well, but this

1. Listen to an interview with John, British Library: https://sounds.bl.uk/Accents-and-dialects/Banking-and-finance/021M-C0409X0057XX-0001V0

was different. It was a curious mixture of "big city America" and also, in downtown, had quite an intimate small-town feeling. It was possible to jay-walk on Michigan Avenue without getting run over!

Chicago was, in some ways, although not necessarily instantly obvious, a natural home for the growing financial derivatives industry. Sitting at the crossroads of the Midwest, Chicago had always been, from the earliest of days, a trading post. As the new settlers arrived and agriculture grew the need for a marketplace for farmers to sell wheat and maize and cattle grew. By the 1870s grain trading with standardised agreements called "futures" contracts with a clearing house able to guarantee trades was well established along with the familiar octagonal futures trading pit.

The Chicago Board of Trade (CBOT) one of the two big Chicago institutions – always believed itself to be the superior exchange. They traded corn and wheat and created a futures market for US Treasury bonds. It is mostly run by Irish Americans with their Johnny come lately downtown rival the Chicago Butter and Egg Board later renamed the Chicago Mercantile Exchange (CME), a much flashier operation trading live cattle and hogs and currency contracts. They were cut-throat competitors until they decided to merge and conquer the world.

The Board of Trade building is in the Chicago Loop – the area bounded by the "L" (elevated railway) – and sits looking down LaSalle Street. It is capped with a 9.4m tall, faceless, aluminium statue of the Roman goddess of grain, Ceres, holding a sheaf of wheat in her left hand and a bag of corn in the right hand. This beautiful, art deco, 1930s building was the tallest building in the neighbourhood until 1965. The statue is unusual in that the sculptor omitted to give her a face – interestingly as the model was allegedly quite beautiful – but if you are the tallest building in town, no one was going to be looking that closely. The Merc was flashier, had started currency futures and had created a subdivision called the International Monetary Market (IMM), designed so that when they came to cities like London and Frankfurt hopefully people wouldn't think of them just as Chicago hog traders. A sort of early Toyota/Lexus sleight of hand trick.

The market I had left in London was a very different kind of market – one that was dispersed amongst its participants – connected, gossamer-like by the wires that ran between the counterparties – it was what was known as an OTC (over-the-counter) market. In OTC markets, trades are negotiated between counterparties sometimes directly, often through a broker, without going through an exchange. The other side of your trade is your counterparty – and your risk. The foreign exchange market that I had left behind was the world's largest OTC market.

The marketplace I had arrived in was a proper physical marketplace. It was an "Exchange". In this exchange the traded products had all been standardised around size, delivery dates and price increments. At the Merc they were mostly futures on hogs, live cattle and lumber and, what I was interested in, financial contracts on Eurodollar deposits and currencies. Your counterparty was, once the trade was matched and cleared, the clearing house.

The method of trading was "open-outcry" where traders standing in an octagonal "pit", a sort of modern-day amphitheatre, call out bids and offers. The Merc built an amazing trading floor. From the viewer's gallery it was, quite simply jaw-dropping in both size and ambition, with its kaleidoscope of multicoloured jacketed traders dressed in a sort of Hawaiian camouflage busy flashing complex hand signals to one another.

The yellow jackets were the "runners" taking the orders on slips of paper into the pits to be traded by people who had a trading seat, which they either owned or leased. Exchange officials wore pale blue. Each house had distinct colours. I always remember the Sinclair traders – they were dressed like nineteenth-century European generals, with dark maroon uniforms, gold cuff rings, and epaulettes. The external manifestation of the pride of the house; the great Jim Sinclair's boys. The pale blue exchange officials would hand-signal the prices out from the pit – the bids, the offers and the price of the last trades. This was typed into "the feed" which drove the shimmering, mechanical "departure board" showing all the activity which clicked and clacked as the trades arrived and departed. The faster the shimmering the busier the market. The feed also fed tens of thousands of terminals in remote offices. For a trader on the floor, his – they were nearly all male – "office" was his jacket; ergonomically evolved over time with a perfect shape in lightweight material and pockets in just the right places ...

I was a yellow-jacketed runner entering the visceral floor, as an actor enters the theatre in the round. Suddenly you're in the middle of the action. You could be a principal, maybe a "local" – someone willing, with their own money, to add liquidity and depth to the market, or a broker, executing client trades. The trading floor was always buzzing. The running jokes were that if one person got a cold in the pit, they all did, and if somebody died in the bond pit down at the Board of Trade, nobody would notice until the end of the day.

My mission in Chicago was to find out what we would need to do back home when LIFFE opened to make a business from this opportunity.

I always find it curious when I find something I wasn't expecting, I tend to be surprised ... naturally if you aren't expecting it, it's not unreasonable to be surprised. But still, I'm often surprised. What I discovered that I wasn't expecting in Chicago were mysterious "dark arts". These dark arts were practised by many followers. Traders would be seen with folded sheets of paper that they carefully opened to study. The well folded paper was treated with the kind of respect given to a treasure map of old – and rightly so, as these people believed that study of these patterns and symbols could predict the future. In a marketplace where fortunes can be made or lost, having a treasure map that can predict what is going to happen next is very useful. Like every dark art, it had its rituals, symbols and special lexicon. Enter the world of Technical Analysis. Many believe its modern origins to be in the writings of Charles Dow – yes, he of the index and The Wall Street Journal – at the end of the nineteenth century. For traders, whether they were following simple graphical patterns looking for "flags" or "pennants", "support" or "resistance" or the breech of a "trendline", a picture was certainly worth a thousand words. For those who dug deeper, there was an even richer world of exotica available: Gann Fans, Fibonacci sequences and Japanese candlestick charts – with their "hammers", "spinning tops" and "dojis".

I went for a few weeks and stayed for over three months and enjoyed this very different, stripey jacketed world of camaraderie. I set up a business for Marshall's back in the UK. My overall mission, in the end, was unsuccessful – non-bank customers wanted to buy the sizzle and not the steak. They wanted someone to create products that brought the benefits for them, not to have to build them themselves – and brokerage had no real profit margin; the days of Merrill Lynch charging $50 a clip were long gone. However, for me, something profound had happened: suddenly for the first time in a decade I hadn't been tied to the desk. I had tasted freedom and it was wonderful, or, as Samuel Taylor Coleridge said, "For he on honey-dew hath fed and drunk the milk of Paradise".

This whole opportunity was amazing. I didn't second guess myself. I was a true innocent, stepping into my warrior self, embracing the energy, being brave and doing it. Daily out of my depth and going back the next day for more.

Accidental leaders appear during moments of crisis.

Who would have thought during the Coronavirus pandemic that Joe Wicks would become the UK's PE teacher running a daily exercise class for children during school closures? When there is a leadership vacuum, someone needs to step in to fill it. Wicks reassured parents and kids with consistency and repetition, showing up at 9am every morning to put them through their paces. You may not be in a formal leadership position, but that does not mean you cannot have influence over others. As Allan R. Cohen and David L. Bradford explain in their classic *Influence without Authority*: leadership is a mindset and revealed in your behaviour and actions. Come the moment, come the man. As Margaret Heffernan says: "Pop up leaders will emerge".[2]

Brave by design – wisdom

It was dawn at the edge of the glorious California desert, the view was magnificent, the early heat haze shimmering all the way to the horizon. Unfortunately, the reason I had such a good view was that I was stuck clutching the top of a telegraph pole with dozens of participants below waiting for me to get on with it. The task was to climb up the telegraph pole, get onto the top, then grab the "thingy", and abseil back down. In my planning, I had missed a critical step – that of getting from the position of clutching the top of the pole to standing on top of it. I hadn't analysed the task correctly. Now I had the ignominy of dropping like a dead man into the safety net below. Tony Robbins hadn't envisaged this type of mastery!

Of course, I came to the desert to see the giant motivator do his massive action thing, billed by Tony as my "Date with Destiny" but also because, amongst the impressive group of speakers, Stormin' Norman was due to speak on leadership. I really had to be there. Fortunately, Stormin' Norman hadn't seen my pole mastery earlier in the day, so I felt emboldened to approach when I spotted him wandering in the hotel gardens. We chatted briefly. He was a genuinely amazing, great bear of a man. Curiously gentle. I believe it's this strength with compassion which made him so attractive. He had a reputation, in word and in action, as someone who took care of his people. He hated sending home body bags. American parents knew that their boys were as safe as they could be with him.

When he spoke to the amassed group that evening, he paraphrased Carl von Clausewitz, and said that the purpose of the military is to

---

2. Margaret Heffernan in conversation with the author.

enforce a political will. Someone questioned, "Why don't you sort out Yugoslavia?" He replied to laughter: "We do deserts, we don't do mountains." And added: "Seriously, when there's no political will you can't send us in to sort something out."

The wisdom to be brave comes from analysing the task, planning and understanding your role in the big picture.

Schwarzkopf also told a story about when he was a young army officer, his first weekend in charge at the Pentagon was during a Labor Day long weekend. He was march-walking in rhythm with his general, seeing him out of the building, and asked: "What should I do if something happens at the weekend?" "Happens, Schwarzkopf?" "Yes Sir, happens?" Without breaking a step his general said, "Rule one, Schwarzkopf, rule one." "Rule one General?" "Yes Schwarzkopf, when given command take it."

This may have been a turning point for the young Schwarzkopf, when he fully understood that his training had put him in a leadership position and now it was his turn to step up. He was there by design and had to step up to take the command he had earned.

It upsets me when I come across people in leadership positions (PILPs) who are not really leaders, they're just people in leadership positions. People are looking for leadership. When you are asked to step up into a leadership role take it. Don't create a vacuum. These PILPs, with their tidy desks and focus on internal politics, betray the role of leader. We'll look more at PILPs in Chapters X and 8.

Through history there have been many thoughtful, wise warrior leaders, for example Elizabeth I of England, the "Virgin Queen": *I know I have the body of a weak and feeble woman; but I have the heart and stomach of a king.* Or Mansa Musa who ruled Mali in the fourteenth century and used his wealth to enlighten his people by creating a great body of written material[3], attracting some of the world's great-

3. https://www.historyextra.com/magazine/who-greatest-leader-world-history/

est thinkers to his new centre of knowledge – Timbuktu, a city located on the eastern fringe of his empire.

So not all historical warrior leaders were Viking axe swingers.

The darker side of warrior leadership shows up in oversized ego, *I'm in charge*, indulging their lust for fame and glory.

Being a warrior is not about being an asshole.

There are other modern, more thoughtful warrior leaders. General Sir Mike Jackson, nicknamed "Darth Vader" and "The Prince of Darkness" by his men, commanded instant respect among his troops. In 1999 he took charge of the Kosovo Force in the successful operation to end the ethnic cleansing of Albanians in the former Yugoslav republic. During the mission he clashed with his American commander General Wesley Clark (who wanted to show the Russians who was boss and block Pristina airport) saying: *"I'm not going to start the Third World War for you."*

I mentored the Fleet Commander of the Royal Navy. One of the youngest ever Vice Admirals. A very inspiring, comparatively unassuming, thoughtful leader. I'm not sure that he really fully understood the power of his office, a little like CEOs underestimate the implications of what being the Chief Executive Officer means to the organisation. He told me a story of when he "turned up" to "pop in" and see the captain of one of his ships. Not ceremonial, just knocking around the dock yard. Of course, the officer on duty nearly freaked out as he got an admiral of the fleet coming on board unannounced! As George W. might have said "Never misunderestimate the power of your office".

You have to understand the power and potency of your leadership position. Not abuse it, nor fall to the dark side of ego and dominance. Even a dictator can explain why being a dictator isn't all that bad. An article in the New Yorker[4], from 1998, opens with: *"I was only an aspi-rante dictator," General Augusto Pinochet said – a candidate for dic-tator.*

With the honour of the warrior, and the power to command armies or companies, comes responsibility. There's a time for consensus and a time for benign dictatorship – knowing which one and when is the secret.

Have you fully appreciated the power of your office?

Alain Dromer understood the power of his office while CEO of Aviva Investors. He could have walked away from the challenging situation and hoped for the best. He chose to take responsibility.

Take the terrorists out – Alain Dromer

I decided to sack my US colleague. He was successful, very much liked, CEO of the American business, but unfortunately really entrenched in his model. He believed that everything I was doing and advising was wrong, or it was interfering with his own organisation. He was a member of my executive com-mittee, and he was a rebel. At all meetings he listened but rarely participated. Whenever it was time to make a decision, he was always against. I made up my mind that I had to get rid of him. It was difficult, because his team loved him as did his local boss in the matrix, the head of Aviva America. It was a risky decision.

I planned for that confrontation with great detail. Every minute was accounted for. I knew who would replace him. I could not implement my plan unless he was gone. I managed

---

4. The Dictator, The New Yorker, 1998: https://www.newyorker.com/magazine/1998/10/19/the-dictator-2

to convince my boss that I was right, and he should trust and support me. There was little space for improvisation; I had my plan, I would sack him, and security would escort him from the building. It all went as planned except he asked if he could stay for the rest of the day. I looked him in the eyes, and we had a real man to man conversation for a few minutes. I trusted him. It was against my meticulous plan, but my instinct said he would do the right thing and he wouldn't betray me. As a result, I gained in the eyes of his troops, that I was treating him with respect, and that would be in my favour.

When I came back to the UK, my worldwide Executive Committee were very happy. My leadership position was enhanced.

With responsibility comes advocacy. If you're going to be an advocate, you have to believe in the cause you are championing, the people you are advocating for, or the ideas you are challenging. To be an honest advocate you need to be authentic, and this is where the crossover from the innocent comes in. Think about Greta Thunberg, the Swedish environmental activist who has gained international recognition for promoting the view that humanity is facing an existential crisis arising from climate change. She may come across as a bit quirky, but she's authentic: She lives, breathes, feels, and takes action, fighting against criticism, for a cause larger than herself.

Margaret Thatcher, love her or hate her, at least she was authentic, and you knew what she stood for whereas today's flip-flop politicians swan out of a focus group and they've changed their opinion. Tony Benn, the veteran British politician, used to categorise politicians as either "signposts" or "weathervanes". Signposts indicate the way ahead, resolute and unchanging in the face of criticism or challenge. Weathervanes spin around, responding swiftly and unthinkingly to shifts in mood or what the newspapers are saying. Boris Johnson's former special advisor, Dominic Cummings said of the Prime Minister[5] "'We cannot keep changing your mind every time the Telegraph writes an editorial on the subject.' No one could find a way around the problem of the Prime Minister [being] just like a shopping trolley smashing from one side of the aisle to the other."

Being a warrior is not about running a mafia operation.

A warrior leader is passionate and may appear somewhat detached. They use their warrior energy as a natural part of their growth until those levers don't work anymore. They believe in their cause and are willing to fight for it. They are champions for their team, people, or idea. Steve Jobs, the co-founder of Apple, was very creative and clever, but more importantly he was a real champion for his ideas and principles. He was the embodiment of his belief, and that's what made him successful.

My friend, Kevin, the special constable, is the most mild-mannered, charming, delightful person in the world. But Kevin steps up frequently. He has the authority and the power of uniform. He is protected by the subtle deal we, as a society, have made in which we agree to be policed. In the UK we are policed by consent. Which is why, although Kevin refuses to admit it to me, I believe the first lesson police officers are taught is: you can't nick everybody for everything. Otherwise, the system won't work. He is trained and conditioned to step up, because he's never really off duty.

Do you believe in your cause? Are you the champion or advocate of it? Will you take your Viking axe and chop anything in sight? Or will you wield your rapier with finesse? How are you going to choose your battles? Is this a battle or is it just a skirmish?

5. Commons Select Committee Hearing and widely quoted in the media, May 2021.

Brave by action – just do it

After one steps out of innocence, into warrior energy, **you may still be quite young in your journey, and your bravery can be a little foolhardy.** Your wisdom may at this stage be a very conscious process, as you think: "What would X do? What would Y do too?" You may even find a comfortable willingness to take advice, to get help. Early on, there is a very strong energy of "can do" probably without necessarily understanding the full implications of the action. Time is needed to gather experience, to learn, to accumulate knowledge, and to feed well on the offered wise counsel. It's like a series of checks and balances. There's a potency in potentiality.

Alexander wept when he heard Anaxarchus discourse about an infinite number of worlds, and when his friends inquired what ailed him, "Is it not worthy of tears," he said, "that, when the number of worlds is infinite, we have not yet become lords of a single one?"[6]

Alexander succeeded to the throne at the age of twenty-one, after the assassination of his father, and spent most of his rooting years in unprecedented military campaigns through western Asia, and northeastern Africa. At the age of thirty he had the largest empire in the ancient world stretching from Greece to north-western India. He was awarded the generalship of Greece and used this authority to launch his father's Panhellenic project. He was undefeated in battle. Tutored by Aristotle, Alexander is considered one of most successful warriors in history.

When a lion roars you know about it. It does not meekly meow. The lion's roar comes from inside. It's primal, an embodiment of their very being. A lion knows what he stands for. Alexander, young in the journey, stepped up and took command. He roared.

---

6. Plutarch's essay On the Tranquillity of Mind, speaking about Alexander the Great, the King of Macedonia, translated by Philemon Holland.

Warrior leaders, like Thatcher (warrior queen and housewife), Thunberg (a surprising voice for activism) and Trump (polarising, as popular as he is unpopular) are unlikely to regularly win contests for charm. They may, and frequently do, receive grudging respect. Eric Heffer, a British Labour MP, didn't agree with anything Thatcher believed in, but he respected the fact that she was a woman who, against the odds, was leading the Conservative party and was Prime Minister of the UK.

I had a young entrepreneur as a client. His business partners were trying to steal his business from him, and he asked me for my advice. I said, "Lee, never take a knife to a gunfight." He asked: "Are you suggesting I turn this into a gunfight?" I said: "No, I suggest you get yourself a tactical nuclear weapon and just take 'em out in one go."

He got a top lawyer and took them out. He didn't incrementalise the problem. He resolved it. Boom.

Sometimes there's a need for complete aerial domination. But there's a price to pay. It's not free. So, how do you keep the potency of the primal energy, but directed as appropriate? If you use it all the time then no one pays attention any more. You're just an old-fashioned paper tiger or a sabre rattler, nobody is fooled.

Being a warrior leader is not about being angry.

Of course, it has to be fair. The warrior energy has to be just and appropriate. It shouldn't be wielded against the innocent. There's a difference between the warrior energy versus being semi-permanently angry. One of them needs teaching how to use their power, the other needs therapy.

As a child learns to walk, they don't give in when it gets a bit tough or they fall. They courageously get back up, try again, fall again – seventeen times an hour[7]. Maybe there's a difference between bravery and courage – I suspect courage is quieter. Nobody ever told little fat, non-aerodynamic bees that they can't fly. So they do.

That innocence of forging ahead that children and young leaders share can be shattered with the wrong or little encouragement.

Step up as a warrior leader

How do we recognise a warrior leader?

When you're led by strong warrior energy, instilled in a good leader, you feel safe and you're willing to do things, even if there's risk – because you know the risk has been thought about. When you are in the presence of a warrior leader you may feel a little prickle in your skin, they give off a particular kind of energy that says, don't mess with me. I saw Dennis Healey (the Labour Secretary of State for Defence who kept the UK out of the Vietnam war) in person and there was a charge around him like static electricity.

People who've served in armed conflict are remarkably cautious about getting involved in wars. Smart soldiers don't like wars, because all of them know it's pretty easy to start and pretty difficult to finish. Military power is always relative. To quote the former US Defence Secretary, James Mattis, *"the enemy gets a vote"*.

One of the concerns in the world is that there are virtually no leaders anywhere who have any experience whatsoever of being in armed conflict. What does that mean for the world?

I watched the film "Tolkien" about the author's early life when he

---

7. How Do You Learn to Walk? Thousands of Steps and Dozens of Falls Per Day: Karen E. Adolph, Whitney G. Cole, Meghana Komati, Jessie S. Garciaguirre, Daryaneh Badaly, Jesse M. Lingeman, Gladys Chan, and Rachel B. Sotsky - https://pubmed.ncbi.nlm.nih.gov/23085640/

served in the First World War and the scenes in the trenches are shocking. If you hadn't been there you really wouldn't have had any idea of the conditions. People wonder why we didn't just deal with Hitler at the beginning? Nobody who had been through the Great War wanted to go through anything like that again. Their fathers, brothers, cousins and sons had been killed. The fortunate ones, disfigured, disabled and dismayed upon return, would never wish to go back.

Everybody talks about how Churchill was a marvellous prime minister. In many ways they are wrong. He was completely unfit and unsuited for the role of Prime Minister of the UK. Then the job spec changed, and he stepped up into the leadership role. My colleague, the author Margaret Heffernan, uses the phrase "pop up leadership" about those people – like Joe Wicks – who "pop up" when the times demand them. She says, "It is so much about context. In the same way that someone who is a loser in one job can be a superstar in another. Or even with just a different boss..."[8]

Leaders come in many different shapes and sizes, as we'll see in Chapter 8.

Is the warrior leader an outdated concept?

It depends on the definition. The warrior *energy* is certainly not about one-dimensional roaring.

Compare and contrast the Viking warrior or lightsaber wielding leader. You can be a Viking, axe swinging warrior leader if you want. Or use your attacker's energy against himself. Or maybe use something a little more elegant. As Obi-Wan passed the baton to Luke: *"Your father's lightsaber. This is the weapon of a Jedi Knight. Not as clumsy or random as a blaster. An elegant weapon for a more civilized age."*

Viking warrior leaders are probably a bit out of fashion now, for all sorts of reasons. I think, older, experienced leaders doing "warrior" now

8. In conversation with the author.

look out of time, out of place, not right. A young warrior hero still has touches of innocence and we forgive them, appreciate the potency, and the drive to succeed. Warrior leaders have an ability to create followers because you can see who they are and recognise them. They are visible. They are not subtle. Their positioning is very clear.

Being a warrior leader is not about responding to every single stimulus.

When you're an older leader, you have many more things to consider. While you possibly have baggage – parental inculcation, from your education, your friends' behaviours. You also have the benefit of experience, observation and trial and error. So you've got some sort of developed internal compass. Now is the time to finely calibrate your compass and decide how you want to move through the world.

This can be a thoughtful, deliberate process or an unfolding. Some calibration will come from learning what not to do. Einstein allegedly[9] said, "The definition of insanity is doing the same thing over and over again and expecting different results." This warrior leader can be the phase when you learn to stop doing the same things as others and learn to be brave and courageous in your own unique way. Be willing to be seen in the world. I stepped away from my innocence when I decided to step from behind the pillar and shake hands. I became visible.

Being visible is the first sign of the bravery of the warrior. The leadership journey doesn't come in tidy chapters. And not always with clear signposts and waypoints. But there are signals to be observed.

There's something deeply attractive (and also slightly scary) about warrior leaders. If the going gets tough, they are going to be there. Not just for themselves, but for you. With great warrior leaders there's a

9. It's widely disputed: https://www.history.com/news/here-are-6-things-albert-einstein-never-said

degree of self-sacrifice, compassion. This strength with compassion is deeply attractive.

A danger for warrior leaders as they bravely march forwards is that they look behind to find nobody is following, or the rest have fallen behind. A platoon commander needs to develop a sheepdog characteristic of bringing the troops with them.

Don't be a "one club golfer". Make sure you're bringing the right weapons, attitude and tactics to the task, rather than automatically relying on your "go to" manoeuvres or just doing one thing again and again.

In order to be brave, you either have to have the energy of the innocent, a hobbit on the journey, hoping it will all turn out right in the end and stepping up when the mentor dies, carrying the ring alone. Or, the energy of a modern samurai, wielding the sword with wisdom and integrity, championing a cause, leading with action and just the right amount of force. The thoughtful, precise Samurai is more attractive and relevant than gold epaulettes and clinking metal of past warriors.

Courage and bravery come in different shapes and sizes. There are the strong and brave, characters Sylvester Stallone can play, action heroes rescuing children from burning buildings. Or the 100-year-old Captain, walking with his frame around his garden acting as a beacon of light in times of darkness and stress. Captain Sir Tom Moore, who received his knighthood from the Queen in his own personal ceremony in July 2020, raised more than £32m for NHS charities. The real warrior heroes put others before themselves. They advocate for others. They are the champions for the voiceless.

We had an issue with a staff member who was planning to take us to an industrial tribunal. He was wrong, we were right. I was up there on my high horse, demanding this matter of principle be righted. My lawyer, advising me on the situation, agreed: "Piers, you're quite right. It is a matter of principle. **I should also remind you though that prin-**

ciple can be an expensive commodity." He wasn't asking me to dump my principles, but to be aware of the price, and select the right battle. We ended up writing a cheque. It was easier. As Sun Tzu said in *The Art of War*: **"The wise warrior avoids the battle".**

As a warrior, it's simple. It's about stepping up. When you are in a leadership position what are you going to do with it? What are you going to make of it? How are you going to do it? What do you want to do? Do you really want to do it? Have you just accepted because you think you should? Will this promotion betray those around you? Or are you maybe just sailing along the travellator, waiting for the pay cheque?

In Chicago things were moving on as well. Electronic trading began in Eurodollar contracts in 1992 on the Chicago Mercantile Exchange, the beginning of a twenty-year journey from its traditional physical futures pits to a completely electronic era.

Twelve months after returning from Chicago, I gave in my notice. I was being encouraged to return to the desk and resume my career as a "producer", but I had tasted a different life. My boss refused to accept it: "You're one of the people here with the energy and intellect to go to the very top". I also had the wisdom to know my path lay elsewhere. While my head was tempted, my heart knew it was time to jump off this particular travelator and move on.

Piers in Your Pocket: Are you ready?

Family legend says we have a motto, allegedly handed down through the mists of Scottish ancestry (either that or my granny made it up): *More than a match for the many*. Do you have a motto or saying that serves you, real or created?

Some points to consider when stepping up as a warrior leader:

1. Choose your battles wisely: Not all battles are created equal. Don't waste your energy on the skirmishes, save it for the right battle.

2. Don't be delusional nor deluded: Understand your own reaction, some people are happy to have a fight. Are you? You need to differentiate between a fight and simply calling out bad behaviour. I seldom look for a fight but will fight (and fight tough) when necessary. This can come as a surprise to unwitting adversaries.

3. Call up the cavalry when needed: Gather allies and reinforcements, be willing to call in the strike reinforcements when necessary. Don't find yourself alone at the board meeting without your wingman! Allies and reinforcements are very important. Any corporate warrior leader, if successful, has developed careful and reliable relationships and alliances that they can call upon when needed.

4. Spend time in preparation: It is seldom wasted. Is it only your plan or have you sought good counsel and input from other trusted strategic thinkers on your team?

5. Decide if you can afford the price: Every time you fight, you pay a price. Every disagreement, skirmish and argument uses resources. Standing up for something will win you allies *and* detractors. Is it worth it? Sometimes though, you simply must speak truth to power to keep your integrity and values.

Chapter 3: Be braver than a Warrior (let the unveiling begin)

*"When the best leader's work is done the people say,
'We did it ourselves.'"*
– Lao Tzu

You've been called to a leadership position, now how do you win people over, gain competitive advantage and lead your business to success? Care and compassion is a vital, frequently underestimated tool in the leader's armoury. Used well and wisely it can have as much power and impact as the force wielded by a warrior leader. Taking care begins with ourselves. When we learn to nourish ideas, be generous with our praise and remove our own mask first, we provide a safe haven for growth and creative action. Remember, leaders come at all levels. Unmask your inner hero to provide direction and hope for people so they can confidently follow your lead.

Come the moment, come the idea, come the man

The tablecloths were white starched, sparkling and expectant. The guests were, what you could best describe as "mixed", that curious combination of locals, retirees, businesspeople and, of course, tourists. The location was impeccable, up amongst the treetops in the outskirts of Cape Town (the Beverly Hills end). It was the end of February 2020, we were in La Colombe, one of the finest restaurants in Africa. The handwritten pescatarian chef's menu promised eight courses, including mussel and passion fruit curry, aubergine and tomato with pine nuts and Kerala style prawns with labneh. Each course accompanied by its carefully selected wine.

I'd travelled to the restaurant by Uber. My driver, a Rwandan expat, commented that his president, Paul Kagame, was: "Tough, but good for the country." I was intrigued, some people think Kagame's a war criminal. Why was this young guy impressed with a warrior-type, sword wielding leader and General of the Rwandan Patriotic Front? Because Kagame is a charismatic leader, a businessman, and a master marketer of ideas. He offers stability in a continent often in turmoil.

I was having lunch with Gavin Dalgleish, CEO of Illovo Sugar. He had flown in from Durban to catch up and pick my brains while we picked over the delicacies. Each course was presented, more elaborately than the previous, with rocks and flowers, large plates and small portions, foamy ambrosia and crunchy savoury meringue appearing. I even had the chance to open my own tin of La Colombe tuna – prepared to perfection with herbs and baby flowers. As the dry ice swirled from the table we got to work.

Covid-19 would become especially worrisome for the CEO of an African, socially responsible business of considerable agricultural and manufacturing scale sitting in the heart of a semi-feudalistic ecosystem. Gavin was a former client. A wonderful, world-class leader: open, strong, compassionate and with just the right amount of unrealistic optimism.

My advice was simple (and this was before a single case of Covid-19 was recorded in South Africa): segregate teams, put a plan in place, prepare for the worst and step up. He didn't need telling, and his response to the pandemic was compassionate, considered and swift.

He led with a heartfelt, authentic, easily remembered message[1]: "It's in our hands". Followed with a series of measures demonstrating his firm

1. https://www.illovosugarafrica.com/UserContent/documents/Announcements/ Illovo-Sugar-Africa-Our-response-to-COVID-19.pdf

commitment to the safety of his staff and their loved ones, and service to consumers and customers across all of their African and international markets. Perhaps most importantly, he promised to communicate with employees through a dedicated information campaign and provide regular updates to all of their stakeholders.

Provide enough information so people could manage themselves – Gavin Dalgleish

My first impulse was to provide people with information because, people were probably scared. Even if I was scared, I didn't have the luxury of showing it. Little accurate information existed in the public domain in South Africa. 'Patient Zero', the first patient who came back from a skiing holiday to Italy, was, by coincidence, an ex-Illovo employee; we closed our building on the precautionary principle of safety first.

People were panicking. My impulse was to provide information for people to manage themselves. Then to **communicate, communicate, communicate.**

I tasked my people with a responsibility to tell their friends outside of the organisation what they had learned. To take that responsibility to be the one who informs.

Then we went into crisis mode, with cross-functional morning meetings daily, seven days a week. I was sitting in on conversations at levels far below me, it was great to get everything so unfiltered. **Our roles as leaders became un-blockers for other people. It immediately flattened the organisation.**

I'm really proud of what we've done. Everyone has been paid. We haven't laid off anybody.

It's been an incredible time of all interests aligning around outcomes, devoid of clutter, pushing aside the normal stuff. The time interval of your action is much shorter. You do something and you see results tomorrow. The time horizons became

> compressed, the organisation became flattened, and everybody's autonomy increased. Everybody felt the ownership. **Everybody owned the actions they were undertaking.**

Gavin's desire to communicate well and frequently was well-founded. The psychological impact of the pandemic impacted people's sense of security, safety and fairness. Everyone was working under increased threat and anxiety, and the best way to deal with it was through transparent communication, acting as a role model and creating clarity.[2]

He emailed me a few weeks after our lunch: "You were very prescient. It's all unfolding with horror, as you predicted. Our wonderful lunch in Constantia now feels a world away and sadly your call on the Coronavirus has been hauntingly spot on". My ability to spot the signals in the system helped him prepare for the worst. It was his **ability to step up, and stay stepped up**, that meant he could lead his business through one of the most challenging times in history. He was prepared for the moment when he would be called to subjugate himself for the greater good of his people and business. He led with a simple and effective idea. He stepped into his compassionate, warrior leader role.

The power of vulnerability

In the last chapter we explored what a warrior leader looks like. It can be both attractive and a little off-putting – and probably doesn't fit so well with today's world. The swashbuckling and sword wielding might have worked well for Jack Welch, Chairman and CEO of General Elec-

2. IDEA REPORT – The Mind in Crisis: Understanding employees' needs in a changed workplace: https://f.hubspotusercontent00.net/hubfs/1927708/ Idea%20Report_COVID_US_Digital.pdf

tric, the Titan of Wall Street, but it doesn't fit so well now. So, what do you do with that strength? What do you do with that energy? What do you do with that drive? Well, you can use it to bring ideas to life and you can add a dash of compassion and be willing to fight for what's right when necessary and then, in the process, become irresistible.

There is something very attractive about a leader who has the strength of the warrior but is also compassionate, caring, open and vulnerable. They are able to use their strength and power as a force for good in the world. They are just and noble. They are warriors with swords *and* words, their pen is often mightier than their sword, their strength and compassion deeply attractive.

When the government in the UK seemed missing in action as the Covid-19 pandemic accelerated in the spring, the nation almost relied on Joe Wicks to lead the way. Fortunately for South Africa, Gavin was ready and able. **Not all heroes wear capes.**

I have a hypothesis: it's that if we are willing to be vulnerable, and open, it's a magic key for ourselves, our businesses and our colleagues. There's a horrible misconception that vulnerability is weak, when in fact, the reverse is true. To be vulnerable is saying, I'm really very comfortable with myself so I don't measure myself by being perfect, by knowing everything.

Vulnerability is attractive, but it's not always easy. Greg Simidian says: "I was a reasonably vulnerable leader, but it comes with age. We think we're supposed to behave in a certain way. There are very few role models for open, vulnerable leaders. The problem is if you're a really nice, warm, vulnerable person in an environment with too many shit-bags you get annihilated, you get eaten, and that's what happened to me after we were bought. The CFO hated me because I was vulnerable, and I called him out on some bad behaviour. It's not always easy being nice."

This bravery, altruism and the ability to make profoundly important decisions for the greater good in the face of confusing, challenging times is what sets the compassionate warrior leaders apart. There is something deeply attractive about leaders who consider the greater good, are brave and vulnerable. McKinsey[3] suggest that: "Four qualities—awareness, vulnerability, empathy, and compassion—are critical for business leaders to care for people in crisis and set the stage for business recovery".

Vulnerability is the key that opens a second world of possibility, a willingness to trust. Alain Dromer believes that, *"Vulnerability is the key to opening new worlds"*. At different times in our career, we tend to feel more optimistic, more open, more expansive. In certain environments, surrounded by special people we flourish. When we land in fertile soil we grow better.

My handyman, Lee, is a master artisan. Given the right level of autonomy (high autonomy is fertile ground for him) he produces stunning results. We have hand mixed paint colours together to get just the right shade. When there is a challenge, I know Lee will find a way. In addition to the house, he has helped me transform my garden into an oasis. I have happily spent hours working alongside him, planting, pruning, perfecting. It's such a pleasure to work with someone who knows what they are doing and takes the time to do it properly. Lee is working in an uncertain domain, he can't force the rhododendron to flower, nor the bulbs to peak through when we want them. He has the right tool for every job, an eye for perfection. He passionately speaks about his work, brings me into his domain, shares his knowledge: he is authentic.

The French novelist Jean Giraudoux quipped (repeated later by George Burns): *"The secret of success is sincerity. Once you can fake that you've got it made."* You cannot fake authenticity. If you try to fake it, you will be found out and found lacking.

---

3. https://www.mckinsey.com/business-functions/organization/our-insights/tuning-in-turning-outward-cultivating-compassionate-leadership-in-a-crisis

Greg Simidian: *"I didn't know what an MD or CEO said or did. I was asking myself, literally, do MDs sit like this? Do MDs walk like this? All of a sudden, because I was the MD, I should know everything. There was this crushing pressure to be clever and erudite. The single best mindset I could have had was 'just be yourself, Greg'. I should have said: 'I'm probably going to be a bit crap for a while. Forgive me, I'm only human.' It's okay not to know."*

If we have a pain we go and see a GP, and often we get referred to a specialist. We find that the specialist is incredibly focused and only does, say, left elbows or corneas but not retinas. It strikes me as interesting that in the medical world people go from generalist, to choosing a field, to specialising until they become the world's top specialist in a subset of their field. In the business world, we seem to go in the opposite direction, usually we start as a specialist, and we end up as generalists who are supposed to know everything about everybody and make good decisions. In earlier parts of our career, we become specialists and because we're specialists and good, and we've got strong vertical knowledge and experience, we suddenly get promoted. Ironic, isn't it? Congratulations you're going to feel useless for the next few years and probably screw up and maybe get fired.

Peter Drucker, the godfather of modern-day management thinking, shared his 4 Cs of excellent leadership: competency, character, compassion, and community. He believed these four qualities are needed from every leader, in every situation – don't wait for a crisis to step up.

Build the fairy-tale castle first

So, what do you have to do to become a compassionate, inspiring leader?

You build the fairy-tale castle first.

It's widely quoted (although maybe apocryphal) that, when Walt Disney was constructing Disney World in Florida, he insisted that they build the fairy-tale castle, modelled after Neuschwanstein Castle in Germany, first. Right in the middle of the swamps. Why? So every builder, gardener, artisan and bricklayer could see what they were aiming for. They had a visual representation of what was in the mind of their visionary leader.

The fairy-tale castle acts as a flag in the ground for people to head towards. It provides the directionality everyone seeks.

It inspires and pulls people towards a north star ... you must build the idea so clearly that everyone can see it, believe in it, get behind it.

It's not like the lure and lunacy of goal setting (which we'll look at in Chapter 7), it's a distant landmark, one might never reach it, but it's there ... It allows you to set your compass and deal with what comes up on the route.

The fairy-tale castle provides inspiration, encouragement and incentive. At this stage, the direction is more important than the outcome ...

*"If at first the idea is not absurd,
then there is no hope for it."* — Albert Einstein

The power of ideas that can be easily remembered and communicated cannot be over emphasised. It's how Simon Sinek appropriated the phrase Start With Why, why Martin Luther King will always be remembered for his "I have a dream ..." despite saying many other interesting things, and also why, even though many aviators claimed the first manned flight, it's the Wright Brothers we all remember.

Being shy at heart, I don't usually talk to people on planes.

Well, I'm introverted – and I also may not want to get stuck talking to a fellow passenger for the next twelve hours. Recently, I was in Miami on holiday and I popped up to New York to see a client. Returning from snow to beach, about twenty-five minutes out of Miami, I somehow found myself in conversation with the guy sitting next to me. When he asked what I did. I said, "I help leaders thrive in uncertain times." He said, head spinning my way, "Oh, how do you do that?"

All ideas should trigger an action, should generate a reaction, and stimulate a "how" if you want to create ideas that people want to follow.

Bernice McCarthy in 1980, developed the 4MAT model, based on research and synthesis of findings from the fields of learning styles. The 4MAT model covers: Why? (the meaning), What? (the concepts), How? (the skills), If? (adaptation). When you develop and communicate an idea using this format and **sequence**, you are able to lead people, to encourage their participation, and keep the message very clear. Through experience, I would say it's pretty universal for all audiences.

Ideas are dangerous. Sonderaktion Krakau was the codename for a German operation against professors and academics of the Jagiellonian University (and other universities) in German occupied Kraków, Poland, at the beginning of World War II. As part of the broader action plan, the *Intelligenzaktion*, to eradicate the Polish intellectual elite, 184 professors, lecturers, doctors and academics were imprisoned. The Nazis naturally also imprisoned senior military leaders because of their ability to command. The fear of ideas being executed, indeed at some level, the very fear of independent ideas themselves was threatening to the regime.

"There is one thing stronger than all the armies in the world, and that is an idea whose time has come." – Victor Hugo

Chile's government finally acknowledged in 2015, that Nobel-prize winning poet Pablo Neruda might indeed have been murdered after the 1973 coup that brought General Augusto Pinochet to power. The fear of Neruda's ideas being propagated, amplified and acted upon meant he was probably murdered for the strength of his pen.

Ideas need a hat stand, somewhere to be hung or flung, from where they can be retrieved and used. When you build a fairy-tale castle to illustrate the idea you set the direction for all to follow.

Directionality not rigidity leads to integrity

Compassionate, open leaders have an accurate compass. They know where their true north is. They are not easily knocked from their path or swayed to the dark side. They firmly plant a stake in the ground, their flag for all to see, and lead towards the goal. They set the direction and provide compassionate directionality for their team.

And, at the same time they are able to see and sense the signals in the system. They are FIFO – fixed on the inside, but flexible on the outside. What does that mean? It means they know who they are and they don't break under pressure. Imagine a building built to withstand earthquakes. There is a firm structure, it has a strong foundation, and is practical. When the earth moves, that fixed inner flexes on the outside to withstand the exterior pressures. When the wind blows the tall building will sway, but not fall. It is solid, yet flexible. I have 70ft (21m) tall pine trees in my front garden. In 1987, when the UK had its "great hurricane", I was woken in the early hours by the sound of the wind. Looking out of the window, the pines were swaying like palm trees. They survived. Whereas my neighbour's oaks – strong but rigid trees with a shallow root system – were blown over by the wind.

Unfortunately, many leaders can be a slushy mess on the inside, often full of doubts and worries, yet they project a fixed, solid exterior. When stress arrives, as surely it will, it breaks the illusion.

The person with the greatest outer flexibility will always win, they will respond appropriately to a VUCA[4] environment.

4. VUCA is an acronym based on the leadership theories of Warren Bennis and Burt Nanus, and stands for Volatility, Uncertainty, Complexity and Ambiguity. It was the response of the US Army War College to the collapse of the USSR. www.vuca-world.org

How does a leader go forth in, for example a crisis, in "command and control" mode, to provide confidence and reassurance, but at the same time not be oblivious to new inputs?

Followers are reassured when their leader knows who they are, what they stand for and provides true direction. The pilot's sonorous, calm voice, "Ladies and Gentlemen ..." as they fly 250+ souls across oceans and mountains, encourages you to dig deeper into your book as you sip your tipple of choice. You know you are in safe hands, that will make hundreds of tiny adjustments to deliver you to your destination. As Napoleon Bonaparte said: *"A leader is a dealer in hope."*

The law of the instrument, or, as its colloquially known, "Maslow's hammer" is a cognitive bias that involves an over-reliance on a familiar tool. Abraham Maslow wrote in 1966, in *The Psychology of Science: A Reconnaissance*[5]: "I suppose it is tempting, if the only tool you have is a hammer, to treat everything as if it were a nail."

For the leader holding a hammer, every problem is a nail. A compassionate warrior leader creates frameworks and systems, so that they can choose the right tools for the job.

Compassionate, warrior leaders are competent, confident, courageous and potent. They do not charge forth with the madness of a MacArthur or Patton. They are open to new inputs, are scanning for the signals, but they stay the course. Where a warrior leader commands the troops a compassionate leader uses inspiration, direction and delegation. Delegation takes time, it's an investment and a demonstration of care and consideration. Compassionate delegation is why the people say, *"We did it ourselves"*.

It's all about integrity.

Structures that withstand earthquakes have integrity. Leaders who

---

5. The Psychology of Science: A Reconnaissance. Harper & Row. ISBN 978-0-8092-6130-7.

withstand pandemics have integrity. It's not about personality, adornments or awards. Compassionate, warrior leaders are not petty, rigid or bombastic. They will fairly reprimand and are idealist and pragmatic.

Greg Simidian is an example of a fine compassionate leader, always encapsulated in my mind with the expression 'the ugly chat'. Greg: *"It took me a long time to have the ugly chat – the honesty required in order to deliver what is perceived as the tough information. Which is actually just honest, direct, unfiltered feedback. That sounds tough, but ultimately, it's a kindness, because when you don't give real feedback, you're lying to the individual, you're certainly lying to yourself, and essentially you fail. You end up perpetuating the problem and then you go away with a bit of self-loathing for your weakness. In Arabic there's an expression that even a donkey doesn't fall into the same hole twice. I'm now the one that says what everyone is thinking. The ugly chat is not easy, but it is necessary."*

I was always envious of Greg's ability, because I felt that I never had the graduation that he had. I think I only really had two modes: pleasant or nuclear. I never managed the middle part very well. Because of my natural care and compassion, I am sure I often didn't deal the intended blow effectively. They went away with what they thought was just a mild telling off, or, the complete other end of the scale, the threat of being fired on the spot.

It's about good construction, inner solidity, outer flexibility. You know when you see a leader with integrity, they move through the world in a special way, it's almost as if they walk differently to the mere mortals. It's as if they say: *"Let me be certain and open to not knowing."*

I've always spoken about "inverting the pyramid"; encouraging decisions to be taken lower down the organisation – by the person closest to the customer. The US Airforce has recently re-written their basic doctrine (without any input from me) to emphasise "commander's intent".[6] The Air Force Doctrine Publication-1 on 22nd April 2021 *"...defines the concept of mission command as a return to the philosophy of mission accomplishment guided by the commander's intent, while operating in environments characterized by increasing uncertainty, complexity and rapid change"*. The US Airforce, facing complex and dangerous battles, wants commanders to push decision-making to "the lowest competent, capable level" to create flexibility in execution.

Lee McCormack: *"I may not know all of the stops, the pathways and the routes to take, but it's really enjoyable learning and listening. I trust I'll innovate my way through it."*

To lead in a non-Aristotelian thinking way, leaders are not bound by black and white thinking, they are able to direct and flex. We must not fall foul of the law of excluded middle, where for every proposition, either this proposition or its negation is true. Leaders need to have the culture in which to be flexible.

Follow the Ranger

Followers are looking for a safe pair of hands to protect their lives and livelihoods, while offering inspiring visions of possibility. They will follow a leader who demonstrates integrity, compassion, confidence, competency, character, and community. Don't blame the followers if you, as the leader, find yourself alone on the mountain. It is your responsibility to create engaged followers.[7]

The Rangers in Lord of The Rings possessed keen senses and the abil-

6. US Air Force rewrites basic doctrine, emphasising 'commander's intent': https://www.flightglobal.com/fixed-wing/us-air-force-rewrites-basic-doctrine-emphasising-commanders-intent/143446.article
7. https://www.gallup.com/workplace/260561/engaged-followership-foundation-successful-leaders.aspx

ity to understand the languages of birds and beasts. Aragorn, also known as Strider, was a war hero, reluctantly flung into the battle for Middle Earth, to protect the innocent and lead the Fellowship. He is the mythological epitome of our compassionate, warrior leader.

People follow a compassionate, warrior leader because:

1. They know the territory. They have walked this way before, mapped the terrain, found the obstacles.
2. They know what to do when the going gets tough.
3. This isn't their first time in battle.
4. They adjust rapidly to incoming and new information.
5. They are always tracking the signals in the system.
6. They don't tell you what you want to hear, they tell you what you need to know.
7. They hold themselves to a higher purpose.

To become a truly compassionate leader you could do well to follow the lead of Aragorn.

When I was in Chicago, my boss gave me a clue where I might find talent and support. He spoke of a quiet leader, someone knowledgeable who knew his way around. I found him. He was a wonderful man called Lou Skydell, a classic, old school, floor trader. He had built a successful business by fair dealing and good heartedness. I'm not a big fan of the water and when Lou invited me to go on Lake Michigan in his boat, after saying "yes" I thought of a thousand reasons why I couldn't go. Lou was an authentic compassionate leader. He first had me put on a life jacket and got me helping with ropes – so I didn't have time to worry about the water. We pottered around near the shore on Lake Michigan for half an hour, and, after I felt comfortable, he gave me control of his boat and we headed out. Lake Michigan is like an ocean, its name is derived from the Ojibwa Indian word *mishigami*, meaning very large lake – they were not kidding, this is not a pond. We bounced on the waves, I didn't have a second to be worried, I was too busy steering. Returning and by now fast approaching the harbour, Lou asked: "How far to the entrance?" I replied, "A thousand yards and closing."

One afternoon and I'm a sailor now! Lou's integrity, authenticity and experience made me feel safe, I felt emboldened in his presence to do something I wouldn't normally do.

A leader has to develop compassion for themself, their people and the wider community. Then they must lead with compelling ideas, set a direction, show the way. Finally they have to be able to inspire others.

The sixth president of the US, John Quincy Adams, said: "If your actions inspire others to dream more, learn more, do more and become more, you are a leader." Are your actions inspiring others? Perhaps, more importantly do you know who your followers are, who your audience are?

You might be aware of the phenomenon that was *Thunderbirds*, a British science fiction television series from 1965 filmed with puppets in "Supermarionation", telling the story of "International Rescue". In a later episode, Parker, Lady Penelope's Cockney butler and chauffeur is breaking into a safe. Click a click with his stethoscope for two and a half hours, mopping his brow until finally there's a round of applause. He's broken into the safe of the Bank of England – as a challenge. When he succeeds the Bank decides to upgrade the safe and alarm system.

Coincidentally, an old mate of Parker had just escaped from Wormwood Scrubs. During the installation of the new, airtight security vault at the Bank of England, one of the employees is accidentally locked inside, and International Rescue are summoned to open the safe before the air is used up. Parker does all he can to slow the operation down thinking he is protecting a former safe cracking rival. When they finally arrive, Parker is asked to open the safe to save the employee. He asks Lady Penelope for a hair pin. He opens the new safe in two minutes.

In the car on the way home (a six-wheeled amphibious pink Rolls-Royce), Lady Penelope asks: "Parker, the old safe took you four and a half hours to crack and the new one, two minutes. Can you tell me why?" Parker: "Well, M'Lady, for the first one I 'ad an audience."

The antipodeans (and fictional chauffeurs, butlers and safe crackers) have a way of cutting through the BS, to get to the important point of an idea, with as few words as possible. As reported in the *FT*: "No room for bullshit in the time of coronavirus"[8], the Commissioner of Police in Victoria, Australia, was asked whether an employee at NAB who had falsely claimed he had coronavirus meaning the entire building had to be evacuated would face any charges. Commissioner Graham Ashton replied on radio 3AW: "Oh, I don't think so. It's not against the law to be a dickhead."

The prime minister of New Zealand, Jacinda Ardern, took office on 26 October 2017. Following an unexpected victory, she led her country in the aftermath of terrorist killings, quickly tightening the country's gun laws, then handled forest fires and pandemics. Many of these while pregnant. She was hailed as the most effective leader on the planet during the Covid-19 pandemic by *The Atlantic*.[9] Ardern is authentic, a compassionate communicator, confident and firm. She is a safe pair of hands when other leaders are panicking. Ardern is the epitome of a compassionate, warrior leader, the Ranger one wishes to follow. Come the moment, come the idea, come the *woman*.

As Stalin's missiles, sorry, I mean Putin's missiles rained down on Babi Yar[10] as he began his war, sorry, "special operations" to de-nazify Ukraine (oh how Shostakovich must've been laughing in his grave at the irony of this) it was left to a former Jewish TV comedian,[11] who had

---

8. https://www.ft.com/content/06e58582-704b-11ea-89df-41bea055720b
9. https://www.theatlantic.com/politics/archive/2020/04/jacinda-ardern-new-zealand-leadership-coronavirus/610237/
10. Throughout his career, Shostakovich used Jewish themes in his music, but his boldest statement of solidarity with Jewish causes was the Symphony No. 13, "Babi Yar". Some historic context: In 1941, Nazis and their sympathizers murdered nearly 34,000 Jews in two days at Babi Yar, a ravine near Kiev. For years, Soviet authorities suppressed any acknowledgement of the atrocity, did not erect a monument, and even went so far as to arrest Jews who prayed at the site.
11. Immediately before he was elected president in 2019, Volodymyr Zelensky played a fictional Ukrainian president in a television show "Servant of The People".

campaigned for presidency wearing a red clown's nose, to be the voice of the Ukrainian people. Refusing an offer from the Americans to air-lift him to safety after Russia invaded Ukraine on February 24th, 2022, Volodymyr Zelensky said: "The fight is here; I need anti-tank ammo, not a ride." Zelensky is prepared to defend the fairy-tale castle, shoulder to shoulder with his people, who will follow this compassionate ranger in a battle against a larger, fiercer villain. Two days later, on Twitter the brave Ukranian leader: "We will be defending our country, because our weapon is truth, and our truth is that this is our land, our country, our children …"

Piers in Your Pocket: The only way to lead is to follow

As we're talking about leadership and compassion, we should also spend some time thinking about personal leadership and looking after oneself. Stephen R. Covey in his book *The 7 Habits of Highly Effective People,* talks about production and production capacity and our own need for nourishment and care of ourself: *"Effectiveness lies in the balance – what I call the P/PC Balance. P stands for production of desired results, the golden eggs. PC stands for production capability, the ability or asset that produces the golden eggs."*

Self-care supports how you turn up and has an impact on everything. I encouraged a client to start running again as I knew how much it suited him, in our next call I asked him if he'd been running. He said with a smile in his voice: "Oh yes, I'm running like Forrest Gump."

Ask yourself:

1. Have you walked the territory?
2. Have you built the fairy-tale castle for all to see?
3. Are you showing compassion and care to yourself?
4. Have you built your own personal, strong foundations so you can be flexible and brave?
5. Are you worth following? Would you follow yourself?

Chapter 4: I'm an Imposter get me out of here

"Not all those who wander are lost."
– JRR Tolkien

Questioning, and hopefully some self-doubt, are part of the human condition. Those without self-doubt tend to be rather scary. If you're beginning to question if you're in the right place, doing the right thing, at the right time, well done! Over the years, in my coaching and mentoring of exceptional leaders I hear these doubts frequently. You are in good company, and a healthy state of growth where your ambition and identity are being formed. This is your opportunity for self-reflection, which will almost certainly generate more questions than answers, as you seek the right path.

Are you a real imposter?

I was in the Gulf on a mission to find customers and drum up business. Operating a classic, but often dubious strategy – when you can't find customers at home ... try further away. I was sitting with a director of the KIO – Kuwait's Sovereign Wealth Fund. I was completely out of my depth, with a deck I didn't understand. I'd been winging it, a prophet in a foreign land. The director was very charming and patient with this young man who had accidentally crossed over from the edge of his knowledge into the scary abyss of idiocy. The endless miniature cups of sweet tea churned in my gut. His short prayer break gave me a little respite to gather my thoughts. My mouth was working away (unfortunately well ahead of my brain) to explain how to use complex derivatives to hedge non-matching instruments. Or some such nonsense.

All that saved me from complete ignominy was his graciousness, and that I knew slightly more about financial derivatives than he did.

At different times in my career, I felt very much that I was the right person, at the right time, in the right job. And other times, I've thought, well, I interviewed okay but was this really the right job for me. In Chapter 1, when Derek Scotchbrook asked me if I could do mental arithmetic, I was surprised there might be some involved in the job, and for a long time I found doing the calculations on an overcomplicated calculator that I never really learnt how to use ineffective and overcomplicated, so I just gave up and did them in my head.

In Marianne Williamson's book, *A Return to Love,* perhaps we are inspired by her poem – the one Nelson Mandela quoted on that optimistic day in 1990 when he stood a free man in front of the world:

> *Our deepest fear is not that we are inadequate.*
> *Our deepest fear is that we are powerful beyond measure.*
> *It is our light, not our darkness*
> *That most frightens us.*

We have seen the progression into compassionate leader, as we discussed in the last chapter, is about being strong in the world and showing compassion and vulnerability by taking care of people. I personally think this is the pinnacle of leadership. We've been given power, authority, we've won that battle and now we want people to follow us in the quiet time and be ready for the next challenge. So how do we do that? How do we care for them around the campfire? Perhaps tuning into our sensitivity to be intuitive, then combine it with rational logical processes and a storyteller's heart is what sets special leaders apart. Greg Simidian: "Sensitivity is a blend of innate ability and training to put judgement to one side, resist your bias. It's a superpower."

So, you've read all these lovely chapters about warriors and bravery, but maybe you're thinking: "I don't feel like that. I don't feel brave. I don't feel like a competent leader. I feel like an imposter." I believe that's very interesting, and in this chapter, we'll investigate why you might feel that way. Maybe you're not an imposter at all and it's just beginner's mind, and a state of not knowing? Or, perhaps it is true, you are an imposter. The question remains, what are you going to do about it?

Should you expose yourself?

Perhaps the bigger question we should ask ourself is: are we really inadequate? Or are we afraid of exposing ourselves and sharing who we could truly be?

Firstly we must differentiate between the beginner's mind and the imposter's mind. While they might look and feel the same on the surface, they are totally different. As a leader, perhaps moving up in the organisation or taking on more responsibility, you may find yourself with feelings of inadequacy. Things are changing, the environment has shifted, expectations are high. How do you know if you're up to the challenge?

Beginner's mind refers to having an attitude of openness, eagerness, and lack of preconceptions when studying and working at an advanced level, just as a beginner would.

Beginner's Mind	Imposter's Mind
Feelings of curiosity, anticipation and excitement	Feelings of fear, panic and trepidation – is today the day I'm going to be unmasked?
Say: I can learn this	Say: This isn't important
Think: Who can help me get better faster?	Think: I need to hide my inadequacy
Are open and eager to learn	Are closed and avoid learning
Have no preconceptions of their ability	Pretend they understand
Think they're a learner	Think they're an expert
Are excited by all the "baby steps"	Are plagued by the primal threat of being thrown out of the cave/tribe which could be life threatening
The learning is in the doing	

In *Zen Mind, Beginner's Mind,* Zen teacher, Shunryu Suzuki, says, *"in the beginner's mind there are many possibilities, in the expert's mind there are few."*

Carol Dweck studies people's minds. In, *Mindset: The New Psychology of Success,* she asks: *"Why hide deficiencies instead of overcoming them? Why look for friends or partners who will just shore up your self-esteem instead of ones who will also challenge you to grow? And why seek out the tried and true, instead of experiences that will stretch you? The passion for stretching yourself and sticking to it, even (or especially) when it's not going well, is the hallmark of the growth mindset. This is the mindset that allows people to thrive during some of the most challenging times in their lives."* Dweck's growth vs fixed mindset comparison is well worth a read.

In 1933, Alfred Korzybski wrote *Science and Sanity: An Introduction to Non-Aristotelian Systems and General Semantics,* where he introduced the idea of the map is not the territory. My own version is the idea is that "the meal is not the menu". Just think about how many times you have read the description on the menu and you're surprised, maybe disappointed, when the meal turns up and it's not what you expected. The experience is nothing like the description. **All learning is in the doing – the map is not the territory.**

When you can sense the possibility, are curious about your own abilities and the challenges you face and adopt a confident stance in the face of not knowing, you are **not** an imposter, you have beginner's mind. So learn how to access the beginner's mind state, which is the basis for all truly effective learning.

Not knowing is a healthy state to master.

Fully formed competence doesn't just arrive; it is a journey from incompetence to competence in a skill.[1] The four-stage model of competence relates to the psychological states involved in the process of progression. The model has frequently (and incorrectly) been attributed to Abraham Maslow.[2] It's like tying a shoelace or a tie. The first few (dozen) times it's complicated, confusing, and you get it wrong. Now you do it without even thinking about it. Except bow ties – where I'm still between "conscious incompetence" and "conscious competence" at best.

Stage 1. Unconscious incompetence – this is when you do not understand or know how to do something and don't recognise your deficit. This sometimes leads to denying the usefulness of the skill. To move on to the next stage you must recognise you own incompetence, and the value of the new skill. This is where our imposters get stuck. ***Wrong Intuition***

---

1. Management trainer Martin M. Broadwell described the model as "The four levels of teaching" in February 1969 and Paul R. Curtiss and Phillip W. Warren mentioned the model in their 1973 book The Dynamics of Life Skills Coaching
2. Conscious Competence Learning Model: https://www.businessballs.com/self-awareness/conscious-competence-learning-model/

Stage 2. Conscious incompetence – when you recognise the deficit and the value of a new skill but do not understand or know how to do something. This can be considered beginner's mind. *Wrong Analysis*

Stage 3. Conscious competence – you know and understand how to do something but need to concentrate to get it done. *Right Analysis*

Stage 4. Unconscious competence – when you have had so much practice that it has become "second nature" and can be performed easily. This stage is mastery. Indeed, this is the point when the apprentice, after producing his "Masterpiece" transforms from Apprentice to Master Craftsman. *Right Intuition*

Additionally though, I believe there is the possibility of another stage.

Stage 5. Aesthetic Beauty – when there is an exquisite beauty where skill, practice and art combine and produce an almost transcendental experience – often for both participant and observer. *Whole Form Embodied Experience.*

Feeling like an imposter is different to the feelings one gets during the "first time" or being a beginner. It's totally different. Being a novice or beginner changes with experience and practice, because "**all the learning is in the doing**".

My client George was a country manager – a local CEO for a multinational energy company. He was asked to go to head office, a good promotion. In his previous role he was responsible for everything. Everyone reported to him, and he could shape and mould the business mostly as he wished. In his new role he would have multi-department responsibilities. It was taking George a while to get his head around what was actually happening in head office, a whispering campaign began and the board was worried they may have overpromoted him.

The Group Chief Executive was replaced and the new guy liked George, they got on well, and he said: "Tell me what you think is really happening around here. I'm ready to listen. I'm ready to understand."

George explained how everything was overcomplicated, almost deliberately, to keep everybody out and keep fiefdoms secure with pockets of knowledge in place. Pricing was wrong, distribution and marketing channels were confused and overcomplicated. It was, for example, possible to buy services more cheaply through comparison sites than it was directly through the company's own website. George was relieved to understand that he was *not* the stupid one. As the new CEO removed layers of unnecessary hierarchy and complication, George was asked to sit on his new ExCo of seven, the leadership team, and help make the needed changes.

It's perfectly reasonable, as we're pushed onto the stage, to feel some fear. It serves us well to remember that this is our time of biggest growth.

My great friend, former colleague and client, Robbie McDonnell, with a very successful career in FinTech (he was the APAC CEO of Trading Technologies), has great inspirational insight: into his own career, his personal and professional development and his ability to thrive in sometimes infertile ground.

Robbie McDonnell: *"It's like music. You pick up the guitar, practice the chords, learn the words, listen to the original recording hundreds of times. You play along, gaining confidence, rhythm and speed. But there comes a point when you have to play in company. It's a progression. You have to perform it for real. The easiest part of running a business is getting things moving. The magic happens when everything lines up. One deal leads to another. The excitement of walking into a serious closing meeting with a major house like J. P. Morgan for a big deal after you've set it all up. The moment beforehand, when you should be concerned and nervous, you remember that the person sitting across the desk is just another man or woman."*

Of course, to get to that magical moment you must have served your time. You have to go through the good and bad performances before you can make a song your own.

There was a time, earlier in my career, that I call the "Carlyle years" because I'd stay in an apartment opposite the Carlyle in New York and enjoy listening to Bobby Short play the piano in the Café Carlyle. Sometimes I would travel to New York on Concorde (I was working for rich folk). Just as the plane is getting close to the sound barrier it becomes very bumpy. Then boom, boom, as you go through – and it's suddenly incredibly quiet and smooth. The turbulence and noise leading up to the event is followed by quiet progress.

We all once had beginner's minds. We started out ignorant, we gained competence. Our knowledge can sometimes trick us into thinking we're an expert and that we know it all. Getting comfortable in not knowing, in being your ignorant self, ensures you are not an imposter, but a true learner and leader.

I've been working as a coach and mentor in the C-suite now for twenty years. To this day, there are times when I feel I am out of my depth or not sure where things are going or if I'm truly adding value. I'm reassured by my slight misremembering of a quote by Wilfred Bion, the great psychiatrist, "When the work is really good, there should be two anxious people in the room."[3] **It's in those times that we stretch and grow and are prepared to be brave and 'not know'.**

You may be asking, what do I have to do to be comfortable in being my ignorant self? How do I come to terms with the feelings of inadequacy?

The scalpel versus the chainsaw

Aristotle did a good job teaching the boy, Alexander. He turned out all right. The idea that came to be called the "blank slate" or "tabula rasa"

---

3. 'If there aren't two anxious people in the room, the two being both the therapist and the patient, then there was not much point in turning up to find out what you already know'. Wilfred Bion 1961

appears in the writings of Aristotle (*De Anima or On the Soul*). He says when you're born, you're a blank slate – tabula rasa – and that it's your upbringing, life experiences and education that makes you the person you are and allows you to reach your potentiality. In Western philosophy we cling to this idea that nurture is of prime importance to the development of the personality.

Contrast Aristotle with the romantic ideas of Plato who believed that the human mind pre-exists somewhere in the heavens before being joined with a body on earth. A prototype, as he described it, and it is your job to *become* and fill that perfect body. I like to imagine the Michelin Man, an as yet fully filled space of potential.

Some personality traits would seem to be inborn – passed down from the parents to the child – while others seem to be more shaped by the physical and social environment. While the nature vs. nurture debate probably seemed once to be central to ideas of personality formation, I suspect it is now viewed as a rather naive attempt to simplify the many influences on personality development. Indeed, Donald Hebb the great Canadian psychologist, influential in the area of neuropsychology, was once asked, *"Which, nature or nurture, contributes more to personality?"* Exasperated he replied by asking (rhetorically of course), *"Which contributes more to the area of a rectangle, its length or its width?"*[4]

My clients are generally well-functioning, smart and capable. I usually only need to wield the scalpel, seldom the chainsaw, unless someone is being an absolute idiot.

I find the idea that individuals are teleological in nature, striving towards a desired objective, fits well with my coaching philosophy and seems logical – but I also understand the paradox of the idea in that in some ways the goal or desires themselves may possibly have been cre-

---

4. This may be apocryphal, and of course Darwin made the connection first in The Eugenics Review, Heredity and environment: https://www.ncbi.nlm.nih.gov/pmc/articles/PMC2986957

ated as a reaction to past events. I see in many of my "driven" clients a set of strong current goals and objectives that, upon examination and enquiry turn out to have been created by a wish to compensate for perceived deficits. We'll come back to this idea in later chapters.

It's this idea of potentiality that piques my curiosity. Why hasn't that potential reality been fulfilled yet?

When thinking about being an "imposter", I suspect that these feelings of inadequacy trigger anxiety, and that activates the amygdala. I don't think it's an intellectual question of "Am I good enough?" being discussed in the prefrontal cortex. I think it's visceral, a gut-wrenching nagging doubt.

The irrational terror of being unmasked

David Rock's SCARF$^{®5}$ model – a brain map model – helps us to understand a little of what's happening when feelings of inadequacy are triggered. SCARF stands for five of the key "domains" that can influence our behaviour when our amygdala is triggered by modern-day stimuli: remember, our amygdala is part of our "ancient brain" designed to protect us. There are pretty much only six things it can trigger: fight, flight, freeze, feed, faint and fornicate. In modern times, our likelihood of meeting a literal sabre-toothed tiger in the board room or the high street are small, but our amygdala is triggered by modern sabre-toothed tiger stimuli.

- Status – our relative importance compared to others.
- Certainty – our ability to be certain about the future.
- Autonomy – our sense of relative control over events that affect us.

5. SCARF: A Brain-Based Model for Collaborating With and Influencing Others
   https://davidrock.net

- Relatedness – how safe we feel with others.
- Fairness – how fair we perceive the exchanges between people – and how we are treated.

The model is based on neuroscientific research implying that these five triggers activate the same threat and reward responses in our brain that we rely on for physical survival. It's our instinctual response to the social surroundings.

David Rock's SCARF Model®

What does it feel like when the imposter syndrome is triggered? For Robbie McDonnell: *"It's a physical discomfort. The butterflies, tightening in the chest with shortness of breath. It's a rise in temperature, getting hot and it's not just a passing moment in time. It's visceral. You have to breathe your way through and try to rationalise the feelings and recognise that you've been here before. And it passed."*

When you are triggered into feeling like an imposter you need to pause and ask yourself: where is the evidence? Are you really an imposter or were you maybe previously an imposter?

Being asked to pause when the trigger is via the amygdala is difficult to begin with – but practice helps. In this situation we need the Buddhist approach of "participant and observer". It's necessary to learn to be able to rationally calibrate the feelings, triggers and stimuli while they are happening in real time. We will have primal triggers activating threat state through the amygdala while simultaneously attempting to rationalise through, for example, the prefrontal cortex and hippocampus.

Malan's triangles – the triangle of conflict and the triangle of persons – were developed in 1979 by the psychotherapist David Malan. Psychologists talk about this two-triangle model, and the concept of transference. **What's happening now is what was happening then.**

When I get antsy it's usually because my freedom is being limited. When I'm told that I can't board the plane yet, I think: "Don't you know I'm a Super Golden Shamrock Royal Flying Kangaroo member of your airline club." It's not about the airline employee not letting me on. It's about my dad or my headmaster telling me I can't do stuff. **What's happening now is what's happening then.**

Inspired by the work of David Malan
What's happening now is
what was happening then

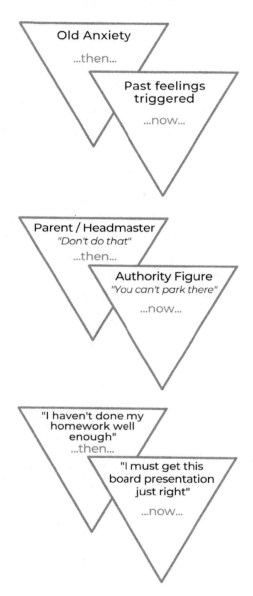

Old Anxiety

...then...

Past feelings
triggered

...now...

Parent / Headmaster
"Don't do that"
...then...

Authority Figure
"You can't park there"

...now...

"I haven't done my
homework well
enough"
...then...

"I must get this
board presentation
just right"

...now...

I had a client who desperately wanted to be on the executive committee of a major high street bank. He suggested I meet his boss to get another perspective. My client pushed himself hard and was hungry for the next position. His boss was elegant, old school, tall and languid, the kind of person who played cricket at school, and always got the girls. We were talking about my client and his boss said, "He's clever and very competitive. He's like one of those northern grammar-school boys. All elbows and barging."[6]

I encouraged my client to be more adoptable, to relax and be nicer. He said, "OK, but I'm not wearing a green tie, and I'm definitely not going to the opera."

Sometimes, we might have to change our dress and learn to use the right knives and forks to fit in. Or not change, to protect our identity. The question I had was: Why wouldn't he change? At that table did he feel an imposter? Did he not want to be exposed? Or did he really believe he shouldn't have to change to fit in? Maybe he's doing all the right things, in all the right ways, but he's in the wrong place. Real meritocracy hadn't quite landed there yet. Of course, some people will never have a seat at that table, even if they know the correct knives and forks to use.

Greg Simidian: *"If you've got that 'screensaver' going in the back of your head saying, 'I hate this. I'm rubbish at this. I'm no good,' that self-judgement is like self-flagellation? It's ridiculous."*

> *"What disturbs men's minds is not events*
> *but their judgements on events."*
> – Epictetus's Enchiridion 5

I've got a fancy name and sometimes people make assumptions – often inaccurate. Piers is old Saxon English, Fallowfield is an agricultural name, for the fields left fallow during a crop rotation. And Cooper, for the barrel makers. My family were in India for a couple of centuries,

---

6. Yes, the English class system is, regrettably, still alive and well.

they were Raj, but by the time I came along my parents were card carrying members of the Labour Party, Fabians. I'm kind of a tweener, I'm in between. I'm a modern, Technical High School Boy, with dyslexia. I was lucky. I was the first wave that came up through meritocracy in the City. It was good. Before my generation, you became, for example, a blue button boy on the stock exchange floor because of your uncle or family ties. I was just a not very well-off dyslexic boy from almost the wrong side of the tracks, but things worked out OK.

Where do you get the self-permission to step up? To do it. To be it.

The Four Million Pound MBA – Greg Simidian

I had come up through sales and marketing and been offered the MD's job. I was in charge, young and didn't know anything. That was me, twenty years ago. I was in panic, absolute panic. One minute, I was this sort of sales superhero with a cape and his team all doing great. Then all of a sudden, I had all these disciplines I knew nothing about with no support whatsoever. It was a sea change. Overnight I went from being the Jedi to the Padawan, but with no Obi-Wan. It was horrific. So, I bought a small company, you know, because I thought that's what MDs do. When the acquisition went sour, and I didn't get fired, Geoff Wilmot the wonderful human being who was my boss said: "Let's just call this your four-million-pound MBA." And that was it. He supported me completely.

The real question is how did you get your list of things you can be, what you can do and when you can step up?

Is this list from your parents? Is it a list from your peer group? Is it a list from school? How are these ideas colliding? Who filled in your "tabula rasa" for you? A classic coaching question that may help uncover your true feelings is: what if this belief you have isn't true?

I am impartial – with no vested interests except for my client's welfare and success. Recently I helped change the relationship between a CEO I'm working with and his board chair. I met his chairman who told me after the formal part of our discussion, almost as an afterthought how thrilled he and the board were that they hired my client. "He is absolutely the right person for the job. We are so pleased." My client hearing this unsolicited via a third party made a profound difference.

How much external confirmation or external validation do *you* need? Are people reassured when they get feedback from their team? From their boss? It's not about being a gung-ho leader and getting everyone killed. I'm much keener on the directionality a leader creates. On their vulnerability and humility.

My mother was a teacher, a head teacher, a university lecturer, one of the UK's leading specialists in the teaching of reading to pupils with learning difficulties. One day she said to me, "You know, some days I think, today's the day they're going to find out I don't really know what I'm doing."

I believe this fear manifests even more often with women. I'm not sure I can make that as an empirical statement, but it's a statement of belief. Every female leader I've worked with has been better than her male counterpart at the same level, because she had to be to get there. But still the doubt was often present.

A study by Christine Exley, an assistant professor at Harvard Business School, and Judd Kessler, Associate Professor of Business Economics and Public Policy at Wharton[7], showed that: *"Women systematically provided less favorable [sic] assessments of their own past performance and potential future ability than equally performing men. And our various study versions revealed that this gender gap was not dri-*

7. Why Don't Women Self-Promote As Much As Men? https://hbr.org/2019/12/why-dont-women-self-promote-as-much-as-men

ven by confidence or by strategic incentives, and that it was robust both in the face of ambiguity and under increased transparency."

The deeper question, which I don't know the answer to is: what is the video that's playing inside your head? What's the soundtrack? It's the irrationality of the imposter's thinking (to the observer anyway) that is so interesting. Even people who are truly successful – by any measure – are often plagued by this nagging feeling of self-doubt. A friend of mine, a very senior female leader spoke to me about that feeling of being found out.

I still think I'm going to get found out – even if I work hard enough: Mary Jo[8]

I was very influenced by my grandfather, the first non-family member to be a director of the company where he worked. He had progressed his way up through sheer hard work. His direct boss was a woman. I didn't know that there was anything at all unusual about a woman being the boss. He told me I could do anything with my life if I worked hard enough.

I did very well academically at school. I thought that I'd probably be able to get to university, even though none of my family had been, if I worked hard enough. My parents wanted me to do medicine, and therefore I didn't. I decided to go into engineering. People said women don't do engineering. And I said, well, of course they do. It was suggested that I might apply to Oxford or Cambridge. Just going to university was another world because I didn't know anyone that had. But, going to Oxford or Cambridge? That's not for the likes of me. Getting to Oxford or Cambridge was such an outlandish idea that I decided to just go for it and do the preparation at the same

---

8. Name changed at my friend's request - she prefers to avoid the limelight.

time as doing my A levels. I didn't want to waste time, because I was going to fail anyway.

I got offered a place. It was genuinely a surprise. I went to the interview, I got on well with the professor's dog. My family were excited, and very supportive, but it did feel as though I was going to a different world. And indeed it was. I suddenly realised what a closed world I had been living in. I was meeting people that had been to public schools, who had whole different lives to me. It was a massive learning experience not just academically, but in terms of life.

I felt as though I would be lucky if I got an interview when I finished at university. I applied to a dozen big engineering companies, and I got a dozen interviews. I was surprised. Then I got offered a dozen second interviews. I was surprised. I decided that of all the firms I applied for IBM and Hewlett Packard were the most interesting. So I decided to narrow it down to those two. Then I was offered a job at both. I was surprised.

I chose IBM because they offered me 100 pounds more. I didn't feel very capable, I'm "just little me". I didn't say how I was feeling, I decided to just give it a go. That's what I still do when I see these other people who are far more qualified than I am, far smarter than me, who have these great thoughts, and my thoughts are pretty trivial and boring compared to them. But I'll give it a go anyway. That's what I did at IBM. And at every company and role since.

People spotted stuff in me that I didn't know was in me. I was lucky, because people spent the time to realise I had the potential. Whenever I was offered an opportunity I would give it a go. I still think I'm going to get found out.

Sometimes I also have this fear of being unmasked.

This is not just about the willingness to be yourself. It is primal, and there are two risks:

1. The hunter who can't hunt is useless to the tribe. So, don't be noticed for your shortcomings.
2. Don't upset the tribe or you will be rejected. Rejection results in no food, no protection, no sex and you get eaten by the neighbourhood sabre-toothed tiger.

What or who is the real villain here? We may think it's the archetypical "bad guys" of the world, those who know best and charge ahead with their own agenda. But are they really the villains? Or is it conformity and orderliness? This desire to conform, to fit in, to be the same and smooth the edges, to create well-rounded people – could "fix the weaknesses" be the real villain?

Do we really want well-rounded people? That sounds like a bland evening drink. I'm not a fan of Horlicks or Ovaltine myself.

Some people live with the terror of being unmasked. Of being found out as a charlatan, a rogue, a fraud. They never become brave enough to ask the right questions of themselves, their peers, nor their bosses. They limit their own growth. These self-limiting beliefs are based on stimuli being seen as dangerous. When "confirmed" the amygdala runs riot, activating the autonomous nervous system.[9] Before the prefrontal cortex even gets a chance to do its job the amygdala needs to be addressed.

Are you the only sane one?

I facilitated the ExCo of a FTSE100 industrial business, which was going

9. Sathyanarayana Rao TS, Asha MR, Jagannatha Rao KS, Vasudevaraju P. The biochemistry of belief. Indian J Psychiatry. 2009 Oct-Dec;51(4):239-41. doi: 10.4103/0019-5545.58285. PMID: 20048445; PMCID: PMC2802367.

through some very big challenges. I stood at the front of the room and, unpremeditated said, "I do not know who I am to be helping you through this." And truly, I didn't know if I could help or be useful, or if I was the right person to facilitate them. I had a slight jitter inside, a feeling of being a long, long way from the shore, on my own.

I didn't find out until afterwards how appropriate that single sentence was. The last person they'd had to try to help them with their thinking kept telling them how he had all the answers. He didn't.

We are all on a journey. A personal one, and a public one. We are all a work in progress, never the finished product.

I worked with a wonderful woman running a high street fashion business that was by then owned by a private equity fund. We started with an off-site retreat, and she was telling me about the business and what was going on. She described the problem and how tough it was, and she said, "What should I do?"

And I said, "I don't know."

Her response was tough, delivered sharply in a particular tone that somehow always triggers a defensive response in me. "What am I hiring you for then?"

I said, "I don't know, I really don't know, this is very, very complicated. It's very difficult." There was a little pause and time stood still, and then, literally, she completely relaxed. Her shoulders dropped, and in that moment I liberated her. She didn't feel stupid or inadequate any more. It was indeed a very difficult problem. A brand facing challenges, now owned by a PE company who had paid too much for the business.

This (probably accidental) bravery, exposure, willingness to not know had unintended beneficial consequences.

Mary Jo again: *"It's quite good to say, I don't know. I go in with a non-arrogant, questioning position, what do I need to know? If you put yourself forward and you don't get what you wanted, what's the worst thing that could happen? The worst thing is I'd be upset, a bit of a bruised ego. Well that's okay. I'll probably learn a lot from doing it. I can live with that. Just have a go."*

Robbie McDonnel is clear, right before you break through to a competence level comes the point of highest stress. Robbie: *"Frequently imposter syndrome hits when you're doing something for the first time. A rational thought afterwards is to look back and realise that of course you felt that way, it was completely normal. You'd never done that thing before; you'd never experienced it.* **The learning isn't in the feeling, the learning is in the doing.** *After the event, you can remember how it felt in the middle. Then the feeling dissipates, and you can accept the learning. Of course, it doesn't go away. It will come around again."*

Vulnerability and openness creates other possibilities. **Remember, the menu is not the meal: the learning is in the (eating) doing.** During the opening months of the pandemic in 2020, I would have been much more comfortable if the UK government had said, "You know, we honestly don't know exactly what to do about this virus," rather than Bojo doing his am-dram Churchill impressions. **Vulnerability and openness opens the door to the world.**

High achievers often have a perpetual whisper of discontent.

Let's imagine that you've taken over a business and you came up through one side (the technical or marketing for example) and you don't know the other side of it (manufacturing or ops). You have two ways of dealing with it:

1. Pretend you know what you're doing, let the gossip run, and hope you don't get found out

or:

2. You can say I don't really understand this area, I'd like to know more, I want to make sure we've got someone who's an absolute expert, top of their field ...

This T-Shaped leadership takes a little getting used to. When first promoted to a leadership, ExCo or board position they've probably been promoted because of their incredible vertical expertise or competence. Now they have to do the other thing – horizontal leadership. The biggest shift for them is to stop giving answers and start asking good questions.

T-Shaped Leadership

Sector specific,
master of *the* game

Generalist,
good questioner, broad

T-Shaped Leader:
Master of the *whole* game, generalist,
broad, good questioner and also, able
to dig deep when necessary.

There's the dilemma. Leaders are supposed to be competent, all powerful, and knowledgeable. So, we have to ask ourselves, as followers, are we comfortable with someone a little less knowing? Personally, I like people who have some certainties and say when they don't know the rest. I'm very comfortable with that. Equally **I'm very *uncomfortable* with people who have the answers to everything.**

Robbie McDonnell: "You just have to be 1% better than the competition. Learn how far you can go and then go an extra yard. The real battle is with yourself. It's not with anybody else. Surprise yourself with what you can achieve. The only way of finding that break point is to never give up."

Newly promoted people have to be taught to shift from vertical expertise into a horizontal breadth and be confident to ask questions. One of the key skills is how to ask questions (without seeming like it's an interrogation), because the quality of the questions dictates the quality of the answers.

"It is not the answer that enlightens, but the question."
– Eugene Ionesco

Remember Lou Skydell, from the last chapter, who took me sailing? He was invited to London by some rich folks to talk about derivatives, so he was flown across the Atlantic and found himself in Claridge's for the night. He was a little peckish but couldn't find the room service menu in his five-star luxury suite in the heart of Mayfair. He rang downstairs and said, "I'm looking for the room service menu." The reply: "There isn't one, Sir."

Lou thought for a moment, this is a very swanky hotel, let's try a different question: "Would it be possible to get some food in my room?"

"Of course, Sir. What would you like?"

The right question brought satisfaction, a nice dinner and a glass of good wine.

When I was a child, during Jersey Royal new potato season we were actively warned of the dangers of injury from piping hot new potatoes and were encouraged to follow the Duke of Wellington's practical advice (which I think may have been useful folklore). Apparently the Duke was having dinner with Queen Victoria and spat out a small, hot potato saying: "Some damn fool would have swallowed that."

Do you become the damn fool who would have swallowed the hot potato? This loops back into the confidence we have in ourselves. Where does that come from? That confidence that allows one to say: "I don't know."

*"The world views you as accomplished,
you view you as just having lucked out so far."* – Dr Erica Crome

Sometimes it's the environment you're in that causes the imposter feelings. In the 1930s, you probably could have been prime minister and run the UK in the mornings and had lunch and spent the afternoon in the Carlton Club. These days we are all under scrutiny, internal and external, twenty-four hours a day. Everybody is questioning everything. We set unrealistic expectations of others and ourselves. Previously the curtains were closed, we could hide our inadequacy (and our peccadilloes) nowadays it's all wide open.

The deeper question: am I the only sane one? You might think you're an imposter, but just maybe it's the company, the department, the job, that's the imposter. And you're the authentic one.

Be more Trump or become the Baron?

There is of course a wonderful paradox at work here for if we believe Alfred Adler's (*Understanding Human Nature: The Psychology of Personality*, 1927) view that children develop in ways that best allow them to compensate for feelings of weakness or inadequacy, then potentially the very things that have become strengths and talents were originally created out of perceived weaknesses.

When I am myself, how do I adapt my behaviour? Remember in Chapter 1, we talked about being adoptable and adaptable. What can you do to be both? How are you willing to be different to fit in? That's a completely different proposition to "just" fitting in. At first glance, they may look the same. Maybe you don't fit in because you are unique.

Donald Trump is interesting, because in his constant inauthenticity, he's actually quite authentic.

There are two types of real imposter – the plonkers and those with panache – the charlatans and the rogues. The David Brent types, from

The Office series, fall on one side. Frank Abagnale, who, before his nineteenth birthday, successfully performed cons worth thousands of dollars by posing as a Pan American World Airways pilot and a Georgia doctor fall on the other side.[10] Do we secretly admire those lovable imposters? What do we admire about them? Do we secretly wish we were that brave?

In *Chatter: The Voice in Our Head, Why It Matters, and How to Harness It*, Ethan Kross, an award-winning psychologist reveals the hidden power of our inner voice and shows how we can harness it to live a healthier, more satisfying, and more productive life. Kross studies the "science of introspection" at the University of Michigan's Emotion and Self-Control Lab, which he founded, and brought together data from MRI scans and clinical observations. We all have these inner voices, sometimes they are helpful and enthusiastic, other times they are critical and destructive. Kross warns that giving in to negative self-talk, the "chatter" of being an imposter, will damage our health, ruin our mood, and cause us to fold under pressure. Maybe it's not you who is the imposter ... maybe it's your inner critic. For example, in the hit TV series, *Succession* (based on a "fictional" family, who remarkably resemble the Murdochs), the family's patriarch, Logan Roy demonstrates an abundance of confidence at the surface, yet he's full of doubt underneath.

In the 2010 British historical drama film, *The King's Speech*, Colin Firth plays the future King George VI who, to cope with a stammer, hires Lionel Logue, an Australian speech and language therapist played by Geoffrey Rush. After his brother abdicates the throne, the new king relies on Logue to help him make his first wartime radio broadcast upon Britain's declaration of war on Germany in 1939. 'Bertie', as his family calls him, found his inner confidence and silenced his inner critic.

10. Catch Me If You Can, a 2002 American biographical crime film starring Leonardo DiCaprio and Tom Hanks

Interestingly, the producer of the film, Academy and BAFTA Award-winning Gareth Ellis-Unwin – who was told by his career master that he "wasn't academically bright enough to work in film" brought his Oscar with him when he was invited back to a school prize giving. Fortunately, Gareth hadn't listened to the career advice although he does admit to times of self-doubt.[11]

On the completely authentic, non-imposter, non-U[12] side of the scale, we have Baron Allen of Kensington, CBE. From a state school in Scotland to chairman of the Labour Party, Charles Lamb Allen, is a British businessman and broadcaster, chairman of Global Radio, 2 Sisters Food Group and ISS. Lord Allen was chief executive of Granada Group and then executive chairman of Granada Media plc, chief executive of ITV plc, chairman of the music company EMI. He was chairman of Endemol, a non-executive director of Tesco plc and Virgin Media. In March 2012, he was appointed by Ed Miliband, the then leader of the Labour Party, to the position of chairman of the executive board of the party. He is authentically himself, and says of his life, "It's been an amazing journey considering I left school at seventeen with no job to go to."

Piers in Your Pocket: Are you an imposter?

"Doubt is an uncomfortable condition, but certainty is a ridiculous one." — Voltaire

Fundamental questions for imposters:

- Maybe, just maybe, am I the only sane one?
- When I am myself how do I adapt my behaviour?

11. In conversation with Clare Balding on Ramblings BBC Radio 4 Saturday 20th February 2021
12. "U" stands for upper class, and "non-U" represents the aspiring middle classes, part of the terminology of popular discourse of social dialects in Britain in the 1950s.

- What's the evidence that I'm an imposter?
- Is the evidence true and accurate? Now?
- If I've never felt like an imposter, have I *really* stretched myself?

Let's presume you're not a con artist, scallywag or imposter. And let's presume that even though you rationally and logically get it, that you're okay, you're not an imposter and yet you still feel that way, you still feel the discomfort, what can you do?

1. **Create your own support committee.** Surround yourself with friends and colleagues, and the right mentors (at the right time) who can help you check your own sanity.
2. **Avoid living a half-life.** In the Australian RomCom, *Strictly Ballroom*, Fran, the overlooked beginner says: "A life lived in fear is a life half lived." Find your own truth.
3. **Ask your gut.** You can also take time to read the signals and understand the messages – are you really an imposter? Where are these signals coming from, and are they (still) true? Review Malan's triangles to help you get in touch with what's really happening.
4. **Take a moment, be open and vulnerable and say,** "Sometimes I feel like an imposter." This is how we often feel at the beginning of something new. Be prepared to expose yourself.
5. **Find a role model.** It could be a leader; someone you've worked for in the past. List the qualities in them that you really admire. Recognise those qualities in yourself.
6. **Focus on what works…** all the time, again and again and again.

In the long term, it's much better if you stop feeling like an imposter. The old adage, "act as if" could be useful here. But in the short term, act as if you know what you're doing and you may find it just happens to work.

Of course, you can be an imposter and still do a good job as long as you are willing to pay a very high price. And remember, unless you're a deluded egomaniac, self-questioning is normal …

Chapter 5: Kill the Grandmothers, and maybe the Poets while you're at it*

"Luke, you're going to find that many of the truths
we cling to depend greatly on our own point of view.
The truth is often what we make of it;
you heard what you wanted to hear,
believed what you wanted to believe."
– Obi-Wan Kenobi

There is great opportunity and profound risk in ideas. It doesn't matter whether it's illegitimate usurpers of Tudor England, the righteous brutality of the Spanish Inquisition or Martin Luther banging on church doors, ideas can be dangerous. Which is why so much time, energy and effort has been spent trying to stamp them out. Ideas are spread from the knees of grandmothers. The attractiveness and seduction of a great idea can lead to death, destruction and new religions – or perhaps peace, passion and authenticity. Movement begins with the utterance of a few, well-chosen words. When you are guided by high values, in a volatile world, you can keep your head (and your heart) and find true authenticity and lead with imagination.

* To be clear, this is NOT a 'call to action'. I'm not advocating you kill poets or grandmothers.

A fool and his dog

One sunny July day, a fool and his dog ran into the road. Of course, I stopped sharply and avoided hitting him and, more importantly, the dog. Unfortunately, the car behind did not stop and drove into the back of my pride and joy, my beautiful Alfa Romeo. The car went in for repair. So, on the following Saturday, rather than drive, I was walking to the station to hop on the train to get back home after a relaxed dinner with a friend. It was a lovely August evening, and I was enjoying my walk when I heard the sound of screeching tyres behind me. A thought arrived in my head, "I'm going to get run over." Everything turned into a sort of slow motion. I momentarily considered outrunning the car but knew that would be impossible. I thought about leaping over the garden wall on my left, but that would be improbable. Time was compressed.

The car mounted the pavement and hit me with a great bang as my femur exploded. You may have heard that when people break an ankle playing sport it sounds like a rifle crack. Well, the femur is a much bigger bone, it makes a big bang. Fortunately, (the first of the "fortunatelys") as he hit me he popped me between the pillar box and the lamppost because then, when his car pirouetted and hit the wall which fell over in virtually one piece, at least I wasn't under that. Everything went incredibly quiet, and of course, there's only one question to ask when this type of thing happens – that's right, I heard the driver utter the magic words: "Are you all right?"

I was not. So I thought: "I'm going to scream", so I did, at the top of my voice. Anyone who hadn't been woken by the sound of the car hitting me and the wall was now definitely awake. The flashing lights and the concerned voices faded as I was taken to hospital in the back of an ambulance. Forget any idea of roadside paramedics with lots of patient stabilising equipment and skills, in those days an ambulance was really only a fast taxi service enabled by a flashing blue light. The only thought in my mind was that my flat was untidy. The registrar, Mr Fernandez, because Mr Lamb the consultant was off sick, took a look at the X-rays and, looking at my femur in nine pieces, came to the conclusion that the middle of the night was not the right time to do tricky surgery. I would have to wait until the morning.

I was very fortunate (the second of the "fortunatelys") in that I was such a smart and fashionable dresser I was wearing brand new, incredibly tight jeans – first day on. It's one of the reasons I kept the leg because the jeans acted like a tourniquet and held everything together. Otherwise, most likely, the femur would have broken through the skin and I would have been in a real mess! Remember what your granny told you: "make sure you are wearing clean underwear in case you are run over"? Well, the jeans were so tight there was no room for any underwear, clean or otherwise. Following a modesty warning to the nurse, my jeans were cut off. The operation was long but the repair went well, and I didn't lose any length in my leg. So, two weeks later, I went home, back to my parents which was wonderful. Unfortunately (the first of the "unfortunatelys"), that same afternoon, I noticed I was doing a wiggly thing with my leg, where the axis of movement was not my knee but in the middle of my femur. It had come apart.

For the next surgery Mr Fernandez pinned it *and* plated it, sacrificed a little length, seeded the area with bone chips taken from my hip (ouch) and harnessed me and it into the air, for three and a half months. Orthopaedic wards are interesting. Apart from broken bones, people are otherwise generally well and healthy and are often "inmates" for extended periods of time. Camaraderie grows. Young lads who had broken something following stupidity involving a motorbike, a wall or a dare could be seen doing wheelies while racing in their wheelchairs on the ward. Healing was slow, the months passed, but the following June I went on holiday to California on crutches. During that period of recovery, I bought a house – a what the Americans call a "do me upper" – and, having no functioning kitchen, learnt to cook my meals at my cream-coloured portable Baby Belling stove,[1] standing on one leg. It's quite a party trick. Still though, the leg wouldn't heal … there was lots of lovely, wispy new bone callous but too many

---

1. Small but perfectly formed, the Baby Belling Type 51 was a 1950's tabletop cooker that attracted a near cult following for its compact size and abilities. It featured a hot plate, fixed electric grill with 6 temperature settings and an oven capable of holding a small turkey – as long as the turkey was the same shape as the oven.

gaps. And somehow, I managed to bend the titanium alloy plate (the stuff they use for making rocket nose-cones) as the bone healed and tried to pull together. As the one-year anniversary of the accident approached and I was still on crutches, time to accept that I wasn't going to wake up one morning and suddenly find my leg was fixed.

Time to find a different approach. I put the word out ... I need the best orthopaedic surgeon in town. Six degrees of separation did its magic work and I was introduced to David Reynolds; head of A&E at St Thomas' and orthopaedic specialist extraordinaire. He was complimentary about the previous surgery but confessed, he doubted he himself would have tried to keep every piece and would reluctantly have given up on some of the nine pieces much earlier on. This time, after taking everything apart, he pinned and plated the leg. After a long and complicated operation (when my mother rang to check how I was, she was told by a young nurse: "He's just come back up from theatre now, he's been on the table for over five hours and he's rather cold." Not altogether reassuring but the operation was very successful. Unfortunately (the second of the "unfortunatelys") I did lose 1½ inches in length but when, finally, fourteen months after being run over I was able to stand on the leg with full weight I burst into tears of relief.

But I did lose a good inch and a half of the length of my left leg. A full year later and it was becoming noticeable, I was uneven. Even using a built-up shoe, when I took my shoes off, I was still listing. I went back to see my surgeon and asked him to even me up a bit and cut the other leg down by an inch. He said he could but advised I should chat with my family doctor, because in those days, family doctors were the route to specialists. My family doctor was great, he wrote, "My patient is intelligent, competent and perfectly capable of explaining what he wants you to do."

So I went back and he did the surgery. It was great. At the post op check-up a few weeks later I asked the surgeon how many height adjustments like this he had done before? This was the first one. I must have looked very surprised as he quickly added: "The only difference is this time I made the cut so we had pieces to join whereas normally I start with pieces." I guess orthopaedic surgery is generally mostly sterile Black and Decker power tool work anyway.

If he had told me he had never done this type of surgery before my mind could have been filled with possible disaster scenarios, the challenges, the chances of failure. His confidence, as a professional, and his omission to share with me that this was his 'first', saved me turmoil and concern. Of course, me being me, even if he'd told me it was his "first go" I'd still have said "yes". A gentleman can't list forever.

There's always a first time – if you accept the risk. But in whom should you trust?

In *The Lexus and the Olive Tree: Understanding Globalization,* Thomas L. Friedman posits that the world is currently undergoing two struggles: the drive for prosperity and development, symbolised by the Lexus, and the desire to retain identity and traditions, symbolised by the olive tree. In this world of spin, alternative facts, social media, conspiracy theorists and influencers, it's becoming increasingly difficult to know which ideas are true, what information is accurate and who are the veracious actors.

Harness the power of ideas to get results

My friend, a lawyer in Brisbane, came to the UK to complete his Doctorate in International Law at the time of the Yugoslavia troubles. He believed the only way to solve the Yugoslavia problem was to kill the grandmothers. Why? Because that's where the hatred begins. The hatred begins on the grandmother's knee. Grandmothers don't like inconvenient truths, they prefer stories, legends, the hurts, and injustice. Until the grandmothers are gone, the stories will live.

Old ideas and received wisdom might need to be killed off to pave the way for new ideas to flourish. There's a tension, a balance to be found – encompass the past but head towards the new and fresh.

The question to consider is how do you bring about creativity, foresight and change without creating revolution? With revolution comes destruction. We'll be looking more at destruction in Chapter 6. There are some very practical elements to get right.

Practical steps for creating change:

1. **Have a very clear vision:** have a really clear sense of where you want to get to, and why. Not necessarily "how" yet. It doesn't matter what type of organisation or who you are, whether you're a politician or a business leader, be able to articulate stages in the journey from where you're at, to the place you want to reach.
2. **Accept the slings and arrows of outrageous fortune:** If you are in a high-profile environment, or in a complex international organisation, you have to accept another bit of poetry, the slings and arrows of outrageous fortune. You're going get hit from all different sides, but you mustn't react in real time to those things as they happen.
3. **Calibrate to stick to the path:** The best way *not* to be buffeted by changing circumstances is to have a clear sense of where you are and where you are going. This is your internal compass, your North Star – this is what you have control over. Organisations frequently react to circumstances, rather than things which they are in control of. You have to configure your organisation to be reactive in a way that doesn't distract from the direction you have set, that doesn't take you off the path that you have plotted. In a crisis, organisations can overreact, over calibrate and that actually prevents progress. Being agile, reacting, calibrating, and resetting the direction keeps you on your true north.

A clear vision can be encapsulated in a slogan. Slogans are short, memorable, striking phrases often used by political parties, companies, and religions to generate movement in a direction. The original slogan[2] was a rallying cry in the Scottish Highlands.

A slogan conveys a whole new idea to encourage people to follow you, but it's important that your slogan isn't a fake attempt at manipulating your followers. Faking a message becomes more of a disaster the more important the required outcome is, the more scrutiny it is under and the amount of pressure there is. A lot of organisations can get away with "faking" in "peacetime", but the minute that they get put under more scrutiny and pressure, that's when it falls apart.[3] **A slogan without heart, without vision, without integrity will not rally the masses. It must appeal to both head and heart.** Here in the UK, and probably elsewhere, in politics, the right always manages to gel around a great slogan, while the left are still arguing about the nuances of a position.

The mismatch of man and message causes the most problems: if you're charismatic you can fluff up any old nonsense and make it sound wonderful[4]; if you're quiet and self-effacing but have a thoroughly worked out plan people will believe it; what scares people is no charisma and no plan.

It's all well and good to create a slogan, but how do you make sure it gets heard, is understood and vanquishes competing messages in such a busy, noisy, complex world? In the midst of the pandemic in 2020, Rachel Grant was the Director of Communications and Advocacy at CEPI (The Coalition for Epidemic Preparedness Innovation). She had previously been Director of Communications in the office of Tony Blair, Global Head of Media Relations for McKinsey, has worked in Number

2. Slogan – from sluagh-ghairm where sluagh was "army" or "host" and gairm meant "cry"
3. This reminds me of the famous Warren Buffett quote: "Only when the tide goes out do you discover who's been swimming naked."
4. No-drama Starmer can win without sparkle – but not without an engaging plan for the country Andrew Rawnsley, The Guardian, 19th June 2022: https://www.theguardian.com/commentisfree/2022/jun/19/no-drama-starmer-can-without-sparkle-but-not-an-engaging-plan-for-the-country

10 and was the head of news at DEFRA during the foot-and-mouth crisis. Rachel says: *"You ultra-simplify. Don't try and meet the fragmentation and complexity of the medium with more complexity. Meet it with simplicity."* She also says, about getting ideas across, *"The poets are the truth seekers. They give oxygen to radical new ideas. If you can harness the power of the poet, of the story teller, you can get established organisations and bureaucracies to innovate and do something new."*

It's not just the good guys who are the masters of the message. The Nazis were expert at using a message to create change, they had an expression *Gleichschaltung* for the process of successively establishing a system of totalitarian control and coordination over all aspects of German society and societies occupied by Nazi Germany. We can roughly translate it to mean "on message". When you look at the Nazi regime, they were the ultimate propagandists. They held rallies, with clear iconography. They created a sense of pride. At the Berlin Olympics they were world beating. From 1934 until the outbreak of war in 1939, the Silver Arrows of Mercedes-Benz and the competing Auto Union team dominated Grand Prix racing. The racing teams' campaigns were funded quite overtly by Adolf Hitler's Nazi regime. All part of the message.

Simon Sinek wasn't the first person to start with why. In 1946, in *Man's Search for Meaning,* Viktor Frankl said: *"Those who have a 'why' to live, can bear with almost any 'how'"*. Sinek was the first to capture the essence of an idea in a phrase that was easily memorable, and shareable, especially for the sound-bite generation.

One man's freedom fighter is another man's terrorist

Galileo's ideas were so powerful he spent a great part of his life under house arrest. His ideas of heliocentrism and Copernicanism were met with fierce opposition from within the Catholic Church. He was tried by the Inquisition, found "vehemently suspect of heresy", and forced to recant. He spent the rest of his life under house arrest.

If you want people to come up with great ideas, you need to create the right environment. People have to be allowed to have them. One of my clients is doing an assignment in Bangladesh, where it's time for revolution, because the political systems do not serve the country or its people well. The government deliberately had not reopened the universities post pandemic – because they don't want people thinking and spreading ideas. They prefer to control the message.

To rally the troops, start with a sense of what you're trying to do together. You need a very clear articulation of where you want to get to – the direction, and a very flexible and open-minded idea of how you're going to get there – the actions. You need the mix of the dreamers and the poets, as well as the doers and action takers, because one can't exist without the other. Sometimes, highly organised structured people in charge kill the thinkers. Those people need the space or the seniority to be dreamers. But those dreamers are often very bad at actually making stuff happen. So you need people who can get you from where you are to the vision in a structured way. Get your idea moving by motivating followers. There's a wonderful video narrated by Derek Sivers,[5] showing a dancing guy who, in less than three minutes, creates "a movement". There is no movement without the first follower. If he can do it, others will follow. Get that first follower! A leader must have a range of successful and flexible skills and tactics to build a coalition of followers whether it's the board or the management team or both – it's essential to ensure that the vision is accepted, lived and enabled but more importantly the coalition can help when obstacles arise.

It often comes back down to the things that are important but not measurable. You create an environment where people feel safe to say

5. For the video and full transcript – First Follower: Leadership Lessons from a Dancing Guy: https://sive.rs/ff

things that are different from the established wisdom. You do that through individual leadership, flexible structures, and from having different types of people working together. Uniform "one size fits all" leadership does not lend itself to that.

You need to avoid the confirmation bias trap. As Obi-Wan Kenobi warned Luke, "... *you heard what you wanted to hear, believed what you wanted to believe.*" Confirmation bias is the tendency of people to favour information that confirms their existing beliefs or hypotheses. People frequently give more weight to evidence that confirms their beliefs and undervalue evidence that could disprove it. Lisa Gansky, serial Tech entrepreneur and author of "The Mesh" says, "*When you create something, you can fall in love with it and aren't able to see or hear anything contrary. Whatever comes out of your mouth is all you're inhaling... you're breathing your own exhaust.*" This is particularly relevant for emotionally charged issues and for deeply entrenched beliefs. New ideas can be killed before they get a chance because of our tendency to recall information selectively or interpret it in a biased way.

How do you give life to new ideas? A leader can cut ideas off or give them legs. The paradox for leaders is that ideas often come from problems and conflict.

It's about mindset rather than structures. You must create an environment where those ideas which are maybe antithetical to the kind of organisational thinking are liked and admired. Rachel Grant: "*You need a space to bubble the unusual ideas to the top. This mindset and culture to allow this has to come from the top down.*"

Even if you don't want to break the system and you're not looking for revolution, it's a good idea to create units within the system, whether it's a government or a big bureaucracy, that are slightly apart from the main business. That way you allow the ideas to develop unhindered. With a problem-solving mindset you encourage people to grapple with problems. Maybe leaders should develop a slightly different mindset – a curiosity mindset and be constantly learning to broaden and widen their thinking. Seek answers from other disciplines. Study outside of your area of expertise. Look beyond the perceived wisdom. Cultivate flexibility.

Rachel Grant on the view from Number 10: *"The problem is that people 'think to their roles' within big organisations, they don't think beyond the structure of their daily tasks. When you're faced with extraordinary circumstances, you need to be able to respond in a different way.* **Do not over plan, leave space for the unexpected.** *You need the ability to be flexible, not overly structured."*

The fixed mindset – we've got to do it this way because it's the way we've always done it – is a massive disadvantage for leaders, especially in a crisis situation. You need to leave space for the unexpected. Eisenhower, Helmuth von Moltke, Carl von Clausewitz, Napoleon Bonaparte and Sun Tzu have all been credited with some combination of the pithy "No plan survives the first shot from the enemy". The reason the "fixed mindset" guys get in a mess is that they don't accept it, and try to play it as a war game, not the real thing. Even Mike Tyson got in on this theme: *"Everyone has a plan 'til they get punched in the mouth."*

Leaving space for the unexpected, for the punch in the mouth, for the anticipated serendipity requires flexibility in the face of changing circumstances. Without that space your organisation and your people can't be creative. If you don't make space for the more creative elements, to challenge thinking, to consider doing things in a different way you will be limited in your ability to respond effectively to circumstances. Make room for empathetic and creative aspects of people. These skills are not easily measurable and very easily get crushed.

To get people to learn, be creative and share their ideas – you need to get them around a metaphorical (or real) campfire. Together you tell the stories, share learnings, and inspire action. You give them context for what you're trying to do. In *Simple Habits for Complex Times*, Johnston and Garvey Berger suggest: *"You need to understand that the future you're moving toward is so ambiguous that you couldn't possibly know what will happen, yet you have to be clear enough about what it is that you can get people off the course to which they have become accustomed.*" You can do this with gentle nudges and experimentation, rather than doctrine and commands. You can start with a shared vision, that establishes a direction that moves your organisation toward the story you want to tell.

Anthony Willoughby is an exceptional man. His work at the Nomadic School of Business has evolved based on what he learnt from his conversations with nomadic and indigenous communities in Mongolia, East Africa and Papua New Guinea.

The Maasai Campfires – Anthony Willoughby

I've spent many years working on a model with the nomads; there are thousands of years of wisdom in these four points.

1. Common Unity: Get everybody around the same campfire. Give people identity, purpose, values and interdependence so they understand their role from an early age.

2. Hard Knowledge: I've discovered the hard knowledge that every single indigenous person has is knowing their territory, what their wealth is, and what the threats are. Once you can get people to agree on the territory, the wealth, the threats and the growth, then you can start to talk about the how.

3. Visible leadership: What does everybody need to know? How do we adapt? Where are the different territories? What are the different ways? Anybody can lead an organisation if they can visually articulate what they're trying to do. Why would anybody follow you if you couldn't do that?

4. Invisible leadership: Once they've got a project they can start to work out how to earn their seat at the table, what humanity and humility actually mean, the meaning of courage and inspiration. Only then can you start to build a community.

Not all ideas are good. Bad ideas usually arise from a misdiagnosed problem. You've got to be very sure of the right diagnosis before you start to think about the remedy. You have to be prepared in the early stages to take on board people's views. Be grounded in *what is true*, not what is ideological. Go broad before you implement, and then when you're sure about it, you've got to be brave.

A contemporary example of a bad idea was British Prime Minister Johnson's handling of free school meals during the pandemic in 2020. Marcus Rashford, a professional footballer whose mum had skipped meals when he was a child to ensure her children didn't go hungry, campaigned to feed children during school holidays. His campaign led to the government changing its policy to allow children to claim free meals during the Easter and summer holidays. He then called for free meals to be provided over the October half-term, with more than a million people signing his petition. Rashford's slogan, his rallying cry, was: *"no child should go hungry."*

Johnson's government got this issue wrong on multiple levels. Despite massive public pressure again, the government refused to give 1.4 million disadvantaged children in England £15 a week in food vouchers. Restaurants, takeaways and businesses, and several local councils got behind Rashford's campaign and provided food for children in need. The government attempted to stamp strong leadership on the issue, then prevaricated and U-turned multiple times. This is a case study in how to run with a bad idea.

Be so brave people can't resist you! When you are brave and stand up for your ideas you will find some people *don't* follow your message. They're the ones who say things like, "Well, there was a big meeting and, you know, we've all agreed we're going to do it, but, personally, I'm not really in favour of it." Those who aren't with you on your journey, get rid of them. Take them out now because they will simply undermine your message, ruin your story and spoil your plans.

The French Revolution began in 1789 when the Ancien Regime was abolished in favour of a constitutional monarchy. In under a 100 years, the French population had increased from eighteen million to twenty-six million. There were massive numbers of unemployed, sharp rises in food prices due to two years of bad harvests, and the country had debts three times the size of its GDP. France had sent many troops to fight in the American War of Independence, to defeat the British. It was no wonder revolution was in the air. There were in fact two groups, one of which wanted to keep the king but with a reduced set of powers. It took four and a half years and the severed head of a king to bring the revolution to fruition with the needed radical social and political changes. But the "story" in most people's mind is of an "event" – the storming of the Bastille, rather than a long-drawn-out affair.

Authenticity is attractive *and* seductive

So with a mindset of curiosity, control of a great slogan, the right environment and a dash of derring-do, leaders can charge ahead and lead their people to new territories, squash competing ideas and forge their own path, right? Well, maybe, but it's a bit more subtle. **To lead you need to be trusted and to trust.**

Stephen Covey in *The Seven Habits of Highly Effective People*, talks about the emotional bank account. You have to make deposits into it. Because if you don't, when you come to make a withdrawal, you end up overdrawn. So people who are continually working on their relationships and making deposits are able to withdraw from it, when needed. A full emotional bank account allows for friction, more direct language, and making amends if you screw up. It also helps with bringing people on board.

Patrick Lencioni, in *The Five Dysfunctions of a Team*, believes that the fear of conflict, and, therefore, too little conflict is bad for your team: *"Teams that trust each other are not afraid to engage in passionate dialogue around issues and decisions that are key to the organization's success. They do not hesitate to disagree with, challenge, and question one another, all in the spirit of finding the best answers, discovering the truth, and making great decisions."*

In Covid (and now post-Covid) working from home times everyone is cheering and congratulating themselves on how easy it's been to move everything on to Zoom. Of course it's been easy, because we've got years of shared relationships. But we began starting to run on empty because no one is contributing to the emotional bank accounts. I encourage my clients to make calls to people and say hello, for no particular reason other than to say hello. Make deposits into the emotional bank account.

Developed From Lencioni's Five Dysfunctions of a Team

One of the challenges for leaders is getting new ideas adopted – with strong levels of trust, it's an easier journey. The process of developing an idea, and then communicating it to shareholders, staff, the press and interested parties is a never-ending responsibility. To inspire trust, communicate a clear direction, admit what you don't know and explain how you feel about it. Robbie McDonnell suggests: *"Don't deny your deficiencies. There's never a perfect system, it will never work perfectly all the time. It's the time when it goes wrong and what you do at that point, that really bolster relationships. That's when the integrity and honesty comes into play."*

During the pandemic lockdowns of 2020, employees have seen behind the curtain, C-suite leaders have been de-masked, de-robed. The genie has been let out of the bottle. Or, as Professor Veronica Hope-Hailey, Professor Emeritus of Management Studies, University of Bath, says: *"All leaders from the 20 businesses interviewed said it had been a time of 'C-Suite Unfiltered', with no corporate communications team able to control real life conversations at all levels with CEOs and their teams."*[6]

Patrick Lencioni and David Rock have both written on the subject of trust and its connection with autonomy. You get the most out of everyone when they are trusted and given the autonomy to act. Larson and LaFasto, in *Teamwork: What Must Go Right/What Can Go Wrong*, suggested that four elements are needed in trust building: honesty, openness, consistency and respect. They interviewed many teams and found that when one of these dimensions is missing trust can be destroyed.

Mayer, Davis, and Schoorman's (1995) model of trust is based on three forms of trustworthiness: ability (knowledge, skills and competence), benevolence (caring about the other person), and integrity (shared val-

6. The Healthy Work Project: Unlocking Empathetic & Emotional Leadership: https://jerichochambers.com/the-healthy-work-project-unlocking-empathetic-emotional-leadership/

ues) – this is the ABI model[7] which was originally developed to address interpersonal relationships within organisations.

Between Lencioni, Rock, Mayer et al, there are a lot of words to play with around trust. I suggest you consider this: On a transatlantic flight, do you know your captain? Does he come and shake your hand? Mostly, I don't even care if he's nice to me, I just presume he is competent and therefore I'm willing to trust him. There's a Dutch expression: "Trust comes on foot and leaves on horseback."

I'm an automatic "truster" – unless my gut says "don't trust this person". In general, I give trust until I find out otherwise. Some people are the opposite. With them, you have to earn their trust. **Trust: are you a giver or an earner?**

These six steps will work to build trust:

Step 1. Align communications and action: Make sure that what you communicate and what you do are totally aligned. That's the first point of authenticity. The message has to go hand in hand with an actual business decision or demonstration of how things are changing. **Don't communicate unless there's substance.**

Step 2. Demand "deep message discipline": Be sure that everyone across an organisation is broadly saying the same thing and understands why. It's much more than just giving people a line or slogan to repeat to the press or staff. The real test of a message is that it can't be faked.

Rachel Grant: *"You need deep message discipline, to ensure that you're not constantly punting new ideas, then be prepared to explain further and not get exhausted. It's a blend of aspiration and relentless rigour."*

---

7. You can read their more recent thoughts here: https://journals.aom.org/doi/10.5465/amr.2007.24348410

You can't fake the depth to which you have thought the idea through. **Communication never makes a poor business decision right. You make a good decision and then you find a really good way to communicate it.**

Step 3. Don't stress it! Especially with the media, get less stressed. The media is a beast that you can never tame. Don't invest so much of your own self and soul in trying to. When Rachel was a relatively junior press officer in Number 10 Downing Street at the beginning of her career, she used to get absolutely infuriated with the Strategy Unit, because some crazy "blue sky" thought would leak from them and end up on the front page of The Daily Mail. Be more forgiving of yourself and others. **This too shall pass.**

"Public sentiment is everything. With public sentiment, nothing can fail. Without it, nothing can succeed." – Abraham Lincoln

Step 4. Have flexible integrity: You can decide to be intransigent, or you can decide to be flexible. You can decide to move with the circumstances, and remain the thing that you are, or you can place yourself so heavily in opposition to circumstances that you either break them or they break you. **The ability to be flexible helps maintain your integrity.** People who can't, burn out and break. In the hurricane, the 80-foot pine trees in my garden were swaying like palm trees, but they survived. The poor old oaks at the end of the road, with wide, shallow roots and strong inflexible trunks, fell over.

Step 5. Be rigorous and relentless: The bigger or edgier the idea, the more important the communication. Be absolutely clear about the vision. Have a proper way of measuring success, be accountable. When the idea is clear and simple, the actions that underpin it to make it happen are rigorous, then you need to be relentless in the pursuit of the goal.

Step 6. Craft a positive, rallying message: Your goals and vision have to be positive, because otherwise it becomes a very reductionist exercise. A negative message doesn't inspire people to rally behind it.

Johnson's government not paying for children's meals during a pandemic was a really negative message. You can't rally people behind that. **Make your message expansionist**.

Nature abhors a vacuum

Killing the grandmothers – killing the stories – creates a vacuum. Nature abhors a vacuum so it will get filled. Maybe by ideas that you don't want to be shared. So it's up to you to decide what stories you want to tell, and tell them. Fill the vacuum.

If you want to stop an idea, replace it with another idea. Ideas that have energy behind them, and change behind them, tend to get more natural legs than something you want to try to take away or stop. Work with what's working.

The attempt to stop an idea, to hide or censor it can have the opposite of the intended effect – in fact this example of psychological reactance has a contemporary name: 'The Streisand Effect'.[8] The unintended consequence of increasing awareness of that information, often via the internet, was named for American entertainer Barbra Streisand. The California Coastal Records Project were documenting California coastal erosion and had photographed her residence in Malibu, California. Streisand objected to this invasion of her privacy and tried to suppress the photograph but inadvertently in the process drew much greater attention to it. When people are aware that information is being kept from them, they are significantly more motivated to access and spread that information.

Generative language is what makes us humans different. We use language, as far as we know, unlike any other species. Humans, in their utterances, create new worlds. When President Kennedy said the US

8. Merriam Webster dictionary. Retrieved September, 2021. https://www.merriam-webster.com/words-at-play/words-were-watching-streisand-effect-barbra

"should commit itself to achieving the goal, before this decade is out, of landing a man on the Moon and returning him safely to the Earth", he created, in that utterance, a potential new reality. Pushing on the open door of ideas, of possibility, of generative change through language is so much easier than trying to stop stuff.

Stop trying to stop things. Oh, the irony ...

By nature I am thoughtful, optimistic and expansive with my language, so I'm very good at the "vision" thing. Now, if I want action, I need to change my physiology and language. I need to use shorter sentences, more abrupt language, move my body differently. Be more directive. What comes first? The language or the physiology. There's an internal trigger that changes the body, and that changes the language. You can hack that. You can change your language, to change your physiology to change the internal trigger and feel more like a person of action.

A probably apocryphal story is that during a visit to the NASA space centre in 1962, John F. Kennedy took a wrong turn and ended up in a service corridor where he noticed a janitor mopping. Kennedy said, "Hi, I'm Jack Kennedy. What are you doing?" The janitor replied: "Well, Mr President, I'm helping put a man on the moon." While the name of the janitor has been lost (or he was invented) the story carries an important message – a positive message rallies everyone because they feel part of a bigger thing. And that message is carried by the story from generation to generation, from grandmother to grandchild. Or from news source to news source.

During the foot-and-mouth outbreak in 2001, Rachel Grant was handling the communications for the UK Government.

Rachel Grant at Number 10

The phones were ringing off the hook. We had journalists ringing constantly. When the phone rang, as a dutiful press officer, I would call the veterinary team to find out if the cows at the farms where the journalists were broadcasting from had foot-and-mouth disease. At the moment of the call the herd were clear, but five hours later, by the time that journalist's piece gets published or goes out, the test has been done, and they have been found to have foot-and-mouth. We had a strong sense that we were not in charge of our own information. We took action. We stopped reacting to journalists' calls. We did two daily press conferences, and we didn't update any statistics in between. We did it to **become a trusted source of our own information.** We were less helpful to the journalists, and much more disciplined around the message. If you seek to feed the 24-hour news vacuum, it will utterly consume you. Use the media as one of your tools to achieve your goals. It's never an end in itself.

You have to call in the experts if you find yourself in the middle of a crisis. Their expertise is invaluable in those circumstances. It's a little bit like skiing. I'm a terrible skier. As a terrible skier you learn that what you do on a slope is exactly the opposite of what you should be doing on dry land. Your whole instinct is to lean back and to not go with the trajectory. In a crisis quite often, you find that what you would normally do will make things worse.

Strategic communicators are able to paint a picture which people can really be inspired by, while the actual nuts and bolts of making that come to life is sheer hard work and discipline.

Leaders tell stories about where the tribe has to go, the vision. Leaders tell stories about journeys a tribe has to go on, making it come to

life. And leaders tell stories about how we defeated the enemies. The language of the warrior is important: Words are powerful weapons. Jainism, an Indian religion, emphasises non-violence against all beings not only in action but also in speech and in thought. They believe that the words you use are as powerful as weapons, and if you use words badly against others, you cause harm to yourself as well.

In *Anthro-Vision: How Anthropology Can Explain Business and Life*, Gillian Tett bestselling author, *Financial Times* journalist, and anthropology PhD, explores how anthropology can shed light on the workplace. When we're able to identify the hidden tribes in the office, and the rituals binding people together as a team we can make better decisions, navigate risk and ultimately lead others. She investigates the connection between "strange" and "familiar", and says that:

1. We cultivate a mindset of empathy for strangers and value diversity.
2. Listening to someone else's view, however, "strange," does not just teach empathy for others; it also makes it easier to see yourself.
3. Embracing this strange-familiar concept enables us to see blind spots in others and ourselves.

A plaque on a statue in Santa Fe reads:

Monument texts reflect the character of the times in which they are written and the temper of those who wrote them. This monument was dedicated in 1868 near the close of a period of intense strife which pitted northerner against southerner, Indian against white, Indian against Indian. Thus, we see on this monument, as in other records, the use of such terms as "savage" and "rebel". Attitudes change and prejudices hopefully dissolve.

To be trusted make the message simple and precise and be true in word and action.

I was heading back to London, it was a trip that seemed normal then, in those pre-Covid days – a day trip to Frankfurt to see a client. It had all been going so well until then. Now a thunderstorm was on the way – a big thunderstorm and we were sitting on the runway, been there an hour. We breathed in the recycled air, sweating in our business clothes. Why wouldn't they just tell us either when we would be leaving or if this flight was cancelled?

The Captain, again apologising for the delay, this time said: *"There is an old pilot's saying, 'It is better to be on the ground wishing you were in the air, than to be in the air wishing you were on the ground.'"* He also invited anyone who wanted to come up and take a look at the radar to do so. In this one phrase and action, he encapsulated an entire message, proved he had nothing to hide and changed everyone's attitude on the plane.

Most government regulations don't pass the "three teachers test". If you want a piece of legislation or communication to be useful then ask three junior-school teachers to read it. They will pick holes in it, remove all imprecision, remove all possible contradictions, uncover all inaccuracies. The school system doesn't work if eight and nine-year-olds don't understand what's required of them. School teachers are conditioned to design ambiguity out of the system.

When Lord Grade was interviewed on BBC Radio 4's PM programme after the Martin Bashir/Princess Diana interview report he said: "The classic case is often, in a crisis, you end up addressing the wrong questions."[9] He added: "It's a sign of strength to own up when you get something wrong."

One of the most difficult things I ever did was when we were selling the FutureSource business. I was identified hugely with the sale plan. When our buyer went into Chapter 11, owing $2.8 billion, we had to turn around and explain: "I know for the last two years, we've been telling you that this was our future. And this was the way forward and this was right for us. And as of today, I'm now telling you that being independent is definitely the best way."

We immediately announced plans to once again invest in the business. Your actions must underpin what you're saying.

9. Lord Grade, former Chairman of the BBC interviewed on PM by Evan Davies 20th May 2021

Piers in Your Pocket: The world is yours

"You can have brilliant ideas, but if you can't get them across, your ideas won't get you anywhere." – Lee Iacocca

The grandmothers need to go, but the poets? We should probably keep them around a little longer.

To make sure you avoid the trap of your ideas getting "socialised" rather than "executed", consider:

1. There's going to be a message, so it might as well be yours.
2. The principle of decision-making is you argue around the table, you decide and when you walk out, you have all agreed. If someone is off message accidentally, then a re-education process is needed, and you forgive them. Deliberately off message, then a conversation is needed, and you have a problem.
3. Think differently by changing the input. Get yourself a twenty-one-year-old mentor – spend time with a nephew, niece or god-child.
4. Embrace the richness of communication.
5. If you're the inspired dreamer, do you have a good executor?
6. If you're a brilliant executor, who's helping you create the dreams?
7. When you've got ideas, work out which are the good ones and which ones you should have killed at birth. Then give the good ones legs and kill the bad ones.

Are you the dreamer, who needs an executer to get stuff done? Or are you the completer finisher who needs the spark of the idea from somewhere else? If you're the amazing combination of both, then the world truly is yours.

Chapter 6: Sacred cows make the finest burgers

"On the border between security and catastrophe lies beauty."[1]
– Nikolaus Harnoncourt, conductor.

There is only one thing more dangerous than change and that is staying the same. Whether it's clearing out the wardrobe or ceasing production of your most successful product, you have to create space for the new. New ideas, new ways of doing, new ways of being. Don't underestimate the power of ideas. Ideas can change the world. Bravely destroying the old to create space to start again takes courage, but it's a necessary part of regeneration that prepares us for creativity and opens the door to new possibility.

Piers and the pimp plan

For a while, becoming a sort-of gigolo was my backup plan.

I'd finished working for the New York bond brokers and I was wondering what to do next. I was invited to come and look at a high value electronics business by an interesting man, Lancelot Mills, who I knew slightly. Mr Mills (it was always Mister Mills, never Lancelot or Lance) was a Jack Hawkins double, both in looks and attitude, an escapee in a grey double-breasted suit and trilby from "The League of Gentleman". He was well in his seventies back then, and he's certainly dead now, so I'm comfortable to mention that the chatter was he'd been a member of the SOE[2] and that he rescued a Princess and her son who he contin-

---

1. Quoted BBC Music Matters December 5th, 2020
2. Special Operations Executive, a secret British World War II organisation.

ued to protect. Mr Mills lived in Jersey and flew into the London operations most Mondays, staying in Lowndes Square. He had a branch of the company in Paris run by Claude, who he "knew from the war".

He wanted me to take over his business because he wanted to retire. I'd been there about eight or nine months feeling less and less that this was a good "match and fit" for me when I discovered his accounting was, how should we put it, "not forensically accurate"...

I was very put out about this; I really wasn't enjoying it. My old stiff neck and shoulder problem returned. The first signs of discomfort for me. Physical, emotional and intellectual discomfort. That winter I went to Thailand for the first time on holiday and it had a profound impact on me because I had never been anywhere where so many people with so little were so content.

I returned to work, went back into the office and within two days the physical symptoms of discomfort were so strong I thought, "Enough of this!" I rang the estate agent to find out what I could get for the house. I rang the dealer to find out what I could get for the car.

I was willing to give it all up, but I also had a backup plan. I was going to buy a 1960s Rolls-Royce Silver Shadow and run historical tours around the UK for rich New York Jewish ladies. We would stand where kings and princes had stood, we would dine in sixteenth century coaching inns, they would be enveloped by the sweep and also the minutia of our history. They would have their photo taken outside the Mermaid Inn in Rye with the words "Rebuilt 1420" clearly visible in the picture. I would be so good at it that they'd recommend me to all their friends, and my pimp plan would be oversubscribed in weeks. I was ready to surrender to the moment.

Within forty-eight hours of being willing to give everything up the phone rang. It was a friend of mine, Alistair. He'd been called by a head-hunter about a job and was wondering if I thought he could do it. I was honest, it was going to be a bit of a stretch for him, he needed a few more years' experience and a bit more seniority. He offered to put my name forward for the role. I interviewed with three Midwestern Americans from Oster Communications Inc. Two weeks later they hired me. At the second interview on the Saturday when they offered me the job, I shook all their hands and, following the advice of a successful colleague: "Once you have the order, get out", so quickly left.

As a Buddhist (well at least that's what it said on my CV – although a colleague had said to me: "You're no Buddhist, you're just a yuppie with a conscience") I had a very interesting and happy career with this born again, Midwestern Christian company – partly because my chairman was six hours' time difference and eight hours' flying time away. If he had been "down the hall", and he had the opportunity to "pop in to see how I was doing" (lighting up my amygdala with the lack of personal autonomy), I think we would not have lasted.

The interview could all have gone horribly, religiously wrong, but I was saved because the chairman found The Book of Buddha in his hotel room drawer, read a few chapters and decided I needed saving. I interviewed wonderfully because I was free. I had surrendered. I was not a hungry shopper. I had choices.

Observe and act upon the signals in the system

There's finite time, finite energy, finite resources, a finite number of people you can spend time with. There's a finite number of projects you can do, so what are you going to do with the finite days you have left? Are you going to do everything averagely? Are you going to get rid of some things so you can do others really well?

The challenge is deciding. When you know how to decide on which things to focus, it all seems rather easy. Know that there are signs to observe, there are signals in the system that can guide you – if you know where to look.

Signal 1: The comfort of closed echo chambers

The danger of conventional wisdom traps us in echo chambers of similar voices. In the UK, I'm spoiled because I read *The Economist*, the *FT*, *The Guardian* and listen to the *BBC* so I think everything's fine with the world. I'm glad I don't read the *Daily Mail*, *The Express* or *The Telegraph*, where, in a parallel universe, immigrants are taking over all the jobs, the EU is stealing our fish, and Prime Minister Boris Johnson did everything he could to protect Christmas.

How can someone who can see the system is broken, that it doesn't work or it's ready for change get started, usually against people who are very comfortable with the way it is? **First, break out of the echo chambers to disrupt your personal status quo.**

Signal 2: The complacency of believing your own BS

I gave a talk a few years ago, called The 20 Rules of Business. It was very simple. Rule number one always look after your boss. Rule number two, never let your boss look stupid.

Rule number five was: the day you begin to believe your own press handouts is the beginning of the end. Be aware of complacency. In his book, *Only the Paranoid Survive*, Andy Grove, founder and former CEO of Intel reveals his strategy for measuring the nightmare moment every leader dreads – the moment when massive change happens to you. **When massive change occurs a company must, virtually overnight, adapt or fall by the wayside.**

When you find your business strategy is based on the newest sound bite from the latest celebrity business leader podcast it's time to pause and read the signals.

Signal 3: Getting lost in the noise of the crowd

In this incredibly noisy world it pays to pay attention to the *actual* signals too. Some of these signals are internal to your organisation: older products and services that need retiring because they're not profitable any more, slowdown in new customers, new hires not sticking around, incumbents moving on. Others are external: industry disruptors, consultants telling you to kill the tail, regulation, clients demanding new products.

A lovely concept I heard on the radio was the idea of a newspaper which was published once every 100 years. Just imagine what would go in it, and more importantly, what would be left out. When you can tune out the noise of the day you can hear the signals better.

Sometimes the signals are obvious: things aren't working. It's more challenging when things are working. So, clear the space in your head Mari Kondo-style, but be careful because nature abhors a vacuum. Make sure you fill it with some degree of useful intention.

This is what happens when you ignore the signals in the system.

I went to Oman with Fran, an old and dear friend – I'm godfather to her two daughters. On the plane Fran told me I must be very present during the trip because I needed to look after her in what she felt was going to be a very "foreign" country. It was her first Middle East trip, and she was, naturally, both excited and apprehensive. After a couple of days in Muscat touring the sights we collected our giant, long wheel-based, Toyota Land Cruiser with an acceptable small dent just underneath the bumper. The hire company rep wrote it down on his checklist, then told us, in not very good English, that to go through the desert we should let the tyres down a bit to manage the sand dunes. The colour drained from Fran's face. We set off on our adventure. Heading towards our desert encampment. She began to relax as she realised that the desert didn't begin ten kilometres outside Muscat city centre and the road we were on was the equivalent of the A23 to Brighton.

We stayed overnight in a beautiful desert camp at A'Sharqiyah Sands and after dinner watched the camel dancing or something underneath the stars. The following morning we headed onto the next leg of our trip, up to the mountains above Ad Dakhiyah. Fortunately, the car had a satnav (GPS for those readers whose countries prefer initials to descriptors). Unfortunately, it was a coordinates system, literally map reference coordinates. We input our coordinates and headed towards the hotel in the mountains, overlooking the religious bit of Oman. After driving for a while with each road becoming progressively more rural, the satnav told me to turn right. So I turned off a pleasant good quality road and immediately onto a much smaller, narrower road. My instinct said "stop and reverse back out of here" but there was no easy place to turn, so I didn't. I was now in a sort of Middle Eastern version of "sat-nav shortest route". You know the one where you feel you are being taken through people's back gardens. The narrow road got narrower. There was sweat on Fran's upper lip, despite the blasting aircon. The narrow road continued to taper. Now there was sweat on my upper lip. Although there was nowhere to reverse, I kept thinking I should stop and try to reverse. That's a lot of Toyota to reverse. I persevered.

"Look, Fran, it's beautiful. We're in a date plantation." A futile distraction technique as the archway ahead beckoned me through its threshold. I was sure we were too big to go through that archway, and we didn't have a "drink me" potion to assist. We can crash into that archway later; right now our most pressing problem is... oncoming traffic. I'm on a single track "road" in the middle of a UNESCO World Heritage Date Plantation, with an enthusiastic Omani trying to come, what felt like, through me. I stop. I try to reverse just a little bit. That's very close to that palm tree. Let's try forward a bit. Crunch. Nasty sounding crunch. Now I'm hanging over the edge into the drainage ditch by the side of the road. The local is somewhere between disbelieving and cross. Fortunately, Omanis are some of the most pleasant people in the world – it's like the world hasn't really caught up with them.

What should a guy do? Apparently, I have a lot of equipment in this giant jeep. One button is marked "crawl". I get the manual out, and wave jauntily to the bead counting bearded gentleman who has exited his vehicle. "Press crawl, do not touch the accelerator, and the vehicle will get itself out of any terrain." Excellent, I thought, escape is imminent. Unfortunately, it only works in forward gear. And I need to go backwards.

So, there we are, stuck in a ditch in a UNESCO World Heritage Date Plantation. How are we going to be saved? Who is going to arrive to rescue us? Maybe a nomadic Bedouin warrior? Fran called the hotel and tries to explain who we are, where we are and what our problem is.

The darkest hour is always just before dawn.

A man on a bicycle on his way home stops, tut tuts, assesses the situation, and heads off. Gesticulating that he will return. Ten minutes later he returns with friends. By then I am frankly quite chilled. What else can you do? You're in a foreign country, don't speak the language, and you've got your Land Cruiser permanently stuck in the middle of a date plantation. You don't know where you are and you have no idea how to get out of the mess you've got yourself into. So, you wait for something new.

The little man with a bicycle brings his two teenage friends who have a Jeep Renegade. They have no fear, no worry, and no regard for the World Heritage Date Plantation Site. They get the Land Cruiser back on the track. Now the hotel management turn up with supplies of tonic water, a packet of crisps and a chocolate bar.

I ask, "Who is the best driver?" Mohammed from the hotel steps forward smiling and jumps into the Land Cruiser's driver's seat, Fran and I pile into the back, and we head towards the archway. He clicks a button and the wing mirrors close in, I'm thinking "we aren't going to get through this", somehow we sail through the archway. Then he handbrake turns us to the right and zips us through people's houses in the ancient city, as tourists gaped.

Arriving at the hotel, we are looking forward to a drink. As we sit down for dinner, we notice there is no wine list, well, there wouldn't be in a *dry* hotel, not even a tiny bottle to be seen. We are in the religious part of Oman after all.

The signals are useless unless acted upon. A dullard will often not notice nor act upon obvious signals. Don't be a dullard.

What to do next: intention and execution

You've read the signals, maybe paid attention or, like me in Oman, read the signals but then failed to execute on them, now it's time to execute on your new intention. Imagine you're at a restaurant, there's one waiter driven by perfection, you get silver service, he doesn't drop a single pea. While the execution is perfect, it's cold. He's doing his job, going through the perfect, mechanical motions. At the other end of the scale, you get the well-intentioned waiter, very friendly, but then they forget to bring you half your meal. It's not that they have too many of the unwilling around here, it's just that they excel at the well intentioned.

There are always two components of a situation: There's the intention *and* the execution.

High Intention

Low Execution	**Dreamers, hopers:** Hire and train (or buddy up with someone to execute)	**Magical:** Get out of their way, follow them
	Dullards: Avoid at all costs, they might be a little hard of learning	**Gung ho:** Destroyers without a plan (but can be useful)

Low Intention

If I'm forced to choose, I'll choose good intention over perfect execution. Unless it's something medical.

When you get good intention and good execution, you get something very special, bordering on the magical. I'm always more forgiving of good intention and clunky execution, than really great execution, but not particularly thoughtful intention. When you go to American chain hotels, they're on autopilot at the front desk – "Welcome to the XX Hotel, how may we serve you today" finished with, naturally, "Have a good day!" If you look in their eyes there's nothing going on, they could be a robot. In the bottom right corner we have the dangerous destroyer, the man *without* a plan.

To prevent a forest fire, set the forest on fire

Sometimes the destroyer comes along of its own free will and you're out of a job, or you have a health problem, a midlife crisis, a family emergency, the death of someone close to you – these are the catalysts that catapult you from certainty to uncertainty. The moment when the new sports car hasn't fixed the discomfort, yet we hold on to the fragility of certainty, and then are surprised when we feel discombobulated.

In one scenario you're the protagonist in the destroying. And in the other scenario you're the victim of it. One man's blessing is another man's sorrow. At one point during the Covid pandemic museums and galleries opened, but you had to have a timed ticket, and there was a lot of social distancing. It was the most fabulous gallery experience I've ever had in my life. Victim or protagonist; it's about looking through the telescope from the other end.

Alex Bello, was a successful fighter pilot, loved by his colleagues and commanding officer, and could have continued to have a wonderful career in the Italian Air Force for as long as he wished. Yet he decided to give it all up. Why does someone decide to give everything up?

Chair time versus stick time – Alex Bello

For pilots, once they start to give you more chair time than stick time, then that's the time to change. When I made that decision, I didn't have a wife, kids, or a dog. I had a mortgage, but I didn't have too many difficulties to make a clean cut with my past to explore the future.

I'd always had an itch and a desire for continuous learning, and after a little more than fifteen years in the Air Force I had a good, professional understanding of where I was, I was on solid ground, comfortable. After you graduate as a fighter pilot, which takes about two/three years from joining the Air Force Academy, you have to sign up to a mandatory twelve-year period. They say it takes about ten years to master something, and I felt that I achieved what I could achieve flying-wise. **The suit that I had the honour to wear was starting to feel a bit**

---

tight. I felt curious to explore other personal and professional avenues.

I'm not an unsatisfied person, I don't always need to do new things, but I did feel that a circle was coming to a close.

So the decision was binary: either I continued to play on that same "music disc", perhaps capturing some other notes that I didn't pay attention to much in those early years, or try to play a new disc with new notes.

In matters of resignation, there's a gap between intention and execution. People generally resign twice, once in their head and once in your office, because, by then they have made both the intellectual *and* emotional decision to leave.

Part of the CEO's job is to get stuff out of the way so people can do their jobs. Peter Drucker said one of the key roles of the CEO is to be the interface between the internal world and the external world.[3]

How do you go about destroying the old to make space for the new, *and* setting that forest on fire? How do you master this creative destruction?

---

3. Yet the question remained: Do we really understand the role and the unique work of the chief executive? Drucker believed the answer was no. He argued that people wrongly view CEOs as coaches and utility infielders who jump in to solve problems as needed, and that CEOs indeed have work that is their own. On his death, in November 2005, Drucker left behind an outline of his emerging thoughts on the role. (The Wall Street Journal had published a portion of it as "The American CEO" in January 2005.) In 2004 Drucker said, "The CEO is the link between the Inside that is 'the organization,' and the Outside of society, economy, technology, markets, and customers. Inside there are only costs. Results are only on the outside." Quoted by AG Lafley in HBR https://hbr.org/2009/05/what-only-the-ceo-can-do

1. **Don't be reckless:** My guess is that the forest fire warden, before setting fire to his forest, is going to ask some questions. How limited is the burn? What are the weather conditions? Which way is the wind blowing? What's the environment? What are the risks? What's the safety plan? Has it been done successfully before?

Populist leaders everywhere tend to be reckless chancers. They risk all the institutions, the entire system. I'd generally not risk the entire system. I probably do it on one product. But if you keep on doing what you've always done, you'll keep on getting what you've always got.

2. **Be brave:** It's probably better to do this on your timetable, rather than somebody else's timetable. So plan the disruption, rather than suddenly having to throw away a two year development cycle as your competitor launches something similar ... but does it today.

Remember, we're not just talking about destroying physical things – we're also talking about destroying ideas. You need to get rid of the: "We've always done it this way" types in the executive team or, quite frequently, one layer below – what I call *the permafrost*. Do not underestimate the desire of the system to remain as it is.

Dr Joseph Riggio: *"If you want to make space for something new or different, you need to take something out of the space that you already have in it, because you've filled up all the space you've got. What is it that I am going to have to give up so that I can have something I don't have yet? Am I willing to give up what I have to get what I want? Oftentimes, the 'successful' people have filled up their space with those things that are most acknowledged as leading to what we call 'success' and they have no room left for the things that give them satisfaction or pleasure or fulfil those magical dreams."*

Many companies aren't willing to eat their own lunch. Kodak had the world's first digital camera, but they didn't want to bring it out because they thought it would upset their customers, the likes of Snappy Snaps. In fact, you and I were their customers, and Kodak completely missed out on the digital camera revolution. Kodak didn't know who their customer was. Most of the American railroad companies missed out on the coming of the aeroplane, because they said, "We're railroad companies". Canadian Pacific, who described themselves as a transportation company because they had a railroad and steamships simply saw aeroplanes as another transport mechanism. Canadian Pacific for many years had a very successful airline.

Walter de Silva after he left Alfa Romeo and became chief designer at Audi said **it's always dangerous to change. It's even more dangerous to stay the same.** There are certain plants that need fire to send off the cones with the seeds, in order to regenerate and propagate. And remember, if you don't burn the undergrowth, you may have forest fires later.

"Everything must change for everything to remain the same."
– The Leopard, Giuseppe Tomasi di Lampedusa

In the 1940s, Lockheed wanted to do interesting things, so they set up a "skunk works" across the road, which wasn't part of the mothership. "Skunk works" is widely used in business, engineering, and technical fields to describe a group within an organisation given a high degree of autonomy and unhampered by bureaucracy, with the task of working on advanced or secret projects, thinking the unthinkable, examining the status quo.

What does it look like through the other end of the telescope?

Through the other end of the telescope

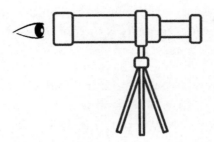

One of the most valuable and interesting things when someone new joins your company is when they ask why you do things a certain way. Pay attention to why they are asking and what answers they get. Frequently the response (while dressed up a bit) is: "Because we've always done them this way." There's a dictum that new employees are most valuable in their first three months because after that they have become part of the system.

It may be that even though you did a thoughtful job of hiring for attitude, you find yourself in the position that you need to fire someone. Don't wait around for the magic firing fairy to do the job for you. Just deal with it. Fire quick, hire slow and you won't go wrong.

Two ways to bring about change:

1. **Revolutionary:** destruction and disruption, overturn conventional wisdom, make space, look at things from the other end of the telescope. What does it look like from a competitor's point of view? From a customer's point of view? It's like a gyroscope, all the creativity is at the edges, but you need the solid centre. Ask: what if I had a magic wand and I woke up tomorrow and everything was fixed? What would it look like?
2. **Evolutionary:** change current thinking, use space, be iterative, sustainable, take another look. You don't have to clear out all the

cupboards today. Evolutionary only works when directionality is strong, and you know where the fairy-tale castle is. Then each day you can ask: is this taking us closer to our vision, or away from it? A former client, Casper de Bono, was quoted in the *FT*: "*I learnt from my father that creativity is the cheapest way to get added value from existing assets.*"

There are inherent risks in either strategy. In the 1960s and '70s, British Motor Corporation (BMC), which became British Leyland, would always have revolutionary cars. They're great. They're all brand new. But they never properly worked. Whereas Ford in the UK, was always evolutionary. The new engine for the next car would go into the final run of the existing car. So the new car starts with an already proven engine and gearbox, it was just a new body. You can argue which is better, but you must have change. This is true for us as humans. **If you keep on doing what you've always done, you'll keep on getting what you always got.**

Raul Vargus says, "*Organisations typically measure the risk of doing something, but very few organisations seriously measure the risk of not doing something. What is the risk of not winning the bet? That is typically not in the map of risk of evaluation of opportunities.*"

How are you going to respond to disruptive technologies? Are you going to risk eating your own lunch? Or are you going to let somebody else eat it?

David Luna from Gamma Digital[4] says: "*When you're the incumbent, it's of utmost importance to decide carefully what you view as disruptive or not. Using a vague definition or calling everything disruptive will certainly not help and could be your last move! Sure, it's to the benefit of every competitor to claim they are disrupting your industry.*"

---

4. Why Uber Is Not Disruptive and What Almost Everyone Around You Gets Wrong About It: https://www.gammabeyond.com/en/blog/why-uber-is-not-disruptive-and-what-almost-everyone-around-you-gets-wrong-about-it

Creating chaos causes untold confusion, especially in large corporations."

Alain Dromer's latest interest and investment is a classic example of turning the whole model upside down. Dromer's recruitment company for interims is wonderful because it views the candidate rather than the hiring company as its customer. The person who's going to deliver the work is the customer. Dromer: *"It's a very competitive market, there are thousands of businesses placing temporary workers with companies so **you have to think differently.** If all the existing businesses have one model, where their client is the corporate client employing the temp workers, then let's be different, not only through the technology, but also by this model. Let's focus on the individual people. In the STEM (science, technology, engineering and maths) industry, people want permanent jobs. The way to get a permanent job is to do good work as an interim. A happy temp worker knows that if they get a good reputation with the recruitment company, it may lead to a permanent employment. It's a win-win situation. So we focus on the individuals, make them happier, help them demonstrate that they are good at what they do, train them better. We rate them and let them rate the companies where they work. **We employ better people, who are better trained and happier**."*

Maybe your company does need to eat its children. Those mildly schizophrenic companies trying to be everything to everybody – like British Airways, with aspirations to be a premium international carrier whilst running an LLC in Europe, with holidaymakers loading 10kg of nostalgia into the overhead bins – will ultimately need to choose who they really are. Or they will have the decision made for them.

The hungry shopper never buys wisely

Is what you do valued? Is it valued around here? Whether the decision is made based on reading the signals, coming up with a strategy and executing plans or a good dose of paranoia doesn't matter. **Cre-**

ative destruction is a conscious, thoughtful process, and can become quite addictive. Cecil B DeMile once said: "Creativity is a drug I cannot live without."

An incredible visionary, Dee Hock was a founding father and former CEO of the Visa credit card association. Going strong into his nineties, until he recently passed away, his wisdom still holds[5]: *"Clean out a corner of your mind and creativity will instantly fill it."* He always hired on character and integrity, motivation and attitude. Hock was particularly interested in forms of organisation that are neither rigidly controlled nor anarchic, a hybrid he called *chaordic*.

Handelsbanken, a large Swedish bank, worked out that it's probably impossible to effectively control an organisation from a head office. You may think you do, but it's a complete delusion. They decided to decentralise and push everything out to the branches. Every branch has what's called the church spire policy, where their customers are as far as they can see from the church spire. The local manager has the authority to do what he needs to do.

An SME I chaired had been banking with RBS, at the time when RBS was packaging a group of branches into a "for sale" company to meet post bail-out European state aid rules. We opened an account as a backup with Handelsbanken. We wanted to buy the building we were in because we had cash – so why pay rent, we might as well buy the building and pay ourselves. It took two and a half months and RBS still hadn't come back with a firm proposal for the mortgage. On the off chance we contacted Handelsbanken. That same evening, the local manager replied, apologised for taking so long to get back to us, and gave us an "in principle, yes". This is the power of decentralisation.

I have always felt the secret of being successful in an international organisation is to be as far away from head office as possible and make

5. http://www.deewhock.com/

your numbers. They always have something closer to home to worry about.

What kind of CEO Do you want to be? Do you want to be a CEO that knows and controls everything? Or are you going to nurture real pockets of experience, real leadership, and let them get on with it?

Some prominent examples of disruptive technology that destroyed the incumbents include: Wikipedia wiping out encyclopedia sales; physical media such as newspapers and books being digitised; personal cameras being replaced by the ever-present smartphone; Blackberry falling by the wayside as messaging apps like WhatsApp stole their final glory; Blockbuster video to streaming Netflix; the everyday mechanical watch losing out to Smart and now the Apple Watch.

The first example of live streaming music is from more than 100 years ago, with the "electrophone" in 1880 transmitting music from Manchester to home telephones.[6] Apple was brave. The iPod was Apple's biggest selling product when they launched the iPhone, they knew that the iPhone would destroy iPod sales. And they were willing to do it. Same invention at different times. Sony should have developed the iPod, because they had the experience of the Walkman and had a vision of the future that had caused them to buy CBS Records and Colombia Pictures. Sony had seen the future of content seamlessly delivered on devices. It worked for Apple but not for them. Sony suffered from fear of disruption and cannibalisation.

Sun Tzu said: "In the midst of chaos, there is also opportunity."

Sometimes, you really have no choice. An article in the *FT*,[7] **How to launch a coronavirus app in one week:** *"It was crazy," Mr Jodal recalls. "We worked as a team, 24/7 . . . On Friday March 13 we had nothing, (two days later the Uruguayan Health Ministry approved the idea)*

6. Electrophone System: https://www.britishtelephones.com/electrophone.htm
7. FT, Michael Stott, December 13 2020, How to launch a coronavirus app in one week: https://on.ft.com/3qQ6ovt

and on Friday March 20 we had the app delivered." Nicolás Jodal assembled a team of 150 people from twelve private companies to deliver the impossible, develop an app to give advice to patients who thought they had Coronavirus – in less than seven days – beating massive teams from Google and Apple. Oh, for the freedom of a tight brief.

So you've got external and internal disruptors, you've got new ideas, the question remains: Are you going to ignore the signals? Or, are you going to make your own move? Are you ready to make a brave decision?

"To continue in one path is to go backward."– Igor Stravinsky

Alex Bello described how he had everything lined up, made an emotional decision, made an intellectual decision, but there was still a chance he could stay if he wanted. But when he went back after his sabbatical he felt like he wasn't quite as good as he had been. What should he do? Walk out without a laid-out future? There is a risk as the hungry shopper seldom buys wisely.

Alex Bello: *"I went back. I didn't tell the Italian Airforce that I was still exploring, they didn't ask any questions. I got my flying skills refreshed, went into the drill, was on the roster, and then I was tasked for a search and rescue mission. It all started out on the wrong foot, the errors were piling up, some things didn't go well, we had an in-flight mishap, but nothing was too bad, and I was able to tell the story coming back. We had some light damage and people were frightened. If I were to analyse the key reason, it's that probably my decision-making process wasn't up to the high level that was required. So I needed to leave. I was leaving security, a job for life, to take a one-year contract. I labelled it good enough to make that transition. It came with a lot of uncertainties. I was feeling quite frightened to be honest. It wasn't perfect in hindsight, nine years later. But it was 'good enough'."*

Tesla has done marvellous work to wake up the world. If you get close to a Tesla you'll see the joins don't quite line up. It depends if that's important to you or not. It's not to Musk. Who's going to get there quicker? Is it going to be easier for Audi and friends to learn to do electric when they understand industrial production? Or is it easier for Tesla to learn industrial production? Or is Musk's "ecosystem" with high-speed chargers just for Tesla drivers the real differentiator. At this point, the disrupter competition is good for everyone.

Thinking about creative destruction and change, it's interesting that although we were very fond of our LPs we were willing to go to CDs and then streaming which shows the relative lack of stickiness. When I was choosing my new career before I settled on mentoring, I asked myself: What is going to become disintermediated by the internet and technology? One that I thought would be significantly impacted and still surprises me that hasn't been fully disintermediated yet is house sales; we still have estate agents and people mostly don't like estate agents – interesting!

Timing is everything

Bill Clinton said: "The price of doing the same old thing is far higher than the price of change."[8]

Timing is everything. I've traded a little on my own account, I made some really good trades and I made money on gold and sterling. The reason I don't trade a lot is that I'm great on direction, but I'm not very good on timing. I mistakenly believe once I've seen it, everybody can see it. And that's not true. As John Maynard Keynes allegedly said, "Markets can stay irrational longer than you can stay solvent."

You can't be everything to everybody all the time.

Jane Garvey, a British radio presenter, and one of the top twenty-five

8. Public Papers of the Presidents of the United States: William J. Clinton, 1993: (ed. Best Books on, 1994) – ISBN: 9781623767907

highest paid presenters at the BBC, bowed out of Woman's Hour after thirteen years: "The reason I'm going is because I could have stayed. I sometimes think the hardest thing is to change when it's the last thing you want to do, but probably the best thing to do. It's the best thing for the programme. I really do mean it."[9]

What are you going to change?

It's a little threatening, isn't it? The positive side of the destroyer is re-creation. But you need to be brave, bold and playful to make space for the new.

"We've all been guilty at one point or another in our careers of boasting of perfect hindsight. It's a terrible sin. If you don't make sure your questions and concerns are acted upon, it doesn't count."
– Jack Welch

The funny thing is, when you decide, when you truly make the decision to change, the work has already started.

Milton Erickson, to modern hypnotherapy what Jung was to psychiatry, said: "Change will lead to insight more often than insight will lead to change." I often say to clients (usually once the relationship is properly established), **"Once you decide you want to do the work the work has already started."**

My boss, the chairman of Oster Communications flew over from Chicago between Christmas and New Year. I'd been CEO for about eight months and I was waiting for sign off on my first budget. We're sitting for a metaphorical fireside chat, two chairs, glowing embers, to go through the budget. You know how every time you poke a log on a fire and a bit drops off, then you poke it again and again until there's nothing left – that's what he was doing with my budget. He was just poking it to pieces in front of my eyes. I thought, I can't take any more of this, what's the worst that can happen? I could get fired. No, it's not.

9. Interview Evening Standard December 31st 2020

The worst that could happen was I'd have to sit through another hour of this. So I moved in my chair just a touch. He was a very intuitive man and he literally stopped mid-sentence and said: "Anyway, enough. What can we do to help you to get this budget right?" He sensed the entire balance of power in the room had changed. All leverage had just disappeared.

If you're a creator, scorched earth may suit you. Jack Welch famously said he was not an entrepreneur. I understand I'm not an entrepreneur, but I am very entrepreneurial within systems, which is a completely different skill set. I would describe myself as an "intrepreneur" I wouldn't want to start a business. I'd have to go out and buy a business and then turn it into the best.

Reinvention can be delicate, or not

"Forty percent of global CEOs think their organisation will no longer be economically viable in ten years' time, if it continues on its current course. That stark data point underscores a dual imperative facing 4,410 CEOs from 105 countries and territories who responded to PwC's 26th Annual Global CEO Survey. Most of those CEOs feel it's critically important for them to reinvent their businesses for the future[10]."
– PwC's 26th Annual Global CEO Survey

Nokia reinvented itself, again and again.[11] They had a culture and tradition of reinventing which worked for them – most of the time. Some people love the excitement of a blank sheet of paper. Others like me, prefer a little bit in place to remodel, reshape and move. I am iterative

---

10. Evolve or die, say 4,410 chief executives in our 2023 CEO Survey. But are they spending enough time on business reinvention? Many tell us no. https://www.pwc.com/gx/en/issues/c-suite-insights/ceo-survey-2023.html
11. From papermill to rubber boots, to makers of cables, televisions and mobile phones.

by nature. So I would be useless building my own house. I would be brilliant at taking a building adding on a wing or two, putting another floor in etc.

"A new idea is delicate. It can be killed by a sneer or a yawn; it can be stabbed to death by a quip and worried to death by a frown on the right man's brow." – Ovid

There's a cost to destruction, are you willing to pay it? This is sometimes a personal cost, other times organisational.

Many people have changed direction mid-career. Lucy Kellaway, former *Financial Times* journalist and creator of Martin Lukes and the world of "a-b glöbâl" retrained and became a trainee teacher in an inner-city secondary school in 2017 at the age of fifty-seven. She is a co-founder of the educational charity Now Teach. She has just written a book, *Re-educated,* about her experiences – including having one's assumptions, about oneself, and others, thoroughly and swiftly dismantled.

My colleague, Geoff Tudhope, has carried out consultancy work with the ForeSight Group in Sweden. He frequently mentions one of their phrases: Think Big, Act Small, Start Now. By accident, I modified it slightly: *"Think big. Start small. Begin today".* It's a great way to think about creating the future.

In the US, most people are interested in wealth creation. In Europe, generally, most people are interested in wealth preservation. These different attitudes are similar to leadership drivers: are you there just not to screw up? Or are you willing to be brave?

My client Dr Kock reinvented himself. He was a senior executive, successful, with a nice journey to the office, pop on the train with a view of the Rhein and then, watching for the trams, just walk across the road from the Badischer Bahnof. Yet he deliberately reinvented himself. Michael Kock: *"I set myself a ten-year deadline for substantial changes. Even within the ten years you need to be careful that you're not doing the same thing all the time, because you end up in the plateau. I never want to be one of the guys on the deck of the Titanic saying, 'It was an honour gentlemen.'* **You cannot transform a Titanic into a flotilla of speedboats."**

The ultimate re-inventor was David Bowie: *"The truth of course is that there is no journey. We are arriving and departing all at the same time."* I can just about say I went to school with him; we crossed paths, just, me arriving as a first year with him departing the sixth form.

In *Good Business: Leadership, Flow, and the Making of Meaning*, Mihaly Csikszentmihalyi, Hungarian psychologist and professor of psychology at the Peter F. Drucker School of Management says: "It is impossible to survive as a leader in business without enjoying what one does. The job would become too stressful, the hours too long, and the temptation to spend more and more time on diversions too strong." This means that leaders and their employees need to find new sources of motivation – passion, conscience and a sense of duty – rather than just the bottom line, as their main drivers.

Sometimes you need to reinvent yourself.

People make the mistake of thinking they can keep adding and adding and adding. I'm an introvert by nature. I've got a finite capacity of the number of people I can see in a week. If I do more than that I am worn out. If I want to go and meet some new interesting people, who am I not going to be meeting now? "For humans the limit is around 132 individuals," says Dr Harré. Professor Mikhail Prokopenko and Dr Harré have calculated how that limit – known as Dunbar's Number – is reached.[12] Fortunately for introverts like me, "To connect together a group of 132 individuals we estimate the average number of links each individual has to be able to maintain is between four and five," the researchers said. So, it's not necessary to have 500 "best friends" on Facebook. Phew!

12. How many friends do you need to maintain your social network?
   https://www.abc.net.au/news/science/2016-05-18/statistics-reveal-how-many-links-you-need-for-social-networks/7425572

Karl Moore, associate fellow, Green Templeton College, Oxford University, claims in his soon to be published book, *We Are All Ambiverts Now*, that while we should celebrate our natural tendency – whether that's to extroversion, introversion or as an ambivert – to be a leader, you need a degree of flexibility in order to meet the varied demands of the job. The emergent nature of being an ambivert – the listening skills and empathy of an introvert, coupled with the enthusiasm and social confidence of the extrovert – is what makes for exceptional leadership in turbulent times.

It's not possible to measure these qualities on a standard intelligence test. Embedded in what scientists call "cognitive flexibility"[13] are traits such as creativity, imagination, curiosity and empathy. These are needed for humans, teams and businesses to flourish. Leaders with high cognitive flexibility bounce back from setbacks, are more creative, are prone to fewer biases, and have a better quality of life. Someone, Einstein I think, once said: *"Creativity is intelligence having fun."*

Piers in Your Pocket: Too much is too much

Enzo Ferrari allegedly said that the secret to success was to build one car less than the order book.

I suspect people, individually, can have a kind of itch or desire for destruction. It's important to know if that itch is because you're bored and you need some entertainment or it is a calm, inner voice that knows it's time for change. If your "passport" photo is old, and people don't recognise the current you, then it might be time to move on.

Maybe ask yourself the following questions:

13. IQ tests can't measure it, but "cognitive flexibility" is key to learning and creativity: https://theconversation.com/iq-tests-cant-measure-it-but-cognitive-flexibility-is-key-to-learning-and-creativity-163284

1. Are you the destroyer and clearing the space? Or is something else clearing the space for you?
2. Are you willing to be the master of your own creative destruction?
3. Are you able to handle both intention and execution?
4. How are you avoiding falling into the traps of being a dunce or a dullard, a gung-ho zealot, or an escapist dreamer?
5. How are you paying attention to the signals to set intention and then the execution to be magical?

It's important to understand that all the learning is in the doing. It doesn't matter how many books you read, how many lectures we go to, how many people give us advice, we only actually learn it as we do it. It's the turbulence of change with the reward that means, ultimately, that **sacred cows do make the finest burgers.** You may not enjoy the process, but I'll put money on the quality of your results. Consider it managed recklessness.

Chapter X: If I'd done an MBA I would have called this chapter "The Pivot Point"

*"We have two lives, and the second begins
when we realise we only have one."*
– Confucius

By now maybe it's dawning on you, it's not simple. It's not black and white. It's all about nuance. You can't be somebody else. You can only be yourself. You have to be vulnerable. This is a journey.

We can't all be pope or emperor

We've journeyed from our innocence, the time when we step into the world, how we learn we have to be strong, and then we find that pure strength doesn't get us everywhere. Strength plus compassion is a better model, using the power of ideas and beginning to get others to follow us. Now we've got to the point where we're talking about three things, and they're all connected in different ways. The first is about clearing space either as revolution or destruction, chosen or forced upon us. Second, now you've got some space how can you be creative? The amazingly creative people usually do one of two things: build a kingdom for them to be in charge of, or they go freelance, wander and are more nomadic, flowing with the energy of the magician, who takes things and makes the whole always more than the sum of the parts. You've seen the opportunity and the pitfalls of destruction and what it can bring you. Even more so you've seen the dangers of not doing something.

Everything we've seen so far probably feels familiar. That's great. You can have a very happy, successful life, avoiding the challenges and disruption. If that's what you want, **then now is a perfect moment to gently close this book … now.**

Too many people have been inculcated by parents, education systems and peer groups to think that the top of the pyramid is the only place to be, and there are only two jobs worth having: emperor or pope. Maybe you are a really good solid middle manager, and you should learn how to be happy? That was my dad – he was truly content. Continually turning down promotions as he liked (although the term hadn't been invented then) his "work-life balance". Keeping up with the Joneses is a never-ending battle and something he had no interest in being part of. You have to understand there's always someone with a bigger boat. There's always somewhere with an even more exclusive VIP list than the VIP list you're on. If you thought your Gold or Platinum airline card was special, sorry to disappoint but there are VVIP lists – Qantas has its Chairman's Lounge, Cathay Pacific has Diamond Invitation and, made famous by George Clooney's character Ryan Bingham in *Up in the Air*, AA has Concierge Key with a phone number just for you …

So before you become too entranced with gorgeous gadgets, slick slide decks, and mesmerising video displays, let's just remember that information is not knowledge, knowledge is not wisdom, and wisdom is not foresight. Each grows out of the other, and we need them all. There was a glorious moment during my Master's where one of the tutors said, "For this exercise, it's probably best if we leave the gods and goddesses of coaching at the door." So, let's leave the gods, goddesses, popes and emperors behind us at the door.

If you're ready, then what we're talking about next is the awakening, something which is deep in every history and culture. Whether it's a religious resurrection, or an ancient traditional bathing in sacred waters, the age of eighteen, indoctrination into some kind of cult, or becoming a master of an ancient guild.

It's time to become a master. Make your masterpiece. This requires the greatest bravery of all because you must start being really true to yourself. So, do you really want this? Maybe there's a whisper, listen carefully this could be the call to your vocation.

Pilots have an expression: the point of no return. The PNR is the point beyond which one must continue on one's current course of action because turning back is physically impossible, for example, not enough fuel, difficult, dangerous or prohibitively expensive. Likewise, accelerating along the runway, after you get to a certain velocity (V1) it's better to take off or otherwise you're going to go through the fence at the end of the runway and hit all those cars in the car park. It's frequently better to continue going forward rather than turning around to go back. If you've read this far, and you're still reading, and interested, you're possibly at your own PNR.

Gail Sheehy's iconic bestseller, *Passages: Predictable Crises of Adult Life*, discusses how through adult life there are inevitable personality and sexual changes as we pass our twenties, thirties, forties, and beyond. These passages or pivots are probably mirrored in your business life. Who you were in your previous role is different to who you will be in your future role. You don't need to go out and buy a red sports car to make the transition. You might not even recognise yourself on the other side, but you will start to see the path. My friend, Albert, could have been a world-famous concert pianist. He's thirty-something and decided that variety, collaboration and autonomy are more important for him than the straight jacket of only playing ten popular audience pleasing concert pieces. Instead, he explores ways to perform and collaborate in unique ways in exciting and unusual venues. This liminal moment of deciding doesn't come at set ages, it comes at pivot points. But not always smoothly. It's like giving birth, sometimes it needs a helping hand.

It's like that flash of lightning in a dark moody sky. In that second, everything is illuminated, and you can see the path. Even though it goes dark again, it's too late, you've seen it. You know where everything is, you know the shape of things to come. You can't pretend you don't know. It's a revelatory moment – the apotheosis.

"If the path before you is clear, you're probably on someone else's."
– Joseph Campbell

Caspar de Bono is the son of the legendary Edward,[1] who sadly died in June 2021. In August 2021, Caspar decided to re-energise his father's work after serendipitously forging his own way for the previous twenty-five years.

Coming Full Circle – Caspar de Bono

In 1995, I was teaching my father's work as a trainer in public seminars for businesspeople, in London, with an audience of twenty to forty people over one or two days. They were going well, but there was a question that I was asked that I didn't have a good answer to: *How do these ideas apply to business?*

My answer was quite weak. I simply said, "I don't know. I'm a psychology graduate."

I thought this wasn't good enough, so at the end of that day I picked up a copy of the *Financial Times*, because I thought *"they must know about business"* and I started reading so that the next time they asked me the question, I'd be able to say, I'm glad you asked me, let me give you an example.

I struggled to understand the *FT*. Fortunately, there was a quar-

---

1. Edward Charles Francis Publius de Bono was a Maltese physician, psychologist, author, inventor, philosopher, and consultant. He originated the term lateral thinking, wrote the book Six Thinking Hats, and was a proponent of the teaching of thinking as a subject in schools.

ter page ad for a two-year business graduate training scheme at the *Financial Times*. I thought great, *"they must know about business,"* I'll apply, I'll do that for two years, and then I'll be able to answer that question better and bring complementary knowledge instead of simply replicating what my father taught me. It would also be a way of escaping his shadow.

I applied, I got in, and I stayed for twenty-five years.

I left the *FT* in July 2021, and now I'm back working on and developing my father's work. And I've learned something about business, intellectual property and digital transformation in the meantime.

If I'd picked up *The Economist* on that fateful day I'd have travelled down a different path. I'd always really wanted to be a painter, the "career's computer" at school told me I would be a deep-sea diver, I was determined I was never going to work in the City, and I certainly wasn't going to commute. That serendipitous moment when I picked up the *FT* gave me an unexpected chance to apply the creative thinking I'd been teaching in a job that didn't even exist when I was at school (digital licensing). It couldn't have been planned. Now, I'm bringing what I learned back to help with re-energising my father's work.

Caspar didn't sit around waiting for luck to find him; he actively searched for answers without expectation of what he might find. He spotted the signals in the system (the questions) and acted upon them. From the outside it may look like a perfectly orchestrated play where all the doors open and close at the right moment, and the right people step in like actors waiting to read their lines. In reality, there are many "right moments" and "right people"; it's having the flexibility to improvise and change course that matters, because as Edward de Bono said: *"If you never change your mind, why have one?"*

Greg Simidian says: *"A lot of life is about timing. You could have all that other stuff but if you don't have the right timing … You can interpret time in different ways, sometimes you're just not reading the signals, sometimes you truly are, it's a really instinctive, visceral thing. Part head, part gut, part body. You just can't force it, because stepping up is not easy. Be honest with yourself, are you ready for it?"*

So, are you going to go into the forest, into the darkest place on your own? Are you going to come out vulnerable and honest, and whole and human? Are you ready to rise into your Sir Percival role, the original hero in the quest for the Grail? With all your wisdom, knowledge and experience will you be able to keep a childlike sense of wonder and beginner's brain? And hold those two at the same time? Or are you just going to continue to dance around the edges? Because if you're willing, this is the moment where you get your cloak and your sword …

You're shedding the snake of its skin. Its rebirth. You die and are resurrected.

Luke: I won't fail you. I'm not afraid.
Yoda: You will be … You will be.
Star Wars: Episode V – The Empire Strikes Back

The question isn't: what do I have to do to be CEO?

The question is: how do I have to be to be a decent human in service to others? Even if I'm afraid …

Should the leader, as Robert K. Greenleaf believes: "[be] as a servant to their employees"; a "servant leader" focused on growing their people. "Do they, while being served, become healthier, wiser, freer, more autonomous, more likely themselves to become servants?" In Chapter 8, we'll take a look at how you can "rule your kingdom", and why it's important to accept this mighty responsibility as a servant CEO. Real kingship is in service to the people.

You are not just your brain

This is the chapter where it's time to do some thinking. How do you do your thinking? Where do you do your thinking? Do you think you do your thinking in your head? Some of it? Do you do some of your thinking talking to yourself? I would respectfully suggest a lot of your thinking is through conversations with your gut. If you are currently using multiple layers of rationality to explain and justify what you're doing, and your gut says, I don't like this, maybe it's time to start paying more attention to your body.

The mind and body (especially the heart and gut) are inextricably connected, the mind influences the body and the body influences the mind – this is the embodied experience.[2] Many features of cognition – your understanding of concepts and categories, how you reason or judge – are shaped by aspects of your entire body. You may have been ignoring these gut feelings, but aspects of your body are communicating with you.[3] It's time to listen to the whole, to get the full picture. The Greeks had the humours. The inner traditions of Hinduism gave us the Chakras, meaning wheel. The humours and the Chakras tell us that paying attention to the mind and body is nothing new. It's about codifying what we sense – now we choose cognition, neuroscience and gut microbiome to describe what is going on.

Are you in the right place personally, emotionally and physically? Are you in the right company? The right job? The right boss? Do you have the interest, energy and focus to succeed?

2. A Brief Guide to Embodied Cognition: Why You Are Not Your Brain: https://blogs.scientificamerican.com/guest-blog/a-brief-guide-to-embodied-cognition-why-you-are-not-your-brain/
3. In an article in the Irish Times, *Buy bubbles, bet big and backache – Soros's secrets:* https://www.irishtimes.com/business/personal-finance/buy-bubbles-bet-big-and-backache-soros-s-secrets-1.1893639, Soros's son claims Soros Snr makes many of his investment decisions relying on "animal instincts", in particular spasms in his back.

Alex Bello (speaking about being a fighter pilot in the Italian Airforce): "Up to the point where I was starting to seriously explore new avenues, I was motivated. The internal focus on the flying was 100%. In flying, it's like a switch, on or off, binary. Once you know that you don't have that focus, like anything in life, it's a matter of mitigating risk. If you're not 100% focused, but 99% focused, in flying, that's not good enough."

Good ideas come from good places. So, it's best to be in a good place. The only "place" you'll ever always be is in your body. So start there. Look after yourself, be balanced enough to sleep well, eat the right food, take exercise, maybe meditate – or at least get some quiet "you" time. There are signals in the system to track.

Pat Ogden, creator of Sensorimotor Psychotherapy[4] has an elegant model helping us understand how we organise and process experience through five distinct levels of perceptions that she calls "Core Organizers." Each level represents a different way of engaging with experience. Whilst developed as a somatic approach to therapy, it can be used as a practical way to "check in with yourself".

1. Cognition, including our thoughts and the meanings we attribute to ourselves and the world
2. Emotions, including feeling, tones and moods
3. Five sense "perceptions" or what comes to us through our five senses
4. Movements, both large and small, voluntary and involuntary
5. Inner body sensations, such as pain in the heart when thinking of a lost love, tightness in the throat accompanying the wish to cry, or a pang in the gut when overwhelmed by sadness.

This framework is a reminder about how to choose well. Pivot point choices are key, whether it's a change in job, industry or maybe even a

---

4. Sensorimotor Psychotherapy Interventions for Trauma and Attachment. Pat Ogden https://sensorimotorpsychotherapy.org

call to vocation. You can go through these levels top down or bottom up to process the present moment experiences.

What would it take to be the same person at home and at work? Personally, I've never known how you could do anything other than that, but, in case you do, maybe time to drop the mask?

Children don't have this problem. When you ask a child what they will do in their future they say: I want to be a doctor/be a train driver/be a nurse/be an astronaut/be a CEO (maybe not). They don't say they want to *do* things; they want to *be* things. It's a completely embodied, holistic idea. They won't be wearing a mask. I love *being* a coach, I don't *do* coaching.

Some days life really is like a box of chocolates, you never know what you're going to get.

My mum was slightly underwhelmed when, at our family Christmas, I bought her a box of chocolates. I don't think she was completely disappointed by the gift – it was a very large box. And she politely said, thank you very much. I smiled.

Over the New Year when she was back home, I called: "Have you opened your chocolates?" "No." I urged her to try one. Finally, she relented and opened the big box of disappointment, only to find a card inside.

She was quite impressed and wanted to know how the card got inside the cellophane wrapping – I'm an ingenious fellow with a razor blade.

"Open the card!" It was an invitation to a holiday, anywhere in the world, with her one and only son. "So, how did you get the card into the box?" she asked.

I finally managed to change the subject from my sleight of hand, and she decided where she'd like to visit – Switzerland. My mum was great, but, ten days with your mother? As a grown-up? I decided I would do whatever mum wanted to do for ten days. It was perfect. I subjugated myself and became a seven-year-old again. We went to Lucerne, and sat outside in the June sunshine, enjoying afternoon tea by the river. All very Swiss, for what felt like £25 for a cup of tea. There was a march celebrating 100 years of the chimney sweeps of Lucerne. Mum was very mystical and believed in synchronicity; she was bowled over when they gave her a little lapel badge – a good luck forever sign.

Suddenly, the restaurant staff started to tidy things up. They quickly began putting everything away. We could see a bit of cloud coming over the mountain, but it was still far away, and the sun was shining. The waiters and waitresses were acting as if they had heard the two-minute warning of disaster. Lock everything down! What on earth was going on?

Splot. The first drop of rain. By then all the tables, except ours, was under cover. Splot. Splot. Big, heavy, fast fat splots. It was like a tropical storm. We ran and hid under a canopy.

This is what happens when you don't pay attention to the signals in the system. When you ignore the local knowledge you get drenched. When you override the signals you look like a fool and his mother.

It's all very well being able to track the signals, whether internal or external, but you're also supposed to take some action.

Take action, get aligned, recommit or reinvent

If you're not aligned, how can you make good decisions? The brain, the gut and everything must be aligned so you know who you are. What's your narrative? Is it true? Is it aligned?

The MBA folks call this the pivot point, because that's when you're making a pivot or a change. But it may just be a recommitment. All good relationships and good marriages have levels of either overt or covert recommitment. You have to wake up, this is your life. Be honest. You have to wake up every morning and ask the question, do I still want to be here? If I do, am I doing the things that align with this decision? There's a danger, right now, of becoming a person in a leadership position – a PILP rather than a true leader.

Being a coach and mentor doesn't generally include me telling people what to do. They have to do what *they* want to do. It does, though, include me pointing out risks, dangers and potentially "suboptimal" decisions. I was mentoring the CEO of a FTSE 100 company, I said: "Are you really sure that's a good idea?" After a long pause, he said: "You know, I think you might be onto something. As I think about it with you, its not looking so good." You can't be afraid to speak truth to power. Be careful you don't end up with a shiny plaque with empty meaningless words in your reception.

So pay attention, don't pivot into PILPness.

Do you want to reinvent yourself here? Or somewhere else?

> *"The only true voyage of discovery, the only fountain of Eternal Youth, would be not to visit strange lands but to possess other eyes, to behold the universe through the eyes of another, of a hundred others, to behold the hundred universes that each of them beholds, that each of them is."* – Marcel Proust[5]

Are you ready to recommit? Or reinvent?

Maybe look for opportunities to do something new – learn a language or a new skill. Improve your network. Refresh yourself with a makeover or a new haircut. Get the red sports car. Because if you decide you're unhappy with what you've got you have to take action and do something. Don't become a victim of familiarity, of the known. Wake up and smell the coffee.

Your gift could be to create and hold the space for others, so they can

---

5. 'La Prisonnière', Volume V 'Remembrance of Things Past', Marcel Proust, Translated from the French by C. K. Scott Moncrieff

learn to speak truth to power in safety. It's not just about supporting the next generation. It's much bigger than this.

I had a coach years ago, he said: "Piers, the problem is you're too comfortable. You've never been fired. You've worked out a deal where they pay you just a little bit too much and leave you alone. You've got no incentive to do anything different."

He was right. High level of autonomy? Tick. Pay me a bit over the odds? Tick. Treat me nicely? Tick. Treat me special? Tick. My SCARF psychological needs (see Chapter 4 for a reminder) were all met. I had become borderline complacent in my comfort. If these needs are not met – status, certainty, autonomy, relatedness, fairness – you feel the nudge to move on.

Barry Schwartz, in *The Paradox of Choice – Why More is Less* says: *"Autonomy and freedom of choice are critical to our well-being, and choice is critical to freedom and autonomy."*

I always knew I was never going to be emperor or pope, so I didn't have this problem, but I sometimes found my parents early messaging: *"the world is your oyster, make of it what you wish"* slightly scary ... too many possibilities and a sense of unsaid expectations that were not necessarily mine. You could argue that because I'm contented, I never had real ambition. And as I look back, I wonder just what I could have achieved if I'd actually been ambitious. I put the time in, but in some way I feel I've kind of strolled through life.

It takes too much energy for me to be anybody other than myself.

Warren Bennis, who was widely known as being a pioneer in the contemporary field of Leadership studies, believed that: *"Becoming a leader is synonymous with becoming yourself. It is precisely that simple and also that difficult."*

Many people come back off a programme all charged up, where they have been told, set and write down your goals. So they do. They set wonderful goals – goals which aren't necessarily things they want, or things they need, or things that suit them. How to choose wisely, how to adjust, how to recheck in with yourself to see if these goals are what you really want? No one talks about those things. **If you don't choose wisely you will end up choosing again.** This process of reinvention can be quite painful. Greg Simidian: "My reinvention process wasn't a quick one. I needed some space to reset, clear the decks, breathe and make an unencumbered certain decision on the next step."

How do you reach a level of complete self-awareness? My mentor, Joseph Riggio, is writing a book about that very question.

Radical Self-Awareness: Who's asking me these questions that are coming to me from me? – Joseph Riggio

You can't choose unless *you're* choosing. If you're simply carrying out the impositions of others, the desires they have imposed upon you, since the time of your birth, and you've begun to think those thoughts are your thoughts, then there really is no choice involved at all.

You can't make good choices if *you* can't choose.

In my new book I call it going back to the magical child. When you were that magical child, and the world existed for you in all its glory. The choice has to be made to ultimately fulfil who you've decided you wanted to become when you grew up.

That leads you to this decision point – what does that actually mean? The challenge is it may take you wildly off track from what it is you thought you *should* be doing and the last twenty, thirty, forty, fifty years of investment you've made into what you *have* been doing.

The lucky ones figured out along the way that those don't have to be two different things, they can actually do what they're doing – running an investment group, being a paediatric surgeon, riding on the back of a garbage truck in the streets of

---

> London – whatever it is, and they can incorporate those fascinations into whatever they do.
>
> My purpose is to fulfil this dream that I've always carried within me – and every path leads to the possibility of the dream being fulfilled. I just have to remember that that's what I'm doing.

When we sold the FutureSource business I was too young to retire … or probably more accurately, not rich enough to retire and live in the style to which I had become accustomed. So what should I do? That same thought had been nagging me for a couple of years before the sale. After each added responsibility there was an opportunity to move on, I'd already got the itch after running FutureSource for ten years. I was ready. Then we had a three-year buy out deal all set up so I agreed to stay to do the deal; but then my buyer went into Chapter 11, owing $2.8 billion. So suddenly, I wasn't going to get the cheque to pay for my bottom drawer pictures of the villa and the yacht.

I had to rebuild something anyway, so was I going to stay or go now? I decided I wanted to go. I didn't really want another big executive job because I had had the perfect executive job for me. Big enough that it was a substantial challenge, but small enough so there was still some intimacy and it was manageable and enjoyable. I've also lived in my house now for thirty-five years, so why move, it is perfect. I live in an area of great beauty, in a conservation area, on a private road with no through traffic, with foxes and squirrels. I can walk out of the house at seven twenty and be sitting down for breakfast in the City at eight. Why more, why bigger? There are no pockets in a shroud.

In terms of the pandemic, we might have all been in the same storm, but we were not all in the same boat. I am fortunate that my "boat" is really very special.

The great artist, Joaquín Sorolla y Bastida, was a master at painting boats. (Do you like the segue?) In the late nineteenth and early twentieth centuries he was able to capture the sun glinting off a mainsail better than even his contemporaries, Monet or Cezanne. He had such a way with a dab of white paint. That didn't stop him from being another potentially starving painter, and, while he had won a number of medals in his early career, it wasn't until he exhibited in New York that he achieved major financial success. In 1909 he exhibited 356 paintings, 195 of which sold. Of course, he could have stayed in Europe and mourned his lack of success.

Through my reinvention, I became a coach, mentor, facilitator and trusted advisor to senior executives.

So, would you rather be CEO of a small manufacturing business or marketing director of a FTSE 100 company? What's the prestige, the status? In the past directorships were very important. Now the "strive-to place" is being on the ExCo. For me status is much less important than autonomy. When I was a money broker, I bought a lovely silk tie at a jumble sale. A colleague who loved my tie said he was jealous that I was able to openly admit I bought it at a jumble sale. When people start new, tentative careers later in life when asked what they do, they often say, "I used to be X" before adding their new interest. It's interesting and a shame that we have to explain why we're poor artists or pickle makers in Brooklyn rather than a corporate Titan.

Greg Simidian said, when I asked him about his new venture: *"It's wonderful not to talk to investment bankers."*

I wonder how Albert feels when he's in the presence of an incredible concert pianist, enjoying all the trappings of a global life. Does he feel that should be him? Or does he appreciate the different things his choice has brought him? If you've realised that you're not going to be emperor or pope, is that okay? You might end up as the Governor of Palestine, a bishop or a division head – is that enough? We'll see in later chapters how this fear of missing out, paradoxically, wanes as you get older.

Our smallest Piers in Your Pocket: Are you in the right place? At the right time?

"Have no fear of perfection – you'll never reach it." – Salvador Dali

When your thoughts and actions are aligned, recommit to the task, and put yourself in the right place at the right time when you are ready.

I always ask people are you in this job to win? Or are you there to not lose?

Awareness is the beginning of freedom.

Nothing in life is as bad as in our imagination.

And remember our old friend: "signals in the system". Track wisely and take action.

So you're still reading, which probably means that you've decided that you want to do something with your career. So do you know which way you're heading yet?

Chapter 8: My Mother met a gypsy in a car park

"All is as thinking makes it so."
– Marcus Aurelius

Words create worlds. So let's make sure the words we are using and the images we are projecting on our internal video screen are taking us in the direction we want to travel. Most people overestimate what they can achieve in a year, and severely underestimate what they can achieve in a decade. Don't be seduced by the lure and lunacy of goal setting because the risk is you may get your goals. Directionality is much more important, taking you in the direction you want to go and creating the opportunity to react when things come up.

The day they thought they'd lost me

We all enjoyed my mother's memorial service – although seven and half years earlier than expected.

My mother was an enigma; a practical, caring "top of her profession" career woman who organised and labelled everything with the enthusiasm of a good Virgo – who I also suspect had a stationery shop in a previous life. She was a fast driving, wayward, other-worldly type of person who appreciated a late afternoon Martini and enjoyed adventures. She was the only person I knew who didn't return from the dump empty-handed but with newly discovered treasure. She once met a gypsy in a car park. The gypsy grabbed her hand, coins were passed (or, knowing my mother more likely a folded note) and a lifeline was read. The gypsy told my mother, "You will live till you are three years short of a hundred". She believed the prediction, and because she believed the prediction absolutely, I think we also believed the prediction. My sister and I were genuinely surprised when she died a few weeks short of her ninetieth birthday. She had reassured us that she would slow down when she was ninety-five; she was still going strong, living independently, loving life and always with a project on the go right until the very end.

I inherited my mother's certainty – in symbols, synchronicity and connectedness and a little of her waywardness – fortunately balanced with my father's sense of humour, curiosity in the world and healthy scepticism. I was ten years old. It was a very cold, very long winter and I had blocked adenoids. I was prescribed a product called Duranate, a sulphonamide antibiotic, to clear the infection. My lovely lady doctor had succumbed to the pharmaceutical talk on the superiority of sulphonamides in the hope of unblocking my rather infected adenoids. At that time many people had mild penicillin allergies, causing blotches and itchy skin, but there was a very low rate of reaction to sulphonamides, perhaps less than one in a million. Unfortunately, when you are that "one in a million" the reaction tends to be quite spectacular.

Between Christmas and New Year, I started with a fever, getting red and blotchy, and it looked like I was having some kind of allergic reaction. Everyone was getting very worried so I was taken to an isolation ward at the hospital. I was experiencing what's technically known as Stevens Johnson Syndrome, a type of toxic epidermal necrolysis (TEN). In simple terms, the body goes into shock. I went into a terrible toxic shock, my skin started to fall away from my body like sheets of dried parchment; it was as if I'd had third degree burns. I lost 80% of my skin. I'd wake up in the morning, parts of my body sticking to the bed, and as I was pulled away from the white cotton sheets, I'd leave behind the odd toenail or fingernail that had fallen off, inches of skin, matted hair. All my mucus surfaces were terribly damaged.

On one particular day, I remember lying in the bed, my mother sitting in the corner just being with me, as she had done day after day, and I felt like I was floating above the bed, as if I was in a warm cocoon above the bed although the cocoon didn't have any ends to it, so I guess it was more like a tube or a tunnel. Years later during a conversation, my mother told me she knew I wasn't there at that moment; she had said, "Where are you?" I replied, "I'm outside the hospital." She said, "Oh, do you want to come back?" Quite typical of my mother. Apparently, I said "Yes". And so she talked me all the way back down through the avenue of trees, back into the room.

That, curiously, was the day they thought they'd lost me.

What you're projecting on the screen in your head is what you get. While in hospital I made an announcement that I was going to be home for Easter. The typical length of time for a recovering toxic shock patient, of my severity, is six months. I had a terrible case (possibly one of the worst cases in UK medical history) but also the best response and repair time. I was back home within five weeks. In my case, when ignorance was useful, it would have been pure folly to be wise.[1] So you know, there's something about this mind malarkey, and the power of lining up your thoughts, and that's what we're going to investigate in this chapter.

"You can analyse the past, but you need to design the future."
– Edward de Bono

Juggling with chainsaws

A former sales director who worked for me, when describing what it was like to go on a sales call with me said: "It's like watching someone juggling with chainsaws."

He saw in his mind daring and danger, I saw in mine, adventure and fun.

---

1. People casually say "Ignorance is bliss" The correct quote of Thomas Gray is "When ignorance is bliss, 'Tis folly to be wise"

The image we project on our internal screen pretty much dictates our ambition, what will happen, where we go.

The Witch Doctor – Mark Landale

In 1978 – when I was 26 – I was working at Unilever at the time – I was seconded to Accra in Ghana to stand in for an employee of a subsidiary company while he was on a six-week sabbatical. The idea, as well as providing the required cover, was, of course, to give me a better understanding of the company's overseas operations as well as to broaden my experience generally.

Accra was different to anything I had ever known. Hot and sultry. Flame trees and other exotic plants in the gardens. Dusty streets with colourfully garbed women – always women – selling various wares from makeshift stalls on the side of the road. Old Bedford trucks were the principal means of communal transport. These were covered with brightly painted – often religious – slogans: "God will Provide"; "Repent Now!"; "Never Despair" – and one slightly darker message which I remember well – "The Wages of Sin is Death" [sic!]. Some slogans looked at life from a more humorous angle such as "Life is too Short to Eat Bad Ice Cream!" All these trucks had large numbers of locals hanging off every part of them – and almost always smiling – especially when a truck hit a pothole and nearly dislodged them! Accra was a vibrant and colourful place.

My office was a bland room in an equally unexciting building. I had a rickety desk and an old fan turned lazily in one corner. When the fan stopped one was never quite sure whether this was due to an electrical outage or because it had finally given up the ghost! It did, however, struggle on for the length of my stay.

My new position came with a secretary – an elderly and very serious gentleman with grizzled white hair called Mr Adi. Mr Adi had an old typewriter at which he clacked away with the repeated sound of the return to interrupt my concentration as he reached the end of each line.

A few days after I took up my position Mr Adi came into my office one morning looking even more serious than usual and asked if he could take a week off. The leave was not scheduled but he had an assistant so there was no particular reason I should refuse his request. I did think that I should ask him the reason why he needed to take the time at such short notice. His response left me almost speechless. He said that he needed to go back to his village to pay the witch doctor and that if he did not do this he would die! It was not clear whether Mr Adi was suggesting that the witch doctor had cursed him or that the payment was required so that the witch doctor could cast a spell to prevent an otherwise "certain" future event. What was clear to me, however, was that this was nonsense.

There were, to my mind, two possibilities: either Mr Adi was try-ing to take advantage of me to wangle an extra week's holiday or the witch doctor was trying to take advantage of Mr Adi to extract an undue payment. In either case the week off was not justified so I turned down the request. Mr Adi was not happy!

Over the next week Mr Adi came to the office as usual but each day he looked progressively more ill. His skin took on a sallow, yellowy hue. His eyes grew rheumy. His stance was no longer upright and he became unsteady on his feet. He also looked exhausted. In short he began to die on me. After a week I gave up and told Mr Adi to take the time he wanted and settle with the witch doctor. Apparently the witch doctor wanted five chickens!

A week later Mr Adi reappeared. All signs of physical deteriora-tion had disappeared. There was even the hint of a smile. He informed me that he had paid the witch doctor and now all would be fine. We worked well together for the rest of my stay and I was very sorry to say goodbye to Mr Adi when my time came to leave.

I still do not believe that the witch doctor could have cursed Mr Adi or could cast spells to change his fate. What I do believe, though, is that Mr Adi believed he could.

Perhaps things have moved on in Ghana since 1978 but the lesson for me was that certainties in one culture do not necessarily translate into certainties in another and that one should always endeavour to keep an open mind when presented with the unexpected.

The quality of questions and our generative language determine our world. One of the key reasons that humans as a species (in addition to the long opposable thumb) took over the world was that in addition to language being a practical communication tool, we also use generative language – this idea that "words create worlds".

I had a lovely coach years ago, who was great for me and for our team, called Oliver Flynn. He was one of the people who encouraged me to get into mentoring because, as he said: "You're good at it and you could charge more than me." He and his wife had rented a little place overlooking the harbour in Marathon, in the Florida Keys. He got chatting to the chef at a local restaurant, and Oliver, being Irish, always asked people if they had ever been to Ireland. "Yes, a long time ago." said the chef.

Oliver then asked the chef a question in a curious way, "What brought you to Ireland?"

The chef said, "Air Force One."

He had been Jack Kennedy's personal chef.

A standard question, such as "where did you go?" would have received a predictable answer, for example, I went to Dublin. This particularly Irish way of questioning opened up a surprising avenue of conversation and revealed much more interesting information.

As discussed, man is the only specie to use language as a generative tool. Other species pass on messages with their coos and baas, but man is able to create worlds with words. When President Kennedy said: *"I believe that this nation should commit itself to achieving the goal, before this decade is out, of landing a man on the moon and returning him safely to the Earth."* he created a possibility.

Lee McCormack: *"Learn the language of your client. If you're not speaking the "language" of your client, or you're not able to see it from their perspective, then you're just trying to impose your ideas on them."*

Humans are meaning-making machines. The meaning we make can be helpful, useful and directional – or not. The picture we project on the screen in our mind can become our reality. The way we are heading, what we are looking at, the signals we are sensing and making meaning from can set our destiny. Depending upon our frame we can see the signals as an irritation and nuisance, or as an opportunity and direction.

In positive psychology we are taught to work with what works. If the pictures you are projecting in your mind are creating worlds you are excited to be part of, then do more of that. If they aren't, do something different.

If you ask them, usually people tell you what's going wrong. Average coaches fix what doesn't work, great coaches help their clients change their world – great coaches ask: when does it work? It's the difference between just doing stuff and being creative. Choose wisely.

Something was said to me by a former (American) boss, "Son, you know, you can be completely unrealistic in your view on life."

I said, "Do you think I should change it?"

He replied, "Oh, no, stick with it, it has made you really happy and successful."

So, if you have your completely unrealistic image projected onto your screen, now, how are you going to achieve it?

The lure and lunacy of goal setting

Of course, we all "know" that writing down your goals will make you more money, get you promoted faster, and make you irresistible in bed. It must be true, it's on the internet:

> In 1953 a team of researchers interviewed Yale's graduating seniors, asking them whether they had written down the specific goals that they wanted to achieve in life.
>
> Twenty years later the researchers tracked down the same cohort and found that the 3% of people who had specific goals all those years before had accumulated more personal wealth than the other 97% of their classmates combined. [2]

This is fake news. There is no evidence. Harvard, Yale and the Ford Foundation have all been attributed as the researchers. Many studies on the power of goal setting are based on this myth. Books abound from famous authors such as Tony Robbins, Zig Ziglar, and Brian Tracy quoting these "facts". Quite probably 97% of these books were written by people who wrote down their goals.

The desire to believe in the magic of writing down our goals overwhelms our ability to think clearly. Simply writing down your goals is not a ticket to success.

People overestimate what they can achieve in a year but underesti-

---

2. Harvard Yale Written Goals Study – fact or fiction? https://rapidbi.com/harvard-yale-written-goals-study-fact-or-fiction/

mate what they can achieve in a decade. While there might not be a map, there is a path.

It was believed that it was physically impossible for a human to run a mile in under four minutes. Then, on the 6th of May 1954, Roger Bannister ran a four-minute mile. Once this "truth" was shattered, sixty-four days later his record was broken. The "four-minute barrier" has since been broken by over 1,400 athletes. Hundreds of years of assumptions about man's ability were destroyed in three minutes and 59.4 seconds. Bannister went on to become a neurologist, claiming he felt prouder of his contribution to academic medicine through research into the responses of the nervous system than changing people's perceptions of what they were capable of.

Aristotle said: "We are what we repeatedly do. Excellence, then, is not an act, but a habit." Bannister didn't suddenly run the four-minute mile on that "lucky" day, he ran towards it in every training session leading up to the event; it was his process, rituals and habits that systematically led to the result.

BJ Fogg is an American social scientist who is currently a research associate at Stanford University. He is the author of *Tiny Habits*, and is the founder and director of the Stanford Behavior Design Lab. The Fogg Behavior Model (FBM) is a model for analysing and designing human behaviour and describes three conditions needed for a behaviour to occur: motivation, ability and a prompt. Motivation can be influenced by factors like pleasure or pain, hope or fear, and social acceptance or rejection. Ability can be impacted by time, money, physical effort, brain cycles, social deviance, and non-routine. Prompts are also referred to as triggers. Of course, habits can be good or bad.

The pandemic gave us a chance to reset. To set up a rhythm that suits with **R3: Rituals, Regimes and Routines.** It's about daily disciplines. Your habits, the R3, set your direction. Your direction leads to your outcome. If you want a good outcome, establish good habits.

"Tolkien is Hobbit forming."
Graffiti on a wall in East London

Robbie McDonnell found himself in Hong Kong, completely out of his depth, wondering what on earth he'd signed up for. He turned up at Chinese New Year, on a tourist visa, with nowhere to stay to facilitate the biggest financial software deal of his career, with Goldman Sachs. He didn't have "goals" he had "directionality" and he dealt with "what came up".

We're all the same underneath – Robbie McDonnell

My prospect and I worked at a deal, we sat down, had lunch and a conversation. It was a very natural thing. It's the same companies, just a different country. We contacted banks, told them that we're working with their counterparts in Chicago, New York and London, that we had a great system and what we wanted to do next. Then we needed to do the logical stuff of getting an office, a phone line, computers etc.

The weirdest thing of all is that when you stand back and look what has to be done it seems like a gigantic mountain. Within a month we had people on the ground, doing exactly the same things as we were doing in London. The lightbulb for me was just recognising that we have a product that is global in nature, that trading knows no bounds, and everybody's looking at the price of the S&P or German government bonds on the same screens. We had a universal language that's more than English, or German, or French, or Japanese, it's a number. Everybody knows that number.

When you realise that we're all talking the same "language" it's just a series of simple steps. The first step leads to the second and third step – small incremental steps. When you look back six months later you'll never believe you could get there. One hour leads to another. One day leads to another. It's logical.

> You cut the path out for yourself. Find like-minded people who share your beliefs because you can't do it all yourself. Business matters, but the human relationships, the human connections, the commonality of purpose takes all the stresses and pains out of it. You think everybody does this, and then you realise after the event that they don't. Flying what feels like a million miles a year, catching a flight to Hong Kong, going around the world five times a year – you just fall into it. It's not that complicated, really.

Robbie ended up with offices in Tokyo, HK, Singapore and Sydney dealing with different environments, ways of doing business, methodologies and cultures. But they all understood the language of trading and systems and numbers. That's how they trade in Singapore and Sydney and everywhere in between.

How do you create an interesting business that people will talk about? You don't do it by goal setting. You do it with directionality in the face of uncertainty.

In the classic bestseller, *The Discipline of Market Leaders: Choose Your Customers, Narrow Your Focus, Dominate Your Market*, authors Michael Treacy and Fred Wiersema say there are three types of companies: technological innovators, the service guys and the execution people. You can't do everything for everybody. DHL or UPS are the execution people. John Lewis and Nordstrom are the love you to death guys. Sony is the innovator. Sony is the opposite of Panasonic Corporation. Sony always wants to be first to market, to be number one. Panasonic, at the other extreme, just want to let somebody else make the market, and then they will become the brilliant execution guys.

Gavin Dalgleish: *"To have expectations of something can be limiting. Sometimes it's good to suspend the expectations, trust the process, understand the direction. The critical piece around leadership is how you lead through the unknown, being clear on what you don't know, and how you intend to acquire that knowledge, corral all the information and integrate it into some sort of cogent analysis that you can use to sit and explain the direction. Never pretend that you've got all the answers. The purpose of the journey is to find the answers."*

So you're a smart leader and you want people to follow you. You recognise that there is uncertainty, complexity and unknowns. The trick is to simultaneously show confidence, direction, and demand the first next step even though you know things will change. **Address the complexity, don't add to it.** Make sure your simplification is not another's complexity.

"We do what we have to do as leaders. That's our job. Our job is to calm more crises than we create."
From a fictional conversation between Prime Minister Harold Wilson and HM Queen Elizabeth in The Crown, Series 3, Episode 3

Peter Rawlinson: "I didn't do it [set goals or targets] on the Tesla Model S and I don't do it at Lucid. Instead I challenge our engineers to amaze me. Set goals and people stop there. That's why, I think, our drive units are so much more compact – everyone else was just happy their units were smaller than a combustion engine and gearbox."

Forget about goals, focus on directionality and systems. I have completely abandoned goal setting with my clients. The challenge is you can only set a goal to what you know, to what you can imagine. Picture going to the zoo with some youngsters. You say, our goal is to see the lions and tigers and bears, oh my. You have a great visit but find on your return home that there were, uniquely for one day only, four giant pandas in that zoo. Wouldn't it be better to say, let's go to the zoo and see some interesting animals, and be open to the possibilities? When you arrive, ask the zookeeper, "What should we see today?" "Well", says the zookeeper, we have a special treat for you today, four giant pandas ..." This is directionality and intention at play. Of course, you must take some action and actually go to the zoo ...

*"I pretended to be somebody I wanted to be
and I finally became that person.
Or he became me. Or we met at some point."* — Cary Grant

Fake it till you make it, or "acting as if", is grounded in the work of Adler.[3] One of his most persuasive and compelling investigations was around the power of fiction to influence fact, a dynamic articulated in his theory of "acting as if". Influenced by German philosopher Hans Vaihinger's 1911 book, *The Philosophy of As If*, Adler explored the power of exercising mental fictions, a precursor to the later emergence of Cognitive Behavioural Therapy. A constructivist psychological approach, the Adlerian technique of "acting as if" encourages the patient to act out desirable behaviour – for example, empathetic responses, or assertive decision-making – on a daily basis.

It's a belief system collision

If you are to recreate your world you need directionality – what's your directionality? Who chose it? You need vision (your internal screen) and action ... So, if goal setting is banned, how do you decide where to go and make headway? Here are four steps.

Step 1. Create your own film

The images we project on the screen in our head create the directionality in which we travel.

Some people get trapped in life through their set of beliefs, sometimes they're not even their own beliefs. I was on a beach in Bali, the early morning sun rising over a quiet seascape as I finished my constitutional. I sat down on the sand enjoying the peace before all the people arrived. A Balinese teenager approached trying to sell me a wooden

---

3. Alfred Adler: Theory and Application: https://www.alfredadler.edu/about/alfred-adler-theory-application

box. He had his patter prepared, I would have been his first customer that day, and that would have brought me (and him) good luck. His English wasn't bad, so we chatted.

He was selling carved, wooden boxes on the beach in Bali to get enough money to change his name. A priest would be needed. A ceremony would be arranged. His luck, and his life would change.

This young guy was trapped in a world where he believed that he couldn't have good luck, because of the name he had. So, being an enterprising lad, he needed a different name.

I offered to do a name changing ceremony right then and there in the water, but he was adamant that – however well intentioned – it wouldn't work. It had to be a special person. We collided with our belief systems.

An article I wrote, *Psychogeography: How Effective Seating Can Make a Big Difference*, (based on the research of Robert Dilts) describes how the geographical relationship between the members of a group has an important non-verbal influence upon the group's process and interactions with one another. **The environment influences the outcome.** Literally, where you sit your team members can change the direction of a meeting. So, before beginning a session consider the following questions to set the directionality, and visualise how you want the meeting to proceed:

· What sort of environment do I want to create for this meeting?
· What type of interactive dynamic will the attendees need for this session i.e. exploratory, brainstorming, open, focused, reflective, etc?
· What type of physical arrangement of the room will best facilitate that dynamic i.e. presence and position of tables, chairs, flip chart, white board, projector, etc?
· Given the goals for this particular session, what type of psychogeography will most support the individual or team to successfully reach the desired outcome?

"We shape our buildings and afterwards our buildings shape us."
– Winston Churchill

The teleological nature of humans, our "drawn towards nature", means we are always heading somewhere or to something. So how should they set that up?

In just two sentences Siemens CEO Roland Busch, when speaking about their return to work plans after the Covid pandemic[4], epitomised leadership in uncertain times: *"These changes will also be associated with a different leadership style, one that focuses on outcomes rather than on time spent at the office. We trust our employees and empower them to shape their work themselves so that they can achieve the best possible results."*

Focusing on outcomes and trusting your employees might seem like obvious leadership strategies, but they are infrequently implemented. Gavin Dalgleish: **"Trust is the root of discretionary effort."**

Bandler, the eccentric one of the pair who "invented" NLP (Neurolinguistic Programming) had a useful set of directionality questions:

- When you've finished how do you know?
- What would be different?
- What would still need to be done?

In the animation industry, Walt Disney was a creative innovator – he stood head and shoulders above the competition. There were specific elements in the way he organised his creative workforce that tended to guarantee creative outcomes. He used a revolutionary approach to keep his staff coordinated in their thinking. The Disney Strategy (cod-

4. This Company's New 2-Sentence Remote Work Policy Is the Best I've Ever Heard: Siemens's new remote work policy is a master class in emotional intelligence. Inc. https://www.inc.com/justin-bariso/this-companys-new-2-sentence-remote-work-policy-is-best-ive-ever-heard.html

ified by Robert Dilts) involves three distinct phases with three distinct rooms:

- Phase 1 The Dreamer – the place where all things are possible
- Phase 2 The Realist – the place where things are sorted out
- Phase 3 The Critic – where the bits that don't fit are picked up on

Step 2. Determine the vital few and the useful many

Deming[5], Juran and the New Zealander: The 80/20 principal is perhaps the most useful of all mental models, and maybe the most under-utilised.

Joseph Juran, a Romanian-born American engineer and management consultant, was a missionary for quality and quality management. He was massively influenced by the work of Vilfredo Pareto, the 80-20 originator. Pareto, a Swiss Italian, did the analysis and found that 80% of the wealth of Italy was in the hands of 20% of the population. Juran believed that 80% of the problems in an organisation are caused by 20% of the actions – or the rule of the "Vital Few and the Trivial Many". Later he preferred "the Vital Few and the Useful Many".

Tony Barnes, a New Zealander who I knew in his twilight years, had been a young navy officer assigned to Dr Edwards Deming – as his bag carrier and bodyguard – in Japan in the early 1950s, experiencing at first hand the application of new holistic management practices that produced the Japanese post-war economic miracle. Deming's and Juran's philosophy took root in Japan through industrial work on production and systems, known as Kaizen. It was also the foundation of "The Toyota Way". Tony later, when serving in Viet Nam, used Dem-

---

5. Edwards Deming was an American engineer, professor, statistician, lecturer, author, and management consultant who believed that by embracing certain principles of management, organisations can improve the quality of the product and concurrently reduce costs. He's famous for his PDCA – Plan, Do, Check, Act model, and 14 Points for Management. Deming was hired by the US War Department to reduce the time to build and launch their submarines.

ing's principles to reduce the many casualties on the Mekong Delta, by armour plating the river boats in just the right spot. Tony later wrote, "Kaizen Strategies for Successful Leadership", showing the reader how to apply Kaizen to leadership, by developing skills such as active listening, delegation and employee motivation.

I had a temporary assistant for a while; she printed out directions to help me get to an event. In the directions she spent just as long getting me on to the M25 as she did with the final destination – the most complicated bit. I knew how to get onto the M25. I didn't know I had to drive round the back of the church, walk up three flights of stairs and knock on the red door. While I'm driving around the square at 11 o'clock at night looking for the damn place, that's where I needed the help – the final 20%.

80/20 Model

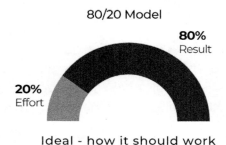

Ideal - how it should work

Unfortunately, what often seems to happen

Greg Simidian when he was working through his new business idea, The Ally Venture, said: *"The irony is that the 80/20 rule is the most overlooked and underused principle in business, and the most effective.*

A couple of calls ago when I started talking to you [Piers] about this new business you said to me, 'You know what, Greg. If you've got a pretty decent value proposition, and a good customer service ethic, and you're really nice, you'll probably be in the top 10% just with that.' That was probably a business book in three lines. I love this sort of simplification."

Some years ago I had been hired to bring FutureSource from the US to Europe. FutureSource was a real-time pricing system with commodity, financial futures and metals prices, and we could do graphs, really good graphs and lots of technical analysis. I worked out that the real value we could bring was twofold. Firstly, in unique content (rather than generic information), believing companies who produce the most content would win – which has been proven since significantly. Secondly, our customers needed a foreign exchange pricing service. The dominant pricing service was Reuters and everyone said I would never be able to replicate the incumbent. I disagreed, because if you work out what your customers really need, the very essence of it, the "20%", and do that really well, they will be happy. You are never going to fulfil the last 20%, the really exotic stuff, but you can do 80% – it's the classic 80/20 Pareto Principle. I worked out how to do it and sign banks up to the process. My moment of glory was when one of my sales team went to work at our major competitor, Reuters. Later he divulged that he'd seen the competitive analysis for the various products available in Switzerland and the GM of Reuters classed FutureSource's FX service and FX database as a significant competitive advantage. It might at first seem unattainable but start asking some different questions and see what emerges.

Step 3. Use leverage to get the maximum bang for your buck.

My early career was in financial markets so I understand leverage, and I'm always interested in getting the biggest bang for my buck. I always tell my clients that I'm not a Victorian coach and mentor. I'm not steam driven. It isn't about how much coal we shovel in, how much steam we produce, how big the pistons are, how many times we get together, how long the meetings are, I don't work like that. They are busy. I want to do the minimum number of things that I can do to help them: the minimum input for the maximum output. If that doesn't suit my clients, or they're measuring things differently, then I'm the wrong person for them.

It is vital to understand and decide where you put your time, where you put your energy, where you put your effort.

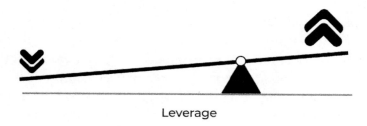

Leverage

The UK did one thing very well during the pandemic – the purchase of vaccines and their rollout. By January 2021, the UK had rolled out more vaccinations than the rest of Europe put together. Later, it naturally levelled up. Not only had we vaccinated a lot of people, we vaccinated the right people – the ones that will die. Which means the lowest number of doses will be to the care homes and the over 80s and it will have the biggest impact. Our old friend 80/20 again. We did it again with the boosters ... get it into the arms of the old and vulnerable first.

The challenge with making good decisions is working out *how* you are making them. Are you making emotion-based decisions or evidence-based decisions? One will lead to saving the most lives, the other will lead to an extended pandemic and a higher death toll. Of course, your decisions might not be life and death, but they will almost certainly be a blend of emotion and evidence. Make sure the balance is right.

Step 4. To be successful you must have vision *and* the ability to execute

So, you now have the focus and you know your direction, it's time to execute. You need vision and the ability to execute, if you only have one of those then you must find someone who has the other. Remember in Chapter 6 we looked at intention and execution? Go back and read it again. It's time to execute.

The funny thing is, like in the legends of old, the gold is already at your feet. Napoleon Hill tells the story in the classic *Think and Grow Rich*, of a young man during the gold rush. After mining away at a Colorado gold mine for many months, he finally quit, just as he was three feet away from striking gold. Everything is just where it needs to be. Your first client is probably an old employer, or the organisation you are leaving.

In *The Fundamental Principles of the Metaphysics of Morals*, Immanuel Kant begins: *"Nothing can possibly be conceived in the world, or even out of it, which can be called good without qualification, except a good will."* Kant believed that there was a supreme principle of morality (The Categorical Imperative) and the rightness or wrongness of actions does not depend on their consequences but on whether they fulfil our duty. But are good intentions really enough? We saw in Chapter 6 (and will see again in Chapter 8) that intention is nothing without action. Having vague goals, hoping for a great outcome, even setting smart goals isn't enough. We must remind ourselves – daily – of our intention and direction. It's our continual choice how we choose to move through the world.

Alex Bello, the Italian ex-fighter pilot says "all pilots say they would prefer a bad Court Marshall to a good funeral: *Sometimes you have to say no, make some changes, put forward the counter argument even though you are aware that it will create stress, and you may have to pay for it indirectly."*

So, I'm going to ask you again: **Have you done everything you could? Or have you just done enough so you can explain why you failed?** The explanations drive me nuts. It's inexcusable.

Dr Urs Bikle is one of my all time favourite clients, an engineer with a good sense of humour. A man who is dedicated, inspirational and builds great rapport with all his clients. I worked with him when he was designing railway locomotives at Bombardier Transportation in Zurich. We recently met up in the UK, he's now head of Engineering for Stadler Rail, a Swiss manufacturer of railway rolling stock. The reason for his UK trip was frustration; frustration that he was unable to truly understand why his trains were still not in operation. The network operator, the train operating company and the leasing company were all sending different messages for the delays. Urs' solution to this problem: fly to the UK, get a hotel in Norwich and work from the train depot for 2 weeks to see for himself what was going on, getting up as early as 3.30 in the morning and often still there late into the evening, because, as Urs says: "You have to be able to look yourself in the mirror at the end of the day and ask if you have you done everything you possibly could."

> *"I love deadlines. I love the whooshing noise*
> *they make as they go by."*
> — Douglas Adams, The Salmon of Doubt

We were getting ready to open in Paris and with our newly hired sales director we had a chance to go and see BNP (Banque National de Paris) and show them our 'kit'. We were determined to show the service at its best. So we lugged our "portable" 20kg PC and, because everything looks better in colour, our CRT monitor with us. We met at the airport, he had the portable, I had the screen, we marched down the Champs Elysees ready to do our best, to do whatever it would take to get the business – not just enough to say we tried. After a successful day, I boarded the plane home and popped the screen nonchalantly in the overhead bin.

Piers in Your Pocket: Are you imagining big enough?

"May your choices reflect your hopes, not your fears."
— Nelson Mandela

So, you've decided you want to go for it, what do you do?

- First, ask yourself how you are going to decide. How will you know what's the right choice for you? How will you know if it's your decision and not still, for example, one of your parents' dreams?
- Make sure your decision is an embodied experience. Use your mind and body to make the best decision.
- Consider what and who you are when you are at your very best.
- Read the signals in the system.
- You've juggled with the chainsaws; you're perfectly happy to operate in the moment because you've done all the rehearsing. Now move through the world in your own, unique way.
- It really doesn't matter anymore the environment you find yourself in, nor the problems you face when you are "ready".
- Remember, "obsessive" is what lazy people call the dedicated.

The big question remaining: if what we imagine is what we create are you imagining big enough?

Chapter 9: Guns or butter?

"Uneasy lies the head that wears a crown."
– The King in Henry IV, Part 2 (3.1.31)

You've now taken on the role of kingship in your senior leadership position. You have control of budgets, people and the levers of activity. I ask you to consider, what levers are you going to pull? What are you going to build? What will you create? Where will your energy be directed? What will be your legacy? You have the kingdom and it is a mighty responsibility. The danger is that you might see this current role as just a stepping-stone to greater power, to another kingdom. Rather than thinking about what's next, focus on what's now.

The Carlyle Years

We first met over lunch at The Savoy Grill – that haunt of UK captains of industry and visiting Americans. Alan Green was a Brooklyn boy made good with a vision to change part of the world of finance. I didn't know, but after that lunch, he wanted to hire me to help him make his dream become real. We met again a couple of months later when he was in London at their offices on Ludgate Hill. I had been offered a job the previous day so when he started mooting the idea of maybe working for him at MKI Securities in New York, I laughed and said, "I feel like flavour of the month." The offer was nebulous but he said, "Think about it and if you're interested, give me a call." I let the idea cook for a few weeks and thought "why not" so I gave him a call. He flew me out between Christmas and New Year to New York. "Do you have a favourite place to stay in New York?" "I do, The Pierre." I thought choosing the most expensive hotel in New York was a smart move as it set the tone for possible future negotiations.

The purpose of the New York trip was to meet his chairman, Arthur Paturick at 61 Broadway. Arthur had been a partner in Tessel, Paturick & Ostrau, Inc but was now the elder statesman at MKI Securities, the archetypal chairman of a bond brokerage who could have been sent up from central casting to fill the role. In his seventies, old school, charming, Jewish, thick rimmed glasses, slightly stooped.

After spending an hour with Arthur, Alan returned. Alan said, "What do you think Arthur?" and Arthur replied, "Lock him in Alan, just lock him in."

I took this as a strong buying sign and negotiated accordingly. After being offered a great job, I even remembered to say, "do you mind if I sleep on this overnight?", I had managed to add 50% to my salary in the first negotiations but then, with a degree of elegance, as we were shaking hands, I pointed out that my newfound opportunity was to be paid in dollars. I asked innocently if we could, "as my expenses are in sterling, lock in the exchange rate?" We did, at pretty much the all-time low of $1.05 – the best trade of my life.

Seizing control is all very well. Sometimes forgotten is that power is useful only when you have a notion of what you want to do with it. Boris Johnson has stumbled upon this truth during an ill-starred tenure in 10 Downing Street. Mr Johnson's personal ambition never looked beyond becoming prime minister. With his hands finally on the levers of power, but lacking anything resembling a prospectus, he has been lost.[1]

I have very few regrets in life. One small one that brings a twinkle to my eye is missing out on winding up a nemesis, Jim Woodhouse. Jim had been our board member responsible for commodities and came from an old family-owned business – Woodhouse, Drake and Carey. He was very cross when I left because it messed up his plans, as he thought I had a great future with them, but I disagreed. Within twelve months

1. https://www.ft.com/content/f029ebf7-557c-46cc-81ca-ae94202d5229

of leaving, I was coming back from New York (after a "Carlyle Years" visit) on Concorde. I was at JFK when I heard his voice boom out "Red-Cap!" as he hailed a luggage porter (all sadly now replaced by nasty little metal trolleys). There he was with his wife, two children, and an overfull luggage trolley, pushed by a RedCap Porter destined for the 10 o'clock British Airways 747 flight to London. I regret, to this day, not walking across to say hello. I'm sure he would have said, "Why don't you pop up to First for a chat on the way home," and in reply, my quip would have been: "Oh, you're travelling subsonic."

Whether you've been made the CEO, Prime Minister, or King of the World there are always paradoxes, choices, difficult decision, and balances to check.

Beanbags or big offices?

What does the business value? What does my boss appreciate? What's really needed at the moment? Your first decision is to work out who you are replacing and what's valued around here, here being your new position or abode.

There's an old sales joke where the happy client says, "Look what I bought." While his less impressed friend asks, "Who sold you that then?" Did you end up with this job as a "who sold you that then" or a "look what I've bought"?

My hypothesis is: it doesn't matter how long you date somebody, it's not until they're leaving a toothbrush in your bathroom cupboard that you actually really begin to know who they are, and whether you want to make a commitment. I think it's also true for work, it doesn't matter how many interviews you go to, how many people you meet, how many people tell you what the job is. It's not until you turn up that you actually find out what it's really like. Day one is when you begin to discover the truth.

Now, it's time to find out what you've got.

There is a concept in business, you find it often in big organisations, of being promoted to the level of your incompetence. Imagine a travellator, one of those travelling flat escalator that you find in large airports. The PILPS[2] jump on at the beginning and if they don't screw much up it delivers them into a senior position at the other end. It means a lot of people who aren't the best get to the top by default. The best leaders often eject themselves from the travellators, they make decisions, perhaps even make themselves unpopular. Why? Because they are brave and have taken the decision to be a leader.

If you don't truly step up, you risk becoming a PILP.

There are many reasons why one might become a PILP:

1. They may not want to be a leader. Maybe they are reluctant leaders; leadership has been thrust upon them. Rather than declining the role, they reluctantly accept the pay packet, without accepting the challenge.
2. There are those who don't want to make any decisions. They will never rock the boat, because it's all too difficult. They are not brave enough to step into their power.
3. Then there are people who would like to lead, but don't quite know how to. They're stuck. They don't have the knowledge, techniques, information, or experience, and often that's where I come in. As a mentor I help them to find and work the levers, to develop their own strengths, to follow their own path.

In the army you may find the commissioned officer theoretically has the leadership position, but maybe it's a sergeant major, advising from the sidelines, who has a real leadership position.

Chief of the German Army High Command, Hammerstein-Equord, who quietly opposed Hitler, wrote about his classification scheme for officers, on 17th October 1933:

2. PILP: a person in a leadership position

I distinguish four types. There are clever, hardworking, stupid, and lazy officers. Usually two characteristics are combined. Some are clever and hardworking; their place is the General Staff. The next ones are stupid and lazy; they make up 90 percent of every army and are suited to routine duties. Anyone who is both clever and lazy is qualified for the highest leadership duties because he possesses the mental clarity and strength of nerve necessary for difficult decisions. One must beware of anyone who is both stupid and hardworking; he must not be entrusted with any responsibility because he will always only cause damage.[3]

It's quite a challenge for a PILP to see that they are a person in a leadership position, and not a leader. They turn up to all the meetings, say what's expected of them, do the annual reviews, go through the motions ... but they are, at heart imposters.

Personally, if I ever find myself the smartest person in the room, I go and find a smarter room.

Assuming you're not a PILP, consider who you are replacing. Were they a PILP? Has the organisation become accustomed to vague, lazy, passive PILP leadership? Or does the person you're replacing have a reputation for being all action and no thought? Does the organisation want more of the same? Or do they want something different?

One client of mine had to go to Bangladesh on a secondment. He told me he wanted to make the environment like Google with open plan offices, decompression capsules, free food and beanbags. I said: "Beanbags, in Bangladesh? Are you sure? From what you've described of the organisation these people want the boss to have the biggest office. You're an engineering business. You have an organisation whose role is to enforce safety and security in clothing factories. You

3. Poller, Horst (2010). Bewältigte Vergangenheit. Das 20. Jahrhundert, erlebt, erlitten, gestaltet [Conquered Past. The 20th century, witnessed, endured, shaped.] (in German). Munich, Germany: Olzog Verlag. p. 140. ISBN 9783789283727.

can't have beanbags." I let him have his open-door policy, but insisted he understand what his people wanted. Did they really want more flexibility and a rotating meeting chair? Or simple, clear unambiguous leadership with integrity. Because, if the latter, then maybe "open plan" could work.

Lou Gerstner, chairman of the board and CEO of IBM from 1993 until 2002, is largely credited with turning IBM's fortunes around.[4] IBM had a reputation for looking inwards, rather than outwards. They always had a "deck" of slides called "Foils" which they used when in internal business meetings. Whenever you asked a simple question a "Foil" would be produced along with lengthy reports bound in smart blue folders. Lou would ask people to tell him about their business unit, and they'd provide a "Foil". The story goes that finally, he got up, switched off the projector and said: "Tell me, what's going on in your business?" They learnt fast.

Find out what kind of pace the business can manage. Can you be a breath of fresh air? Or are you in the kind of place where going from idea to gestation might take a while. If you're a marketing business, you can print a new brochure tomorrow afternoon. If you're building aero engines that are already operating at the very edge of the laws of physics, then you're not going to knock up a new one tomorrow. A business such as Rolls-Royce will be making huge, long-term, 25-year decisions.

When you were enjoying your garden leave before starting this new role you were probably very excited, making your big plans on the back of a metaphorical, maybe an actual, envelope. Then, when you turn up, you maybe find out they don't have any money. All the things you need to do need money, but there's no budget.

If you believe, as I do, that part of your job as CEO, or being in charge,

4. Gerstner: Changing Culture at IBM – Lou Gerstner Discusses Changing the Culture at IBM: https://hbswk.hbs.edu/archive/gerstner-changing-culture-at-ibm-lou-gerstner-discusses-changing-the-culture-at-ibm

is to get stuff out of the way so people can actually do what they need to do, then your big question could be: **What are we going to stop doing?**

Raul Vargas, CEO at Zurich Santander Insurance America has spent more than two decades in international leadership in global life and non-life insurance markets across Europe and Latin America. Raul Vargas: *"I think the main purpose of a leader is to clearly build the vision and support your people in order to build the capabilities to get there. Organisations are living creatures. You don't need the same capabilities, the same effort, in the same things all the time. You need to activate things, but you also need to deactivate other things. You cannot add things all the time – it's not possible nor healthy."*

You could take Alain Dromer's approach: *"Do nothing. Think, explore, find out, talk, interview, and then make your changes."* Or do the classic 100-day plan, and on day one abolish the canteen or something equally rash. You might get points for action, but you lose points for doing stupid things. **You can't undo day one stupidity**. As Liz Truss found out to her cost, only making it to day 49 of her first 100.[5]

If you're considering the 100-day approach, add an extra day, or year. Go beyond the event. Rather than thinking 100 days, think about a couple of years. What will you be handing over? What would it feel like when you've shaped it?

5. Liz Truss, Prime Minister of the UK for just 49 days (the shortest term for a UK PM in history) found that day one stupidity - in her case, her economic project dubbed "Trussonomics" which proposed borrowing to fund tax cuts was not a smart move. After knocking 10 big figures off Cable (the £/$ rate), destabilising the Gilt market and threatening the solvency of parts of the pension industry, the Bank of England was forced to launch an emergency government bond-buying program in an attempt to stabilise the markets. Sacking her Chancellor and reversing most of the proposed tax cuts failed to save her premiership.

Are you the difference that makes the difference?

We might be seduced by being the expert in what we know. We feel good, proud, satisfied – but that's not always very helpful. The question to ask yourself as you gain more "power" is: What is my job? What's the difference that makes a difference?

The X Factor of Leaders: Plays well on teams they don't lead.

David Reimer, Adam Bryant and Harry Feuerstein, wrote an exceptional (pun intended) article describing the Four X Factors of Exceptional Leaders.[6] They concluded that exceptional leaders can:

- simplify complexity and operationalise it
- drive ambition for the whole enterprise
- play well on teams they don't lead
- build leaders

These X factors should be recruited for, cultivated and fostered.

On the subject of recruiting – I find it curious, ridiculous and perverse when leaders recruit people who were "very good at the interview". We should not be recruiting "good interviewees", we are recruiting the right people for the job. Look for good people not good interviewees. And on the reverse, don't be a "good interviewee"; you should be at the interview to find out if it's a great place to work, if they'll value you, if you are who they need, if it's a good match and fit for you both.

This ability to play well on teams you don't lead extends to the board where the number one rule is: No surprises for the board. In my experience, in FTSE250 and medium sized businesses, boards are often quite actively involved. Whereas in FTSE100 companies, they tend to keep a

6. The four X factors of exceptional leaders: https://www.strategy-business.com/article/The-Four-X-Factors-of-Exceptional-Leaders?gko=b971d

bit more distance: they are guardians of shareholders' interests, checkers with responsibility to hold management to account. Maybe they also like a little bit of distance, for a touch of plausible deniability. I'm not sure why someone these days would want to be a non-executive director on a bank board because if the Economic Crime and Transparency bill which is currently at committee stage in the House of Commons goes through, the personal liability for any "failure to prevent criminal activity" will rise dramatically – including the risk of jail.

In *Drucker on Leadership: New Lessons from the Father of Modern Management*, William A. Cohen says Peter Drucker believed leaders need five things[7]:

1. Strategic planning as the first priority.
2. Business ethics and personal integrity are critical pre-requisites for effective leadership.
3. Model the military as they offer the best lessons in leadership development.
4. Effective leadership depends upon knowing what motivates people, so treat employees like volunteers.
5. Leaders should be marketers.

It's quite possible that Boris Johnson, when he took on the leadership position in 2019, managed to screw up all five aspects.

Johnson betrayed the role of ruler – the ancient art of "kingship". You can't just lust after it – when you get it, you must do something with it! Tony Blair spent part of his first term still a bit surprised he had won. Obama was pretty much still campaigning all through his first term, with all his rhetorical speeches rather than getting stuff done.

7. Drucker on Leadership review: https://www.kornferry.com/insights/briefings-magazine/issue-1/86-drucker-on-leadership

"You can't solve the tasks [of government] with charisma." [8]
– Angela Merkel

President Trump was tweeting like crazy ten times a day and you got the impression there was a lot of activity. In fact there probably wasn't a lot – mostly just noise, but you got a sense of activity. It was strange in the first days of the new administration in the US in 2021 – there were three or four days when President Biden said nothing. We were so used to a Twitter storm of random thoughts and alternative facts from a president that Biden's silence was surprising. But, for the listeners/viewers/audience, when Biden isn't busy tweeting, is there the feeling that nothing is happening? It's interesting what you get used to.

So how do we signal "thinking/planning" so our people feel comfortable that we've taken the reins? How do you show you're getting on with stuff? How do you send messages to the system? The bigger and more dispersed the organisation is, the more complex it becomes. The pandemic has probably sharpened our skills in remote communication: virtual town halls, CEO video clips, authentic and empathic messages, but still it's not easy.

Mary Jo again: *"You need to communicate to your direct reports, communicate with the chair and the board – communicate, communicate, communicate. I said to the Founder that I have to communicate ten times more often than I would think, and by various different means – written, verbal, face to face. He said, No, you're wrong. It's not ten times, it's one hundred times. Communicate with the customer, the team, with everybody again, again and again."*

It's about putting their people to work: *"The most valuable assets of the 20th-century company were its production equipment. The most valuable asset of a 21st-century institution, whether business or non-*

8. Told to her biographer and reported by Vanity Fair 'Angela's Assets' January 2015

business, will be its knowledge workers and their productivity." – Peter F. Drucker

What qualities make a CEO different to a regular leader (although naturally, some non CEO leaders will have these qualities)? You'll probably think of all the regular lists you've read in magazines like *The Harvard Business Review*. My list isn't quite so normal.

1. The ability to manage paradox and ambiguity.
2. A willingness to say, "I was wrong," and to make a 180 degree turn on a sixpence.
3. The ability to make decisions without all the information. Leaders out of their depth often ask for more and more information leading to paralysis when action is needed.
4. An ability to "catch the whisper from the quiet one" and hold a space for them to bring what might be vital information to the conversation.

Maybe the single most important thing is to decide ... to do nothing, yet...

As the CEO or senior executive you need the ability to hold paradoxical positions.

How do smart people miss simple things? Danske Bank in the Baltics was money laundering most of Russia's illegal cash.[9] Lloyds Bank had

---

9. €200bn of foreign cash flowing through its Estonian branch was suspicious. FT 20th October 2021

funded exotic instruments from short-term money market deposits[10] and Credit Suisse didn't understand counterparty risk.[11]

It starts with diversity, not just a variety of gender or race diversity, but diversity of thinking. Diversity matters; it's not about being "woke", it's about being smart.

Dr Michael Kock has a strong view on **The Heterosis Effect in Leadership**: *"In plant breeding we would call this diversity the heterosis effect – hybrid vigour is the improved or increased function of any biological quality in a hybrid offspring. **In other words, the more diverse the genetics of two plants are, the more highly performing the offspring.** Formerly a strength in big companies was homogeneity – the cultural state of all being the same. It's a big risk when it comes to adapting to a rapidly changing environment. The changes we see today are so rapid that if you are unable to adapt, you're out of the game. Darwin was right, it's not the strongest that survive but the ones who are most adaptable to change and diversity."*

Recall, Peter Drucker always felt that the CEO's role was to be the interface between the internal world and the external world. I work with a COO in the Middle East who came up through finance. In his portfolio and remit he has finance, strategy and operations. Of course, some of those are really CEO jobs. But his boss, the CEO, spends a huge chunk of his time on external relationships, talking to ministers, investors, and the regulator. So, my client takes the slack. **They are a great team – an**

10. And at that point the banks realised that they were exposed to what we call maturity mismatch: they'd borrowed short to lend long. And the scale on which they've done that turned out to be much greater than they had anticipated ... Many institutions will now realise losses, many of these complex vehicles that were created, into which the instruments were sold, will close down and be sold off, some people will lose money. Mervyn King, the Governor of the Bank of England, interviewed by Robert Peston, BBC Business editor, for a File on 4 special on Northern Rock 6 November 2007

11. How Credit Suisse rolled the dice on risk management – and lost, FT 20th APRIL, 2021

external facing, relationship building, strategic thinker and an internal "completer finisher".

Where will you have the most leverage?

Where can I get most leverage? What's the minimum input for the maximum output?

Spend your time on high leverage, minimum input for maximum output tasks. Pareto didn't come up with the 80/20 rule to look cool. You won't be able to do everything for everybody immediately. You need to decide where to focus your time.

Here are three important leverage points to consider:

1. **Circumvent the catastrophe:** Is there anything catastrophic that you must fix today? If you don't fix it today will the problem grow? If "yes", then fix it. Today.

How are you going to get your information? How are you going to find out what's really going on? Let's not kid ourselves, you're going to get managed. You are managing the chair and the board so don't think it's not happening to you as well. If you came up through finance, maybe you don't need the CFO to tell you things you have probably worked out for yourself, maybe you need to hang around marketing to let them tell you about the challenges they see on the horizon. If you came up through marketing, you obviously need your CFO to tell you how, unless things change, you're going to run out of money in six months.

It's as important to **stop doing things** as it is to start new things. Avoid the desire to make your mark by starting lots of things.

2. **Capture the good stuff:** Find out what the business is good at – really good at. What is it that your customers like? Explore the reasons your customers keep coming back. Focus on the people who buy stuff from you.

Uncover the espoused versus actual values. Some companies have their values on a plaque, posted on the wall in reception. These are the espoused values, such as *We believe in a healthy work-life balance*. It makes you wonder why so many people are still in the office at 7.30pm. Or, *We believe in diverse hiring*. Hmm, where are your black, disabled and female staff?

Another way to define culture is by **"what's the worst behaviour the organisation tolerates".**

I worked with Lloyds Bank some years ago who had a wonderful list of five qualities that made for good team behaviour at a senior level. Five principles that were a sort of "Team Charter". Most people forgot four of them, but the one that was always remembered, especially when it was breached, was *never knowingly let a colleague fail*.

You may have to make changes in the key executive team. Perhaps you need to replace half of them, do you do it in one go? Do you do it over time? If you replace them all at once, that's great, you got rid of them, but then you've lost half your knowledge. If you do it over time, then everybody's waiting for the next shoe to drop.

Do not be seduced into trying to fix all the things that are wrong. Leverage, biggest bang for your buck. Focus on them. Also, go big on the things that are great, celebrate them.

3. **Maybe, cancel the IT project**: Conrad Hilton said there were only three important rules about hotels: location, location, location. If you're inheriting an overdue, over budget IT project there are only three rules: cancel, cancel, cancel.

Now, many of you will come rushing back to prove how you rescued your IT project. Well, lucky you. If you've inherited a terrible IT project in six months' time it is *your* IT project. Don't allow sunk cost thinking to increase the already "invested" $250 million another cent.

So, if you're $250 million into a completely new system that you know is two years behind, maybe the smart and brave thing to do is to write it off and go and buy something that is already working.[12]

We had plans to spend a lot of money on a new IT project – a new database architecture and customer interface. The IT special project team told us, frequently, that they were making great progress. After we had spent somewhere between $8 and $10 million it was time for a first demonstration. They set up their big screens, plonked the hundred-page manuals on the desk, and we watched as a globe slowly spun in the corner showing that the system was receiving real time data. That was the sum of our spend. We were speechless. I truly didn't have any words. The beautiful manuals, they were just "props", blank inside. A genuine Wild West shop front. If that's what we got for $10million, the rest of the budget was fantasy. We cancelled the project.

When there are too many buts for making a decision, then the decision is cancel. Raul Vargas: *"We make decisions when we feel that we did as much as we could in order to evaluate the situation and the context. You could get it right or wrong, but at the end of the day, I did my best effort in a given period of time. The critical part is 'in a given period of time' because otherwise you become the kind of organisation that takes ages to make decisions. Taking ages to make a decision is an awful decision."*

Aviate – **Navigate** – **Communicate:** Pilots are taught[13] that if you have a problem the first thing to do is aviate – fly the plane, keep it in the

---

12. If you think your project is horrible, spare a thought for Australia's Department of Defense. "At least 28 defense projects are collectively 97 years late. Separately, at least 18 projects are roughly AU$6.5 billion over budget" Defence Minister Richard Marles widely quoted in the Australian media.
13. https://www.faa.gov/news/safety_briefing/2018/media/SE_Topic_18-07.pdf

air. Then you can point it back to where you're supposed to be going, you can navigate. Finally, when you're still flying and you're heading in the right direction you can communicate: "Ladies and gentlemen, sorry about that. We lost an engine but we're okay."

So as a leader, the first thing you have to do is take the temperature of the patient, because if the patient has a high fever, just taking them out for a walk, and a bit of fresh air is probably not very helpful.

If you're looking for a blueprint for your first days in a new leadership role here are some things to think about:

1. Do the research – speak to everybody who can give you insight before accepting the position, including all the board members, any consultants, team members.
2. Create your first diagnosis and know the value you can bring. Hopefully, you shared that at interview, so they know who they're hiring, and you know why they're hiring you.
3. Generate a working hypothesis around strategy, people, and execution, which you can only do by meeting as many people as possible before "day one".
4. If it's the CEO role, speak to the chair and set parameters. Speak to everyone and ask a set of questions. Listen. Create your databank. Formulate your 90-day plan.
5. Communicate, communicate, communicate: by asking open questions and listening.
6. Test thinking and refine the plan with the aid of trusted supporters. Formulate your 30-60-90-day plans.
7. You can't do everything. So, set the direction, choose, then focus.

The new CEO continuum

There's a continuum that starts at one end: investigate, ask everybody, interview hundreds of people, meet the entire board, meet the entire previous board. The other end is turn up and take off.

When I was running FutureSource we were the first data vendor in

Europe to use a commercial satellite for data distribution. I had wonderful stickers made: "Quotes from Space".

Half the world didn't get it, the other half did, and those who did get it loved it. I always said if you head out from Liverpool and you're two degrees off the direction to New York you end up in Rio. One degree off on the direction of the receiving dish and you missed the satellite by fifty miles. Day one is when you discover the truth, set your direction aim for the mark and continue recalibrating.

The "no buttocks" rule: Your leverage might depend on whether you're an internal promotion, or you've been hired from outside. If you've been hired from outside, you can make a huge impression in the first forty-eight hours. You can set the tone for how you want to behave, how you want to be, how things will be routed. If they've known you before, then that's a whole different interesting set of dynamics. For a start, you may be burdened with the "passport photo problem" – you have changed, but the picture in their mind has not changed through time. There's a convention in the UK that unless it's an exceptional circumstance, deputy headteachers don't become head of the schools in which they've been deputy. Possibly because of the risk that sometime back in the distant past a photocopy of their buttocks after the Christmas Party exists somewhere. It does rather remove your ability to discipline if the person you are disciplining has pictures of your buttocks.

Frederick Hertzberg[14] explored motivational drivers. Factors for satisfaction include achievement, recognition, the work itself, responsibility, advancement, and growth. For dissatisfaction we have company policies, supervision, relationship with supervisor and peers, work conditions, salary, status and security. Everybody bitches about the stuff they don't like, then you take it away and it doesn't seem to make any real difference to motivation at all. It's what he called "hygiene factors".

14. One More Time: How Do You Motivate Employees? Frederick Herzberg, January 2003: https://hbr.org/2003/01/one-more-time-how-do-you-motivate-employees

I suspect it's linked with neuro drivers in the brain, the excitatory and the inhibitory.

You need to find the levers.

The irony for a leader was summed up by Tony Blair,[15] who said, speaking about his own premiership: "The paradox is that you start at your most popular and least capable and you end at your least popular and most capable".

Remember in Chapter 4, we talked about SCARF (security, certainty, autonomy, relatedness, fairness); well, you're going to be firing all these psychological triggers with your leadership team. You'll bring change, threaten their security, certainty, and autonomy. You'll hire and fire and change relationships. They might not think it's fair. You'll be putting them in a mild threat state, and nobody works at their best under threat of fight or flight.

I recall a client in Dubai who had been working at a local bank, which was very dynamic and entrepreneurial. When she joined a major international bank she wanted to make changes, but all she heard from her team was: "Oh, I don't think Group would like that." Or, "Group prefers it this way." Finally she said, "Who is this Group? I want to meet him." The idea of "Group" had taken over all critical thinking; the culture was determined by "Group", this mythical controller who didn't like anything.

If you're a quoted company, then you need to know what signs and signals your investors are looking for. In one of the first board meetings, somebody will talk to you about those quick, easy, wins. I've yet to find them myself.

In *Good to Great*, Jim Collins: *"They said: 'Look, I don't really know where we should take this bus. But I know this much: If we get the right people on the bus, the right people in the right seats, and the*

---

15. 2nd April, 2021, The Independent

wrong people off the bus, then we'll figure out how to take it some-place great.'"

As Dr Kock says: *"The dilemma is we need to find a solution to encour-age intelligent people to become political leaders. Leaders with vision, who know where to go, and they're not just thinking of their re-elec-tion in four years' time. That's not a vision. It's just becoming re-elected. I would always prefer even a bad leader with a vision than a leader without vision. At least you know where you're going and you can choose if you want to go along for the ride."*

If you're brave (crazy) enough to run a change programme, just make sure it is a *change* programme, and not a reorganisation programme. Unless there is a change in culture, the way people deal with each other, how people react, then it's just a Titanic deckchair reorganisa-tion.

> *"You should take the approach that you're wrong.*
> *Your goal is to be less wrong."*
> – Elon Musk

And maybe don't *empower* people. Should this dreaded e-word be banished? Of course, there's a case for giving the valiant call centre people discretionary power to make £25 payments to annoyed cus-tomers. But do you really want the Rolls-Royce Aero Engines safety engineers "empowered"? Be appropriate.

Focus on the sweet spot

The intersection of these three questions can produce some interest-ing insights:

1. What does the business value?
2. What am I good at?
3. Where can I get most leverage?

That little sweet spot in the middle is where you put your time and energy.

What am I good at?
What energises me?
What do I love doing?

What does the business value?

What's really needed?

What does my boss appreciate?

Where can I get most leverage?

What's the maximum output for the minimum input?

World-class Leaders Know Where to Focus

I never wanted a career. What I did know for sure was I had a very strong "moving away from" value.

The advantage of "moving away from" values is they give you a kick into action. For example, the beaten wife with the drunken husband finally decides it's too much and she's out of there. She may end up staying with her sister, in a hotel or even sleeping in the car. But she is out of there. Moving away from values have no directionality, but incredible energy to move. My moving away from value was "I don't want to work in an office", because the very idea of that seemed like purgatory.

I ended up on a trading floor, which was alright: it's not an office, it's a trading floor. When I later took over a business as MD, I ran it as if it was a trading floor: open plan, quick, open communication, get on with it, take action, fix it attitude. No politics, shared purpose.

A leader must have a line that must not be crossed, and you need to send signals long before you get too close to that line. Mine was always the boardroom table. You were not allowed to put anything on the boardroom table without a coaster. Once, a visitor went to put his coffee mug down on the table, and one of my team across the other side of the room literally whooshed across the table to get the mat underneath it. This was the culture. My mum's immovable line was glitter. She banned glitter in her schools, "If you're head teacher, you absolutely have to have something that you are immovable on so they know you mean business. No glitter at Christmas. Glitter is nasty. It gets in children's fingers and eyes." You must have a couple of things that you're absolutely immovable on. It doesn't matter what they are, it will set the tone. I also always insisted the meeting rooms were tidied as people vacated them, ready for the next user.

It's all about culture.

I once went to the offices of Petro Canada, a big Canadian oil company. The coffee room, which was called a "coffee point" to subvert the planning rules, was immaculate. I asked: "How come the room is impeccably tidy?" "For health and safety." It didn't really compute, but I'm not stupid enough to ask the identical question again, so I said, "Tell me more," which is my get out of jail free card. "We're operating in the North Sea. If we can't keep the coffee rooms clean and safe what hope have we got on an oil rig?"

It was cultural. A colleague told me he worked with Shell as a guest speaker and the first five or six minutes was all about the health and safety, where the exit doors were. The fact they were in a conference room in a beautiful hotel on the ground floor with a lawn outside was immaterial. No fire alarms were expected. Health and safety was part of their culture, their DNA. The good DNA must be respected, but cut out the bad stuff.

Lou Gerstner: "I always viewed culture as one of those things you talked about, like marketing and advertising. It was one of the tools that a manager had at his or her disposal when you think about an enterprise. The thing I have learned at IBM is that culture is everything."[16]

Leaders who think they must stay because they have something important to negotiate, or a project they must finish or a deal only they can do ... don't handover properly. These "hero" leaders are hopeless at succession. You need to know when it's time to hand over to somebody else.

When President Obama was travelling in Africa,[17] he remarked that the African leaders he had visited believed they couldn't go because there was nobody to take over. On the 28th July 2015, the BBC reported on his Africa visit: "Sometimes you will hear leaders say 'I'm the only person who can hold this nation together.' If that's true, then that leader has failed to truly build their nation." If you hang on then you've failed, because part of your job is getting your successor ready.

So, if you think making sure you have at least one internal successor is a job well done, maybe think again. Anthony Willoughby: *"I sat down with the Maasai and asked how they had managed to adapt to colonialism. What was the essence of what they'd done?* **They created a methodology, a model for building sustainable, trusting communities, one leader at a time.** *Everybody is a leader from the age of three or four. You are a leader, you're given a goat, you're responsible for the community, look after the goat. So everything starts with your role in the community."*

Be just a little unreasonable.

16. "Who Says Elephants Can't Dance?: Inside IBM's Historic Turnaround". Book by Louis V. Gerstner Jr., 2002.
17. Obama chides African leaders who cling to power: https://www.aljazeera.com/news/2015/7/28/obama-chides-african-leaders-who-cling-to-power

Negotiation is a fine skill – part art, part science. The ultimate essence of negotiations was summed up to me by a two framed cartoon. In the first frame there's a policeman hiding behind bushes looking up at a man with a shotgun at the upstairs window of a house; he's shouting down: "You're never gonna take me alive." In the next frame a tank has rolled up, and the police shout back: "We don't intend to."

If you really want to negotiate you must be prepared to walk away. You can't just pretend you're going to walk away, because it's an embodied experience. Something that people sense. Think about what side of the table you are sitting on. Are you sitting on the same side of the table as the people you're negotiating with? Or you're sitting on the opposite side of the table? When you're raising money, selling a deal, you've got to be on the same side of the table.

I became involved (because the young founders needed some "gravitas") as chair of the world's first mobile phone payment system using text messages. You could pay for your parking, then go into the multiscreen cinema and buy film tickets (and your can of Coke) all with your little grey Nokia phone.

We needed some cash. I got an introduction to a fund with money. They flew into Dublin to meet us, bringing with them their little carry-on wheelie bags. I said, "Those bags are very small."

"Well, we're only here for one night."

I said, "Yes, I understand but they must be full of very large denomination bills then."

They laughed, but the message was there. We are here to make a deal. It's very important to make sure people know what you want.

I told them I was taking them somewhere very nice for lunch, the wonderful restaurant in the Merrion in Dublin; the two Michelin starred Restaurant Patrick Guilbaud, but that they couldn't have dessert because the fixed price lunch menu is two courses, and a comparative bargain. But the desserts were full priced and expensive. At the end of the second course they were talking about dessert and I reminded them with a smile – no dessert! He said: "I tell you what, let's have desserts and we'll pay for lunch." They couldn't not give me the money after that. In 2001, Itsmobile, a Dublin-based developer of payment applications for mobile phones, raised €2.5 million in the weeks following the dot-com bust. Your sweet spot – where you can make the most difference – might seem unreasonable for others. I'm proud to be on "just the right side of unreasonable". Especially when it comes to desserts.

Maybe modern businesses need feudal monarchs.

In *Zero to One: Notes on Start Ups, or How to Build the Future*, Thiel and Masters write about Steve Jobs: *"Apple's value crucially depended on the singular vision of a particular person. This hints at the strange way in which the companies that create new technology often resemble feudal monarchies rather than organizations that are supposedly more "modern." A unique founder can make authoritative decisions, inspire strong personal loyalty, and plan ahead for decades. Paradoxically, impersonal bureaucracies staffed by trained professionals can last longer than any lifetime, but they usually act with short time horizons. The lesson for business is that we need founders. If anything, we should be more tolerant of founders who seem strange or extreme; we need unusual individuals to lead companies beyond mere incrementalism."*

This authentic "founder", who Thiel and Masters compare to kings and figures of mythology, jumps us back to the energy of the warrior leader in Chapter 2, being brave and unstoppable, mixed with just the right touches of alchemy from our magician leader which we will explore in Chapter 9.

In the FT article[18], *The Man Who Broke Capitalism — did Jack Welch*

18. The FT: The Man Who Broke Capitalism — did Jack Welch destroy corporate America? June 7th, 2022: https://www.ft.com/

destroy corporate America? The author, David Gelles says that a former GE executive quipped: "If Jack jumped off a bridge, half the Fortune 500 would have been jumping off bridges".

We've shifted from the Jack Welsh "I'm in charge, cookie cutter, find the system, roll it out everywhere, then do it again in order to command your market model". To transparency, complexity, and humanity coupled with the willingness to be strong and brave.

During my twenty years as a mentor to C-suite executives I've noticed this change in leadership styles. We've moved to a much more consultative, inclusive style, being flexible to adapt to complexity, and transparent in addressing people, relationships, and diversity. In mentoring there's also been a shift to providing active encouragement to do things, be braver, bolder and to power through old limiting assumptions into the new world. I'm not sure that Milton Friedman's essay "The Social Responsibility of Business is to Increase Profits"[19] would get much traction these days!

Leadership Lift™ - A continuum of counsel

---

19. Milton Friedman's epochal essay, "The Social Responsibility of Business Is To Increase Its Profits," was published in the New York Times Magazine 50 September 1970

To help leaders navigate this new terrain they call upon advisors, trusted mentors and consultants. From the deeply personal, individual through to the organizational. A continuum of counsel. My wedge, my "slice of the pie" is business coaching and business mentoring with occasional business consulting and life coaching.

A powerful antidote to mediocrity.

Piers in Your Pocket: Power through the paradoxes

Oscar Wilde quipped, "*There are only two tragedies in life – one, not getting what you want and the other is getting it.*"

In the face of paradox a leader must decide and be seen.

Your moral compass cannot be private any more.

In macroeconomics, the guns versus butter model is an example of a simple production–possibility frontier, highlighting the relationship between a nation's investment in defence or civilian goods.[20] The nation will have to decide which balance of guns versus butter best ful-

20. With great synchronicity, as I was working through my final personal edit for the book this idea of "guns or butter" suddenly shifted from an interesting intellectual idea for management and something that was, by its very nature quite historical into a very current topic as Russia cut off supplies of natural gas to Nord Stream 1 and the German government was about to be forced into deciding on guns or butter; power for industry or domestic users. During the final edit of the book, the German government has asked both citizens and companies to reduce gas consumption by at least 20% following the Ukrainian invasion and Russia turning off their gas to avoid emergency cuts. The suggested measures include encouraging domestic customers to purchase electrical heaters and install woodburning stoves. The next stage of course will be the question "guns or butter" who will get the gas, domestic consumers or industry?

fils its needs. A leader has to choose between options when spending their finite resources. These are the paradoxes of leadership.

- You are the ruler for a time, not forever. Think beyond the event.
- Think about what you inherited, where you are and what you want to achieve. And what you want to leave behind.
- What do you want to learn?
- Be the difference that makes a difference – today.
- Hold the space for internal and external communications.
- Good for you versus good for the business – get them aligned.
- Long term versus short term – know your cycle.
- Hiring versus firing.

When given command, take it. Take action, lead the team, move firmly ahead, be seen as confident and committed in the face of the paradoxes.

Chapter 10: Dances of connection

"There are things known and there are things unknown,
and in between are the doors of perception."
– Aldous Huxley

Like the alchemists of old, you have the opportunity to create some-
thing from nothing. It's your chance to use your unique gifts and tal-
ents to produce what to others will appear as Arthur C Clarke said
(speaking of technology) "indistinguishable from magic". For you it's
natural. You will be reading the signals in the system, tracking for
opportunities, altering the thoughts and behaviours both of yourself
and those around you with your transformative powers. You won't
make the mistake of waiting until you have all the data. You will be
willing to dance with uncertainty, make unseen connections and be a
catalyst for creation.

The answer is yes

I wasn't travelling with Japan Airlines. I should have been – I'm a
"Oneworld" man – seduced with the business traveller's crack cocaine
of miles, points and status. I had been given an upgrade voucher by
Virgin Atlantic in an attempted seduction so decided to fly with them.
It was my first visit to Tokyo, I had a streaming cold and was taking
Australian bush flower drops under my tongue as a cure. It was winter,
but the weather looked good in Tokyo, so I packed lightly and didn't
take an overcoat. My disappointment began at the airport. The small
print on my upgrade voucher contained the words "providing space
is available at time of check-in". My bed for the night turned into a
Premium Economy seat sat next to a teenager playing Nintendo. As
we taxied away from the gate the captain announced our flying time

and noted that it would be a "nice crisp morning in Tokyo after the overnight snow"! I found the drops comforting and began, I guess, to gently overdose on them.

I was met at Narita and accompanied on the journey into Tokyo, I was dozing and waking in the car thinking that soon, so very soon, I would be sleeping. On arrival at The Royal Park Hotel, which appeared to be a sort of "reverse Tardis" where the inside, especially the rooms, seemed much smaller than the outside of the building. It was chosen, I was later told, because they had the best croissants in Tokyo, allegedly even better than those available in Paris. I thanked my chaperone and explained I would be going to bed. A look of horror and a sharp intake of breath signalled a problem. "But Mr Piers everyone is waiting for you." Knowing Asia, knowing protocol and understanding loss of face, I said, "OK, let me freshen up and we can go to the office." Off we went to the office for a meeting with our local partner – NTT and my Asia-Pacific Director, Tim St George, scion of the Italian dynasty. Tim had an amazing ability to build and nurture relationships across the region. He was very international, appreciated cultural differences and was a huge asset to us. Tim had inherited some of his grandfather's sense of adventure. In 1912 Maximilian J. St. George crossed the Atlantic on the freighter *Anglian*. Once in London, he cycled to Dover from where he crossed the Channel and, over the course of the next sixteen months he cycled and visited "every capital of Europe" with the exception of St. Petersburg and Lisbon. He later wrote up his adventures in: *Traveling Light or Cycling Europe on Fifty Cents a Day.*

Tokyo was, and probably remains for me the most "foreign" place I have ever been. A city of paradox. The taxis in Tokyo, for example, were generally older cars, all wonderfully polished, often black, as if they were just out of the showroom. The rear door opened and closed at the driver's command as a piston expanded or contracted. The drivers adorned with their white gloves sat with their heads poised a perfect inch away from the antimacassar. There was a strange contraption made of wicker containing a ping pong ball next to an early electronic mapping system. Tim was fluent in Japanese. My Japanese consisted of one very simple word, coupled with a very reverent bow – *Hajimemashite* – which literally translates to the very correct: "It is the first time (meeting you)."

Tim told me there was a welcome dinner. For me. Everyone was looking forward to hearing my *Hajimemashite*. I was looking forward to my bed. I'd been up thirty-six hours. I needed a nap. By the way, did they know I was vegetarian?

They decided to take me to one of Tokyo's oldest, very traditional restaurants, "Tofu Kaisei Goemon" – an "only in Japan" experience. The shaded courtyard separated us from the busy road noise, leaving the ornamental carp to their peaceful circling. Kimono-wearing waiters bowed us through to our own semi-private dining "room", *zashiki*-style. A low table was set on tatami flooring. We removed our shoes, and fortunately for us inflexible Westerners with our dodgy backs, we could dangle our legs into the leg wells, to keep up appearances and avoid the agony. Our meal started with tofu hors d'oeuvres in the shape of flowers. Lovely. Then we had the tofu bubbling soup, where you poured your own bowl, which was very tasty. Then came the tofu main course, which was a little less wet. My Japanese hosts are drinking beer, so I have a beer and with my lack of sleep get slightly light-headed. Finally we get to the dessert – fruit flavoured tofu. A little tea, followed by tofu petit fours. Fortunately, I was high on the bush flower drops by then so didn't really care.

The Japanese have a wonderful ability to sit with silence. Which makes it awfully confusing when the translator at our meeting with our partner NTT, the Japanese equivalent of British Telecom, stops speaking several seconds before the person they are translating. The very formal Japanese language accounts for the discrepancy, the translator doesn't need to wait for the final codas.

Later in the trip, we had gone to see the head of trading at Mitsubishi Bank who didn't want to buy our system, he just wanted our data. My colleague was about to tell him, unequivocally, that we never sell the data. I interjected: "What are you going to do with it?"

The head of trading said, "Well, I have a model that needs data."

I followed up with: "I have a couple of questions. How are you going to keep the data up to date? Who's going to clean and edit the database?" "Hmmm," came the reply. "You will need two people to look after it." "Two?" "Yes, someone to cover during holidays. You might be better off buying the system and taking the data out of it."

Afterwards, my colleague said, "I just learned something amazing. I would just have said no we don't do that. You said yes. And you created opportunity out of it."

The answer is yes. Then you work out the details later – you can tell I didn't come up through engineering. That's how you create something out of nothing.

When I was writing this chapter, I became especially energised and excited, because this is, at its core, the chapter about leverage. About making something out of nothing. Taking the wisp of an idea, finer than smoke, and running with it. Hearing in a sentence an echo of a thought, probing gently and then opening doors that moments before had not existed. It's about taking action and not taking action.

We're looking at the archetypal energy of the magician because every ruler needs a magician; King Arthur had Merlin, Sun Tzu had his strategies of "misdirection", wise warriors who avoided the battle and Elizabeth I had John Dee,[1] who encouraged her to think big (and coined the term "British Empire"). Magicians are able to rearrange things, see things differently to how others see them, and create something out of thin air.

---

1. John Dee (13th July, 1527–1608 or 1609) was an Anglo-Welsh mathematician, astronomer, astrologer, teacher, occultist, and alchemist. He was the court astronomer for, and advisor to, Elizabeth I, and spent much of his time on alchemy, divination and Hermetic philosophy. As an antiquarian, he had one of the largest libraries in England at the time. As a political advisor, he advocated for the founding of English colonies in the New World to form a "British Empire", a term he is credited with coining.

Stage magicians follow rigid procedures to surprise, misdirect and deceive. We're talking about The Prestige; a business magician is not a stage magician, following a set rule of things to create an illusion. Business leader magicians are the modern-day alchemists, more biblical than bogus, more enchanter than charlatan, more maestro than shaman, wielding wands not swords.

Magicians solve problems people didn't know they had

In an article in *HBR* in December 2009,[2] *The Innovator's DNA* authors Jeffrey H. Dyer, Hal Gregersen, and Clayton M. Christensen collated five "discovery skills" that innovative CEOs cultivate. They call the combination of these skills the "innovator's DNA", and happily for us, you're not born with it, you can build it. These five skills are: associating, questioning, observing, experimenting, and networking. When a leader has these skills they are like a magician, taking the ordinary, transforming it into the extraordinary ... and making it all appear so simple.

It's not just about innovation. It's about the alchemy of rearranging the pieces, seizing the moment, making the connections; coupled with the discipline of practice, training and acting on the signals. **If you've got some of that magician thinking and ability in you, use it. If you haven't then make sure you've got someone on your team who does.**

Dr Kock: *"I think magician leaders help by looking at your problems in a different way. It helps to change your perspective and sometimes it's necessary to take a step back, look from a different angle. I often give people a different perspective about their situation, the opportunities or the directions they can go."*

2. The Innovator's DNA, Jeffrey H. Dyer, Hal Gregersen, and Clayton M. Christensen: https://hbr.org/2009/12/the-innovators-dna

Kostya Kimlat is a corporate magician who fooled Penn & Teller on their hit TV show, *Fool Us*. He speaks to businesses about how to Think Like A Magician™ to improve sales and customer service. In an article for ISE Magazine,[3] Kimlat shares how thinking like a magician can improve your innovation and lateral thinking, perception management, and social intelligence. He says, *"To be creative and innovative, you have to be able to see existing resources as more than they are, you have to seek methods and technologies unknown to you (and maybe to others)."*

You can't speak about lateral thinking without mentioning the great man himself, Edward de Bono, who wrote more than sixty books on his original and sometimes unorthodox theories. His goal was to free us from the tyranny of logic, allow us to glimpse our inner magicians. De Bono claimed that business leaders came to him because they recognised the importance of what he was talking about: *"It upsets people when I say business is more interested in thinking than universities, but it's true."* In the preface to his book, *The Six Thinking Hats*, he claimed: "The Six Thinking Hats method may well be the most important change in human thinking for the past 2,300 years." He wasn't plagued by imposter syndrome, nor humility. In 1999, he pioneered the online courses genre, and with his brother, Peter, set up the Effective Thinking Course. His timing was excellent, his books and courses were adopted worldwide and made him a very wealthy and successful man.

The magician leader has impeccable timing – which comes from many trials and errors, most of which you will never see nor hear of.

The iPad was Steve Jobs' second attempt. The Newton was the first but the technology wasn't ready for what he wanted to do. Jobs hired John Sculley from PepsiCo to come and run Apple as a proper business, Sculley told Jobs that there was no market for high end con-

3. Want to Wow at Work? 3 Secrets From The Business Magician:
https://www.isemag.com/2018/08/want-to-wow-at-work-3-secrets-from-the-business-magician/

sumer electronics. They were both right. At the time the technology was not good enough for what Jobs wanted to do. According to the book *Steve Jobs* by Walter Isaacson, Steve Jobs and John Sculley, then PepsiCo president, were sitting on a balcony overlooking New York's Central Park. Jobs turned to Sculley and said, "Do you want to sell sugar water for the rest of your life or come with me and change the world?"

It's not just modern-day magicians who must wait for the timing to be right. In the early days of railways, carriages (imagine a wagon) were fuelled by human power, or by horses. During the late 1700s, the shift was to railways that had a static power supply such as a steam engine with ropes to pull the wagons. Later, locomotive engines were developed, using mechanical engineering to create the "iron horse". One later idea, adopted by the greatest engineer of the nineteenth century, Isambard Kingdom Brunel, a true magician,[4] was an atmospheric railway that used differential air pressure carried by a continuous pipe to provide power for propulsion. He was commissioned by the South Devon Railway to create for them an atmospheric railway. After a year of some successes – trains reaching over 60mph – in 1846, the failures increased: most notably rats eating the leather sealing flap, (rubber was not yet available) and the project was abandoned. If Brunel had had access to modern plastics, who knows what might have happened. Timing is everything.

As Otto von Bismarck, chancellor of Germany and author of *Gedanken und Erinnerungen,* said: *"Only a fool learns from his own mistakes. The wise man learns from the mistakes of others."*

Josiah Wedgewood's financial backing of James Brindley to build the Trent & Mersey Canal (before the true potential of canals was appre-

---

4. "We do not take Isambard Kingdom Brunel for either a rogue or a fool but an enthusiast, blinded by the light of his own genius, an engineering knight-errant, always on the lookout for magic caves to be penetrated and enchanted rivers to be crossed, never so happy as when engaged 'regardless of cost' in conquering some, to ordinary mortals, impossibility." -The Railway Times 1845

ciated) in 1764 not only sent his pottery to Liverpool and the world, but also enabled china clay from Cornwall to come via boat to the factory. With canal transport Wedgewood saw a great reduction in breakages of finished product. Previously, his expensive sets of pottery had to include many spares in each consignment due to breakages as the carts were hauled over terrible roads. Wedgewood, the Steve Jobs of the time, attended monthly meetings of the Lunar Society where he met with Matthew Boulton, Erasmus Darwin, Joseph Priestley, James Watt and other "movers and shakers" of the day. Great minds coming together to solve society's biggest problems – what a time. It was called the Lunar Society because it met when there was a full moon so they could enjoy a safer journey home.

It's not just colleagues or peers we can learn from. Some leaders bring together apparent competitors to learn from each other and build something much larger than any one company could achieve alone. In an *HBR* article, The Rules of Co-opetition, Adam Brandenburger and Barry Nalebuff claim that rivals are working together more than ever before.[5] Of course there are risks[6] as well as rewards in co-opetition, *"There are many reasons for competitors to cooperate. At the simplest level, it can be a way to save costs and avoid duplication of effort."* Deals between Ford and Volkswagen, Amazon and its marketplace sellers, Apple and Google cooperating with contact tracing technology, are all great examples of co-opetition. Among the most striking current examples of co-opetition, says Brandenburger, is that between Apple and Samsung. While Samsung's Galaxy and Apple's iPhone are fiercely competitive products, Samsung continues to be one of Apple's main suppliers, supplying OLED screens. Together they can change the world. Dr Michael Kock navigated and pioneered a protected commons to bring competitors to the same table.

5. HBR, The Rules of Co-opetition: https://hbr.org/2021/01/the-rules-of-co-opetition
6. The risks and rewards of collaborating with competitors: https://blog.lboro.ac.uk/sbe/2019/02/18/the-risks-and-rewards-of-collaborating-with-competitors/

Broker commons to create magic – Dr Michael Kock

The International Licensing Platform – Vegetables (ILP) is a brilliant example of a commons. It's the first really successful commons in the area, which turned IP rights from exclusivity to inclusivity built on the principle "free access but not access for free". It's a protected commons, so you can only join if you accept the conditions. Before it existed, everybody was using IP as a weapon, like an armament race; you need to have more to exclude the others. Companies spent a lot of money in devious, unhealthy cycles, because if you don't do it the other ones will and screw you. In the end everybody understood this was unhealthy.

It took a lot of patience, trust building, and more than three years to establish the platform. Then it became a self-proliferating system built on trust. Everybody wants to live in that world, with trust-based relations and fairness. It takes very few to destroy the trust in a system, like a disease. We built the system so you need to behave, with rules against bad behaviour.

ILP Vegetable's main objective is to guarantee worldwide access to patents that cover biological material for vegetable breeding. In the end it came down to the simple principle that if you act unfairly, you get penalised. It's based on a kind of baseball arbitration, where if no agreement is reached on the fair remuneration for using a fellow member's patented invention within three months, the case with the two opposing proposals for remuneration is submitted to independent experts, who then choose only the most reasonable proposal from the two but cannot mediate a compromise. Inherently, there's a very strong incentive to be as fair as possible. Both sides know what fair remuneration is, and the rest is posturing. When you take that out of the game, you have a sustainable system.

The ILP platform (ilp-vegetable.org) has been running for seven years and we've never needed a single case of arbitration. In addition, the concept is now copied and expanded to field crops.

It starts with the culture of the companies, not everybody joined the licensing platform, for example, Monsanto (now part of Bayer Cropscience) didn't join. The next area will be field crops, where Bayer/Monsanto and Corteva have very strong shares. If they don't join, it may never fly. But in the end, they may get there as there is so much pressure. I don't know how long they can resist. The problem is they don't naturally embrace it. It's not in their culture. And as we all know, culture eats strategy for breakfast.

Dr Kock and the other companies needed to leave their egos behind to work together to build the commons. Some companies were unable to take that leap, trust the process and build something larger than their own desires. They were unable to focus on win win win. Dr Kock: *"The past was all about winning and exclusivity. As we move more into an area of integrated innovation and complexity, where one cannot survive without the others, where if you try to kill your competitor you'll kill yourself, it's more about creating commons. Very few leaders can do that, because you have been conditioned to win. **Sometimes if you want to go for the prize and beat everybody, you lose.**"*

Flexibility is required to make the magic happen.

With my mentoring clients, I begin the process with a "Retreat" usually for two days. I take them off-site to get away from the business so they can do some deep thinking. We send them a list of requirements in advance – what they'll need, what I'll need, some assessments to complete, the preparation in advance, find a nice location, a room with a view, some space to walk – a garden, things like that. I flew into Dubai, feeling fairly fresh, with only a four-hour time difference. The night was short but I was good. I was in reception at the appointed hour waiting for my client. It was a lovely location, well selected. When my client arrived, after the initial "chit chat" I asked her what meeting room we were in. "We haven't got a room. No one ever said anything about a room. We've got a garden. You said we needed a garden." So I did a retreat outside in a garden for two days – a first for me.

I could have been irritated, perturbed maybe even discombobulated, and allowed it to ruin the session. But I'm very flexible by nature. I knew how to deal with what we got. I focused my inner magician, adapted as necessary, thanked the weather gods for their kindness and made the sessions in the garden work. I made the client happy. For her, it looked like this is how I always run a retreat. There is, though, an interesting psychological undercurrent worth a moment's exploration. If I had booked the hotel and I'd screwed up, I'd have been very, very uncomfortable; my "responsibility" drivers kicking in. As the client had mis-booked, it was easy to say: "Don't worry, we'll do the best we can with what we've got." And use a little magic to bring it all to life.

Robbie McDonnell recalls working on a deal and reaching an impasse, he was truly in the middle of the deal, with his boss on one side and the CEO of the biggest propriety trading group in London on the other. They reached an intractable point, and both men were hot under the collar. It was going to explode. Robbie: *"Instinctively, just before getting walked out of the room, I said, 'Okay, just one second guys. I know that we want to get a solution, and I know this is a crazy way to do it. But I'm going to suggest that we end the meeting and we come back tomorrow. Let's sleep on this because there's always a way we can fix this.'"*

They were both delighted to walk away because they both needed to win. They couldn't back down. Overnight, they found a solution, and the following day, at the trade show, they shook hands on the deal. Twenty years later they're still working together. That deal was worth 100 million dollars. But in that moment that deal could have died.

Robbie: *"If you really want something badly enough, you'll find a way of getting there. In a negotiation it's a matter of finding either a way* out, or a creative way of doing a deal. That means discovering what the important thing is for the other side. Let the egos go. Call the draw, and then find the solution. **You don't have to be right all the time. You just have to be right at the end.**"

That's the hardest part – the third act. The character, Alfred Borden, played by Christian Bale in the 2006 psychological thriller *The Prestige*, says:

> *Every great magic trick consists of three parts or acts. The first part is called "The Pledge". The magician shows you something ordinary: a deck of cards, a bird or a man. He shows you this object. Perhaps he asks you to inspect it to see if it is indeed real, unaltered, normal. But of course... it probably isn't. The second act is called "The Turn". The magician takes the ordinary something and makes it do something extraordinary. Now you're looking for the secret... but you won't find it, because of course you're not really looking. You don't really want to know. You want to be fooled. But you wouldn't clap yet. Because making something disappear isn't enough; you have to bring it back. That's why every magic trick has a third act, the hardest part, the part we call "The Prestige".*

Magician leaders are able to take something ordinary – The Pledge. Transform it into the extraordinary – The Turn. And make the hardest parts look easy – The Prestige.

My sales director at FutureSource in Paris wanted me to come over for a meeting with a very difficult but potentially important client. On a good day, I have a little French, enough to get me a meal, a glass of wine and a bed for the night but she said they were insisting on doing the meeting in French. I wasn't too worried, of course it would be a little difficult, but my colleague could keep translating for me or ask my questions. As we entered the old Paribas building with its classic French birdcage-style lifts, with concertina doors, our client asked me if I could speak French. *"Je peux parler un peu français, tu parles anglais?"* He replied: "Yes, of course." So, quick as a flash I said, "Perfect. We'll do the meeting in English."

In the moment, I transformed a difficult conversation into a much more comfortable conversation – well for me, anyway.

If you're an ESTJ, with extroverted, observant, thinking, and judging personality traits, what the magician does, really looks like magic. If you're more on the intuitive scale, able to track the signals, then the magician seems quite normal. Lee McCormack has an incredible ability, honed through many different projects, to see opportunity where others didn't, and to almost pull ideas out of thin air.

Unpicking with him how he does it, it looks like a three-step approach to recognise ideas:

1. Input: Initially you need information. Input is absolutely essential to formulate an opinion on whether something is a good idea, or not.
2. Interest: To become better at identifying and recognising ideas, you need to have a general interest in everything. You don't necessarily need to be a specialist, but you need to be interested in stuff and how people live and operate and function and how things work.
3. Insight: To have a level of excitement about something, you need to have insight into it. There's no point getting excited about something you think is great, only to find when you do research, that people have been thinking about that for the last ten years. Your excitement about an idea would be ill-formed and naive. If it has no excitement, it's just another boring idea.

A few years ago Lee took a sketch, literally on the back of a napkin, to some Californian real estate developers and persuaded them to give him money. That idea has become Global Home.

Lee McCormack – The Orrb

Ideas are more like ecosystems, rather than single points; for me, it's like a cluster of components that together create a really good idea. The magic happens when the points get brighter and stronger, and other satellite ideas, nuggets, float around them, and form the level of density.

Sometimes **you have to be brave enough, after you've invested time, energy, passion and excitement in an idea, to let it go.** To be better at coming up with great ideas: **be honest with yourself** in recognising what's a good idea; **be brutal at attacking the idea** that you're really passionate about; **be faster at pivoting and adapting** without knowing where the idea is going; **have a high level of faith in your own judgement**; be true to those ideas to end up somewhere better than where you started.

I was able to translate my idea for the Orrb – a personal "pod" environment within which a person can feel safe, secure, supported, nurtured and improve their performance – and leverage this experience, drawing on what I knew, reimagining what it is, for the home. **It's basically painting a picture without even starting the project.**

I remember being in Singapore on an Asia-Pacific trip and making client visits with my regional director, Tim St George. We were at the offices of Phillip Securities and one of the directors had an enchanting picture hanging in his office – it was pen and ink with watercolours. There were several figures standing around some dying embers and a pile of what at first glance looked like rubbish, some small reptile bones, worn cotton clothing etc – a really beautiful picture. It was painted by a Chinese artist but the figures looked like they were North American Indians. So suddenly I was thinking that the North American

Indians must have walked across from the very north of China through Alaska and down at some distant point in the past.

I visited the offices several times during that trip – after again commenting on the picture, Tim warned me against saying anything else about it saying, "be careful or in a minute or two he will feel obliged to take it down and give it to you." The reason the director loved it was that to him the message was simple: **finding value where others see none.**

He told me the name of the dealer he bought it from, and I went to see him but of course no more of that kind of work of art was available.

Remember, the only way to lead is to follow, and we're not just talking about your staff. You need to enter the customer's world, appreciate what they do, and at some level, understand it, because you've done some research or some reading or gained some knowledge. You connect with them in their space and then you can lead them to somewhere else with a new idea.

It's not just pulling ideas out of thin air

Although magic looks effortless, you might have done 20 years of research to get there.

Clare W. Graves was a professor of psychology and originator of the emergent cyclical theory of adult human development, many aspects of which were later popularised as "Spiral Dynamics". He was influenced by Maslow but didn't think his "pyramid" went far enough. Graves was a professor of psychology at New York University and set up a summer holiday project for his PhD students, which became his life's work, as these things often do. He codified numerically a model of understanding the world. Graves' model has a double helix hierarchy of one to eight, covering both the broad societal progression, and the individual's growth and development.

The odd numbers are all individualistic, and the even numbers are more about groups, teams and together. Number one is very primal – me on my own in the world, there is only the stars and maybe the gods. Number two we get together, in a tribe, we feel stronger together. In modern terms that's the idea of a gang or a club. Number three is about one ruler, and feudalism; war lords and gang leaders. Number four is about following the rules, and rule-based society, law and order, and is the foundation of society as we know and recognise it. Number five is typical robber baron entrepreneurship, with competition and achievement. Number six is about harmony and social cohesion, let's sing Kumbaya, we're all in this together. Number seven is freedom and self-actualisation, with a rifle and tins of beans in the back of Montana and eight is holistic, the good of the whole is much more important than the wishes of the individual.

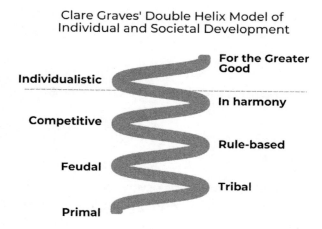

Clare Graves' Double Helix Model of
Individual and Societal Development

For the Greater Good

Individualistic

In harmony

Competitive

Rule-based

Feudal

Tribal

Primal

I know my natural default position, but then I ask the question, "What kind of energy and what kind of Graves position do I need in this situation?"[7]

The classic level sixes are the Scandinavian countries, where people will pay high taxes because it works for social cohesion, and no one person is more important than another. Australia is a classic level four moving into five. When I first went to Australia, twenty-five years ago, no one in Sydney would have jumped a red light. Now some do.

Most people you meet will view the world through the lenses of levels four, five or six. Graves believed there is a glass ceiling at level six, where most people – and current societies – stop. At level seven people unplug, just leave me alone. The extreme of that are the people holed up with their boxes of ammo and tins of beans. My mentor is a classic level seven, doesn't own any property, free living.

Here's the key thing about the Grave's model: if you haven't yet experienced the level, you don't really understand what they're talking about. If you're talking about entrepreneurship to a Grave's level four, which is all about control and rules and thoroughness, then your plan to game/arbitrage the system appears potentially like magic – they won't know what it is because they haven't experienced it yet.

What level is magician? Usually, the level above their audience. Think of a Connecticut Yankee at the court of King Arthur. When Hank Martin (played by Bing Crosby) was mystically taken to the realm of Camelot in the film, *A Connecticut Yankee in King Arthur's Court*, this simple mechanic from 1912 showed his new counterparts technology and gently gave them hints about the future. His back to the future knowledge appeared quite magical. If you've never seen something before, or you don't know how it works, then it seems like magic.

---

7. "Briefly, what I am proposing is that the psychology of the mature human being is an unfolding, emergent, oscillating, spiraling process, marked by progressive subordination of older, lower-order behavior systems to newer, higher-order systems as man's existential problems change." Clare W. Graves

"No great genius has ever existed without some touch of madness."
– Lucius Annaeus Seneca

Elon Musk believes failure is necessary on the path to success, and he should know a thing or two about failure,[8] he was ousted as the founder of his own company Zip2, crashed his new McLaren F1, was dumped from Pay Pal, and not even the Russians would sell him a rocket (maybe due to his uncanny ability to crash them – lots of them). He's still worth (depending on today's Tesla stock quote) over $150 billion – so failure isn't always a problem. Musk: *"Failure is an option here. If things are not failing, you are not innovating enough."*

Really successful companies are not afraid of failure. JP Morgan, the US bank, bought *Nutmeg* an investment platform in the UK to support their plans for a retail banking offering in the UK that may not be successful. Amazon put a billion-dollar bet down on Prime to see if it's worth spending time and energy in the entertainment business and Ratan Tata, founder and Chairman of Indian conglomerate Tata created, near his retirement, a prize for "Best Failed Idea" with the aim to spark innovation and encourage risk taking.[9]

O for a Muse of fire, that would ascend
The brightest heaven of invention,
A kingdom for a stage, princes to act
And monarchs to behold the swelling scene
Shakespeare, Henry V

In the prologue to Henry V, Shakespeare suggests we suspend our disbelief: "'tis your thoughts that now must deck our kings […] turning the accomplishment of many years into an hourglass". The suspension of disbelief was a necessary part of the theatre. The concept was first

---

8. School Of Hard Knocks: Elon Musk Learns From His Failures: https://evannex.com/blogs/news/elon-musk-is-a-failure
9. "Failure is a Gold Mine!" says Ratan Tata. Reported widely including in HBR

explored by Aristotle in relation to the principles of theatre where the audience ignores the unreality of the fiction playing out in front of them in order to experience catharsis. If you want to put ideas into other people's heads they must be part of, and willing participants to, the magic.

When we suspend our adult rational disbelief then we too, can enjoy the delights of the child. There's nothing more exciting for me than to hear, "Ladies and gentlemen, boys and girls ..." I get goosebumps just thinking about it. I'm one of the boys and girls. I'm prepared to suspend my disbelief to be part of the magic. When I was little, about five years old, I was taken to Kennards in Croydon to see Father Christmas. Kennards was a medium sized, mid-level department store, started in 1853, founded on the principle of selling reliable goods at low profit margins. I can tell you I was very excited. We bought our tickets, joined the queue, "travelled" in a submarine/hydrofoil contraption for five minutes being jiggled side to side, with "scenery" passing by; we hopped out of our craft and we were there. The North Pole, with Santa. It was smashing. I had been a good boy; I was full of hope. When I'd finished my audience with Santa, we left his grotto and I was unceremoniously ousted from the North Pole into the paint department. All the wonder was destroyed. If only there had been a journey back to our departure point, the illusion would have been complete, and magic would have happened.

If you're going to do the magic, do the magic.

Right up there with Churchill and Brunel as Great Britons, I place Biddy Baxter, the editor of Blue Peter. You may scoff, but if you've ever coveted a Blue Peter badge, with its tiny ship designed by Tony Hart (yes, *the* Tony Hart, best friend to Morph), then Biddy will have impacted your life.

While at Durham University in 1955 she spotted a career's poster about working at the BBC. "It wasn't that I was being snotty about secretarial work or teaching, I just didn't want to do either of them," she said in 2013 of the options offered to her on this occasion. "All the men were going off to do these amazing things." She did manage to join the BBC and went on to edit one of the most successful and influential children's TV shows. As a child she was bitterly disappointed after writing to Enid Blyton and receiving the same reply, twice. So to avoid this disaster impacting future generations, she introduced a card index system at Blue Peter, recording the details of every child who wrote in, so that they could receive personalised responses.

She was awarded an MBE in 1981 in recognition of her work on Blue Peter. There's a level of excellence that magicians aspire to, and even when they're not in front of the camera they make it look so easy.

Staying with the BBC theme, Jana Bennett,[10] who tragically died young of brain cancer in 2022, was the first woman appointed as director of television at the BBC. She said: "There may be a desire to own everything, but you must not stop the bus and stand in the way of a good idea ... The ecology is less rich if you shape everything in your own image." Her list of achievements included the launch of BBC Three, BBC Four, CBeebies and iPlayer. She understood that her role was to enable others, to encourage the magic, to make it easy for others to be magicians too.

Magicians like Baxter and Bennet have had massive impact on the daily lives of millions of Britons. Yet we barely remember their names.

I did a piece of work for the Old Course Hotel, St Andrews, a five-star hotel with a famous golf course and a luxury spa. I was given a suite overlooking the estuary, wonderful meeting rooms, excellent food, all top class. For one of the meetings, for some unknown reason, they invited me to a sort of "below stairs" exposé; we dined in a mid-level canteen, under flickering fluorescents. All of the mystique had gone. You mustn't do that. If you're going to create magic, create magic. Remember what Joan Crawford said: *"I never go outside unless I look*

10. Jana Bennett obituary, The Guardian: https://www.theguardian.com/media/2022/jan/25/jana-bennett-obituary

like Joan Crawford the movie star. If you want to see the girl next door, go next door."

Zen and the art of sandwich making

I met Lee McCormack at my office in the City.

Lee: *"I thought it was a fantastic meeting, it was brilliant, it went exactly how I wanted. When we met the next time, I realised I hadn't been in listening mode, I was just talking. It was quite an eye opener. You [Piers] have a Buddhist method of teaching where you crack them with a stick, just the right pressure at the right moment so the impact of the lesson is really felt."*

I encouraged Lee to go and work in Pret a Manger, to just try it out for a while. He'd never had a job. Not a proper job. Lee had worked in bars at college; now he got a job sweeping the floor and making sandwiches at Pret a Manger. He did that for two weeks and was planning to quit because he'd learnt enough. I reminded him he needed to give a week's notice or he wouldn't get paid, so why not stick it out for another week. He did.

Lee: *"I learnt a lot about myself. I was surprised how much I enjoyed doing simple things, and even if I was sweeping up I wanted to do it well and took pleasure in doing it. I enjoyed each job. I was given a knife. I enjoyed it. I liked making the sandwiches.* **I thought, if I'm going to make sandwiches, I'm going to be the best at it."**

David Beckham would practice free kicks midweek at his training sessions so he could deliver them flawlessly on match day. When he delivers on a Saturday afternoon, it looks like it's magic. It looks like it's magic because he was practising again and again on a wet Wednesday. Herbert von Karajan when he was chief conductor of the Berlin Philharmonic Orchestra would rehearse the core repertoire of Bruckner, Beethoven and Brahms, stuff they'd been playing (literally) for hundreds of years, every season. He had them rehearsing it two or three times in the morning, so they could play in the evening. That's how you get to be magical, make it look easy, and deliver with panache.

When you've learned all your building blocks, then you can adapt to what comes up. The magician is solid, not a will-o'-the-wisp. They will have put their 10,000 hours in, and then some more. That's how they make it look so magical.

As Malcolm Gladwell explains in *Outliers: The Story of Success*, the "10,000-Hour Rule", the key to achieving world-class expertise in any skill, is, to a large extent, a matter of practising the correct way, for a total of around 10,000 hours. Tom Hopkins, legendary sales trainer, said you should Practice, Drill, Rehearse, Forget – PDRF. It's not just about 10,000 hours of repetition, it's about immersion.

The magician leader is the epitome of preparation meeting opportunity. Luck is what happens when preparation meets opportunity.

During the Covid pandemic, Illovo Sugar were an essential service. They make potable alcohol and the need for hand sanitiser was urgent. They decided the priority was to get this product at scale to the people who needed it most, and the only people who had the ability to do that were their FMCG customers. They contacted Unilever and said, "Let's meet and have a baby." The R&D labs in Europe said no, they couldn't make hand sanitiser with the alcohol Illovo had in in plentiful volume.

Gavin Dalgleish: *"I grasped the nettle, sent an email, 'Look, mate, we can't let excellent get in the way of good.' Three hours later they were able to do it."*

Frank Lloyd Wright, the American architect, designer, writer, and educator, designed more than 1,000 structures over a creative period of seventy years. Wright believed in designing in harmony with humanity and the environment, a philosophy he called organic architecture. Perhaps his most well-known design, *Fallingwater*, was completed in 1939. Like Mozart, Wright's ideas came to him fully formed. He said:

"Early in life I had to choose between honest arrogance and hypocritical humility. I chose the former and have seen no reason to change."

The *Fallingwater* story isn't quite so simple, linear nor straightforward as one would imagine. Wright accepted the commission in 1934, and then for nine months did nothing. Absolutely nothing ... that anyone could see. In his book, *Years with Frank Lloyd Wright: Apprentice to Genius,* Edgar Tafel explains how, with two hours to spare before the patron, Edgar Kaufmann Jr. was due to arrive, Wright, "briskly emerged from his office ... sat down at the table set with the plot plan and started to draw ... The design just poured out of him. Pencils being used up as fast as we could sharpen them ... erasures, overdrawing, modifying. Flipping sheets back and forth."

Wright was in his late sixties when he pulled off this magician's stunt. He frequently said: **"I just shake the buildings out of my sleeves."**

There's a fine line between pulling a rabbit out of a hat at the last moment, and procrastination. Ask yourself: are you procrastinating or are you waiting for the moment? The magician waits for the moment, to deliver the climax, the twist, the reveal, the prestige. Magicians know how to get the maximum out of the moment. The magician seizes the moment.

In *Profiles of the Future: An Inquiry into the Limits of the Possible*, science fiction writer Arthur C. Clarke formulated his famous three laws. The third law is the best known and most widely cited: "Any sufficiently advanced technology is indistinguishable from magic."[11]

You may see the signals in the system, that's great, you may even read them very accurately, that's even better – but you also have to take action. You can't just read the signals.

---

11. The other two laws are: 1. When a distinguished but elderly scientist stated that something is possible, he is almost certainly right; and 2. The only way of discovering the limits of the possible is to venture a little way past them into the impossible.

"When the front of the exchange is full of bicycles, sell" [12]
– Yang Huaiding, Self-made Chinese millionaire, 1950-2021

Magicians read the signals in the system very well. Dr Michael Kock explains how he spots the signals in the system: *"Resonance is a kind of chemistry thing. For some people you get a really positive resonance, with others you get dissonance."*

I suspect two of the key signals may be smell and timing. It's fairly well documented that smell is a key human attractor. But I notice sometimes, when I feel "out of sync" with someone else, its often an issue of timing. I sense when their pace is different, when the conversation is clunky, it's often just because the timing is out. Hopefully I'm flexible enough to adapt. I adjust myself to them. **The only way to lead is to follow.**

I was up a mountain in Glion, a pretty village above Montreux, Switzerland, on a gorgeous spring Saturday morning. I went out for a relaxing stroll around the village to look at the mountain cog wheel train come up with all the fit people heading up to Rochers de Naye. I didn't bother to take my wallet. I was planning to go into Montreux later to buy a copy of the *Financial Times*, when I came upon a little shop, almost as if my mind had created it. On the tiny rack of local Swiss newspapers, there was the *Pink 'Un*, a copy of the *Weekend FT*, amazing. I decided to walk back to the hotel and get my wallet to buy it. By the time I got back it had gone, and I had to take the funicular all the way down into Montreux for my paper. If you're tracking for it, and you see it, **take action.** Do something with it.

Traders often have a rule: always take unexpected profits. If you're leading and receive unexpected opportunity – take it. **It's those signals in the system again ....**

---

12. It drew on the astute observation that when retail investors – especially those who arrived on bicycles because they could not afford a bus fare – flocked to buy shares, it was a sure signal that a rally was nearing its end.

Some people know the signals *to put into the system* to override your own tracking of the signals in the system. I tell this story now with the benefit of hindsight, analysis and reconstruction. I was in the West End of London for a Saturday haircut. I dropped into the Conran shop to look at overpriced furniture and then went to get a paint sample. All very smart and very nice on a sunny summer's day. If you're new to Marylebone High Street (and I wasn't) you can get seduced into thinking you're in a safe place with all the crooks and charlatans down the road in Oxford Street. I'm reasonably aware of my surroundings and pick up on things. I needed some cash, I put my card in the machine, I put my number in. And suddenly there's somebody standing right next to me. He said: "Don't trust this machine, it took my friend's card earlier." He leant over and pointed at the screen, "It was a Maestro card like this." I looked where he pointed. The machine peeped. The screen is now the "home screen" and I think it has my card.

He had pressed the Cancel button while my attention was at the card logos above the screen while simultaneously doing a Derren Brown sleight of hand. "Oh, no, bro. It hasn't taken yours as well? If you put 2222 in, it gives it back to you."

I'm now on full alert. But I'm too late. It's all been done. He's still standing to my right with a handful of folded £20 notes in his hand. The subconscious message he is sending is "I've got money from the machine, why would I need more money?" He's smart, he used the notes to take the card from the machine, so he doesn't touch it and his prints aren't on it. So if necessary, he can just drop it. He's still talking to me. He's got my card. And he's standing there talking to me. "What you going to do? Should you ring the bank? Or will you wait?"

I still think the machine's got the card. I walk away. When you don't have the card in your hand, you don't have the number to call. I get the number to call, but now I've got a bad feeling. After going through security, I find out that my card has been used in the last five minutes to withdrawn four lots of 500 pounds. Another new learning ... I thought it was a daily £500 limit; no, £500 per transaction. He was wearing a mask – not the cops and robbers style – the pandemic style. The bravado of standing there talking to me while he has my card in his hand. Can you imagine how cool you have to be to do that?

Piers in Your Pocket: Channel your inner alchemist

"If you hear a voice within you say, 'You cannot paint,'
then by all means paint, and that voice will be silenced."
– Vincent Van Gogh

When I'm simultaneously slightly trepidatious about doing something and also drawn to it that means we're at a boundary condition. And boundary conditions are where all the excitement happens, where all the creativity comes.

Magician thinking comes from preparation plus opportunity and the willingness to act on the signals. When you channel your inner alchemist you are able to delight people with your creativity. You'll see patterns, wisps of ideas where others see chaos.

Being a magician leader is not a solo sport.

It's at the very heart of leadership to choreograph these dances of connection with your people, the market, ideas and opportunities. To bring the spark, ignite the imagination.

To make some magic:

- Do things other people can't do,
- To get things other people don't have,
- Make it look so easy everyone wants it.
- And, don't practice your free kicks in the UEFA Champions League Final.

Magic appears in all sorts of different places. Sometimes good. Sometimes bad. There can be, like in everything, a dark side of the magician.

Remember though, it's not about party tricks, it's much more special than that.

Chapter 11: When you're in a hole, keep digging

"It is unrealistic to expect people to see you as you see yourself."
– Epictetus

There will be a point in your career and journey where people will now come to you for advice, knowledge and wisdom. This is a beautiful gift that you can benefit from twice. First as you received wisdom from previous sages, and again now as you contribute and put energy into sharing your knowledge with others. The pleasure and enjoyment you feel as you pass on the know-how that has been forged from your own critical thinking and practical application will provide huge benefits.

Are you ready to share your gifts?

When in Singapore I normally stay at the Hilton on Orchard Road. Good location, consistent service, nice lounge with a shower for a late departure. That's all I need. On a slightly extended trip, with the Singapore government backing a hotel promotion to get every visitor to stay one extra day, the Four Seasons was offering four nights for three. It was fractionally more expensive than the Hilton, but what can a guy do? So I went to the Four Seasons, and it was very nice.

I don't trash hotel rooms, I'm a reasonably good guest, but I do leave my things around the room. After my meeting in Marina[1] Bay, I returned to my room and noticed my laptop cable had been tied up in

---

1. Yes, it's Marina like Troy Tempest's love interest in Stingray, not marine as in underwater. Although of course it is reclaimed land...

a cable tie. In the bathroom my lotions, potions and toothpaste were all standing to order, labels aligned. There was a note: "Dear Mr Fallowfield Coo (my long surname causes problems now and then) I notice that your mouse did not have a mat, so I've left him one. I hope he enjoys it. Your room attandant [sic] Jeff."

We're all quick enough to complain, so I decided to say thank you. I went downstairs and asked the man behind the desk if I could speak to the GM. He asked: "Is something wrong?"

I explained that I just wanted to say thanks to housekeeping. He gave me the card of the hotel manager, so I sent him a note so that my housekeeper's boss's boss would hear about it. Singapore's not a tipping culture, so saying thank you is a more appropriate gesture.

Within the hour I had a grateful e-mail reply, and I thought nothing more of it, went out and enjoyed a beer and a pizza with an old friend. As I returned to my room I fancied a bit of chocolate, but I didn't want to go wandering down Orchard Road looking for a shop. There was a knock at the door and a smartly dressed young man in a white uniform and gold epaulettes handed me a small tray. Chocolates with a note. "We thought you might like this with your evening drink." I'm still not sure how they did that thought reading trick! The wonderful service continued with special attention paid to my breakfast guest the next morning. As I was checking out, the front desk attendant said, "I just want to say thank you for your comments about housekeeping. We so appreciate it."

How did he know? Because they talked about it at their morning meeting. Wherever you break that stick of rock, it says Four Seasons Service, from the (minimum wage) room refresher and housekeeping, through to the restaurant and the front desk. Their "hole" is brilliant service. They keep digging.

Feedback frequently leads to over-correction

Sometimes people take feedback, and then over-correct. My mum started to learn to drive when she was fifty-five, after Dad died. I called her after her first driving test to see how it went. "I was a bit fast. I failed. Otherwise, it went quite well so I'll leave it a few weeks and try again." A few more lessons and another test, how did she get on? "I failed again; this time, I drove like a hearse in a snowstorm."

The danger with all feedback is that it becomes a closed loop, an echo chamber of over-compensation and assumption. The CIA have a wonderful model to guard against this. Whatever they are working on they have another team asking: "What if we're entirely wrong?" They realise they're making assumptions, and that they could be completely wrong, so they fight against their internal bias. They question if they are shutting down and closing out the one person who may be shining a light in a dark corner. Because it's uncomfortable the CIA actually pay teams to do that.

In an article on *HBR*, The Feedback Fallacy,[2] Marcus Buckingham and Ashley Goodall explain that there are better ways for managers to help their employees excel, and that constructive criticism, or "feedback", is rarely helpful.

I was working with the divisional head of a major engineering business. He told me: "I'm happy to have contributors, with thoughts and ideas, but I'm fed up with commentators on my business."

Feedback fails for a number of reasons. Research shows that people can't reliably rate the performance of others because over 50% of your rating of someone reflects your characteristics, not theirs – this adds noise to the feedback process, muddying the signal. Neuroscience reveals that criticism provokes the brain's "fight or flight" response and inhibits learning. Finally, who decides what excellence looks like? It's

2. The Feedback Fallacy: https://hbr.org/2019/03/the-feedback-fallacy

not the opposite of failure. Telling people how not to fail is not the same as showing them how to succeed.

There's another issue – the feedback needs to be fast, clear, and in the moment to be effective. The feedback signal needs to be free from noise and bias to be acted upon.

If we assume the "signals in the system" could look like intuition, then maybe the reason we don't always follow them is the feedback is not instant. If the feedback were instant, in the same way that we learn to not touch a hot stove because if you touch it, it burns, don't do that, that's stupid, we might pay more attention. Because we don't have that kind of immediate feedback loop, we discard the data. As we grow older, wiser and more mature (if those three go together) then maybe we become more willing to pay attention to those signals. That's why perhaps we get better at not making the same mistake – not because of experience, but because we're more willing to pay attention to those whispers coming from the data.

I'd flown to Cyprus for an autumn break and rented a car, a Nissan. We got on the road at about 10 o'clock at night; there wasn't much traffic on the A1 motorway. The speed sign said 100. I was doing 100. All was good, we were making great time, we'd be in our hotel very soon. After a while I started to wonder why no one was overtaking us. No one. Everyone was going slow. There wasn't even anyone going our speed. I started doing some logical deduction. In Cyprus they drive on the "correct side" of the road i.e. the left-hand side. This Nissan was right-hand drive, built in Sunderland. I wondered if any modifications had been made to suit local conditions. No. Driving at 100 miles per hour is significantly faster than the 100km limit. It was a different 100. All the information is always in the system.

As a leader, when you see a great outcome, immediately identify it and share your impression of why it was a success. We know that we grow most when we focus on our strengths, not our weaknesses. Make the feedback signals clear and noise free so that transitioning and trans-formation can happen and we can make meaning from the signals.

Meaning-making is a lifelong activity that begins in earliest infancy and continues to evolve through a series of stages encompassing childhood, adolescence, and adulthood. Dr Robert Kegan,[3] a former Harvard psychologist, shows that adults go through five distinct developmental stages. At any point we are in transition from one stage to another, and we may be at different stages in different areas of our life. As we become more self-aware, wise and mature we move up the stages.

Kegan's stages of mature adult development:

Stage 1 – Impulsive mind (early childhood) – Purely reflex driven.

Stage 2 – Imperial mind (adolescence, 6% of adult population) – The person's sense of self is ruled by their needs and wishes. The needs and wishes of others are relevant only to the extent that they support those of the person.

Stage 3 – Socialized mind (58% of the adult population) – Shaped by the definitions and expectations of our personal environment, and coheres by alignment with, and loyalty to these definitions and expectations.

Stage 4 – Self-Authoring mind (35% of the adult population) – Is able to step back enough from the social environment to generate an internal "seat of judgement" or personal authority that evaluates and makes choices about external expectations. Ability to self-direct, take stands, set limits, and create and regulate boundaries.

Stage 5 – Self-Transforming mind (1% of the adult population) – We can step back from and reflect on the limits of our own ideology or personal authority and are friendlier toward contradiction and opposites. We have the ability to align with the dialectic rather than the extremes.

3. Robert Kegan – The Evolving Self: Problem and Process in Human Development

Wherever you think you are, Kegan recommends looking one step lower. He claims we all believe we are one step higher than we are, although we transition through the higher levels with clarity – of who we are, what we want and what we'll do to achieve it.

There are no pockets on a shroud

By now hopefully, you've worked out that the idea of the game is not to be the person with the most when you die. There are no pockets on a shroud. As the buffer generation start getting taken out, you find yourself nearer to the end than the beginning. You've got something nice parked on the drive with all the added options, but you know what, what are you going to do?

Dr Joseph Riggio suggests some leaders are adrenaline junkies, looking for their next hit: *"A vast number of leaders who had great success in their thirties and forties, who are now transitioning to a new role are adrenaline junkies. Satisfaction or pleasure to them means the next hit. They're looking for a different crack pipe. Whether it's bobsledding, or alpine skiing out of a helicopter on untouched paths with fresh powder six feet deep, they keep looking for the next hit. The question for them is are they really finding enjoyment? Relationship and contribution is perhaps the answer."*

It's tempting to keep searching. Going for more. Hunting the next hit.

But really, it's time for some digging into your thinking. **Wisdom frequently comes dressed as the right question.** How are you going to find your real fulfilment? Have you done enough?

The dark side of enough is excess. The rich and spoiled youth of Stureplan in Stockholm, Sweden, were forbidden to spray champagne on each other like winning F1 drivers. Their absolute excess couldn't be stopped though, they were insistent on showing everyone around them how much money they could afford to throw away so they invented *"vaskning"*. They would order two bottles of expensive champagne and tell the bartender to pour one of the bottles in the sink (*vask* in Swedish). **This "one for the sink" thinking will keep you tied to pursuing more.**

The key here is to not become a prisoner of your language. If you believe you are "between a rock and a hard place" in your mind's eye, you are. A prisoner of your own language.

Dr Joseph Riggio warns: *"Be careful thinking about what you want to create, and ask yourself at what point does the success become enough?"*

In conversation with Andrew Dinwiddie, a rising star in the world of insurance, we were discussing an internal role he was considering applying for. He said his dad always applied the three circles rule:

- Money
- Prospects
- Fun

He said, "It's wonderful when you can get all three but often you only get two. For example, great prospects and a lot of money but not much fun, well you can do it for a bit and then use it as a springboard. Money and fun might work while you're young, but without prospects where are you headed?"[4]

Each circle will have greater significance at different stages of your career. At this later stage you may wish to adopt a new three circles model:

---

4. There are many models of three. In options trading, it's time, price and volatility. Change any one of those and everything else changes. In psychology we talk about physiology, language, and emotion. Change any one of them, everything changes. In investment: what's your attitude to risk? What's your time horizon? What's your tax status? Software projects: fast, good, cheap? For chiropractors its speed, force and accuracy.

- Contribution
- Impact
- Enjoyment

Most people find a deep level of fulfilment in some kind of contribution.

You've enjoyed the benefits. How are you going to give back? Are you going to join your local Rotary Club? Help young offenders? Be a mentor? Take a position as a non-exec on a not-for-profit board? Are you going to make a formalised contribution? An informal contribution? Are you going to learn something? **What are you going to do?**

"The only way to make sense out of change is to plunge into it, move with it, and join the dance." — Alan Watts

Not everything is a simple transaction. Lee McCormack intentionally invested energy into areas with no specific sense of what the output might be. *"It bears a lot of fruit. In the worst-case scenario, I learned stuff, I helped someone, even if there's no obvious output result for doing it."*

Coaching and mentoring is the work I was born to do. It's the most fulfilling work I have ever done. I regret that I didn't start doing it ten years before. But if I had, I wouldn't have had those extra ten years of senior leadership experience. So I wouldn't be able to work as easily with the group I work with. It's roundabouts and swings. It would have been nice to do the work for longer, and maybe I'd be even better, but I would have found it less easy to enter the world of the people I like working with: C-suite, ExCo, ExCo-1, and the leaders of tomorrow. And while I'd love the body of a twenty-one-year-old, with the wisdom and experience I have right now – I am, actually, truly fulfilled.

Life beyond the next hole

The benefits at this stage are different. You might get lucky. It might be causal. You might be able to recognise that you spent X time with Y person you got Z result. It definitely requires time and input. But it's generally not linear. I was fortunate I had the opportunity and interest to coach and mentor my top team. It lit my spirit.

I naturally transitioned in the business from leader to leader as mentor which began the journey to my third – and most enjoyable career – coaching and mentoring senior executives.

In 1975, Taibi Kahler, identified five common drivers that motivate us. These can be useful if we are aware of their potential impact but not if we just unconsciously follow them, even when it's not in our best interests. Most people have a combination of two drivers.

The drivers are:

- Be Perfect
- Be Strong
- Hurry Up
- Please Others
- Try Hard

I have a predominance of **be strong** and **be perfect.** My be strong and be perfect combo means I achieve a lot, but I use a lot of energy to get things "just right", and sometimes suffer from imposter syndrome, waiting to be found out. I always help others but see it as a sign of weakness to ask for help for myself, and I can withdraw under stress. I can become the hero in the shadows.

Our drivers can be helpful or hinder us. There's a certain point where things catch up with me. Then I know I need some space, maybe to have a conversation with someone – ask for a little help. My dad died when I just turned 30, I was strong and got everything perfectly orderly and organised as I became "head of the house". But it caught up with me months later when I began to cry … and didn't want to stop crying. So I went to find someone to talk to.

When my mum died in the summer of 2020, there was a moment, a realisation that the "buffer generation" had now been removed. My own sense of mortality was suddenly brought into focus. This time I was smarter and paid more attention to my needs for support and care and quietly rode the shifting emotions.

You may begin to think about your legacy. It could be just a personal legacy to oneself, spending time with your grandchildren, going on that trip you always promised yourself or restoring that old car that reminds you of your first date.

Most twenty somethings don't know they're going to die. They know intellectually, but they don't understand they're going to die unless they've had a fall off a horse or been hit by a car or lost a parent in childhood. They don't believe it. By now, you know you're actually going to die. It's a bit like an old-fashioned reel-to-reel tape recorder; the "adventures to come" tape reel of your life is now spinning quite quickly with not much tape remaining, and the "experiences I've had" reel is quite full.

"It's about living on purpose with meaning, and resolving the existential issues. Time doesn't ask if you care if it keeps going on. If we're lucky enough, we get to be old."– Dr Joseph Riggio

Give the greatest gift of all

At this stage of life, if you are fortunate, it's more about the people you're working with, rather than yourself. The greatest gift that you can give when you're beginning to do this kind of work with someone is helping them move away from that headlong rush into more and more and move towards their greatness and choosing well for the future.

The greatest gift you can give anyone else is to allow them truly to be themselves.

Garma CC Chang, in *The Practice of Zen,* said: "The greater the doubt, the greater the awakening; the smaller the doubt, the smaller the awakening. No doubt, no awakening." If you are doubting your ability to give this gift you are on the right track. Some doubt and questioning is healthy, it keeps you honest; and prevents seduction to the dark side – becoming a manipulative mentor and advisor like Cardinal Richelieu[5]. His position of prominence could be seen as manipulation. There's a distinct line between mentor and manipulator.

> *"No one is more hated than he who speaks the truth."* — Plato

Perhaps the greatest soldier in American history, considered by Churchill as the true organiser of Allied victory in WWII, George C. Marshall,[6] a five-star general who later won the Nobel Peace Prize, has plenty to teach us about being a leader. In a wonderful article, *Leadership Lessons from General George C. Marshall*, Dr Mike Hennelly, who served in the US Army for twenty-one years and taught at West Point for twelve, captured three key lessons from Marshall:

1. speaking truth to power is important, but disagreeing with the powerful is usually dangerous
2. strategic leaders have to be good at interacting with followers *and* other leaders
3. and that empowering others is not a modern concept.

5. Richelieu, known as The Red Eminence, was instrumental in consolidating royal power and building a strong, centralised state in France in the 1600s. Richelieu's decisions to suppress the influence of the feudal nobility and levy taxes targeted (mostly at the commoners) made him a hated figure among both the nobility and the peasantry, and incidentally, one of the clergymen most frequently portrayed in film (the many versions of The Three Musketeers).
6. Leadership Lessons From General George C. Marshall: https://www.realclearde-fense.com/articles/2018/01/11/leadership_lessons_from_general_george_c_mar-shall_112885.html

For me, it's Marshall's strong internal compass that stands out. Despite having his card marked by Roosevelt for disagreeing with his defence plan in 1938, just five months later FDR selected (and rapidly promoted) Marshall to Army Chief of Staff. Great leaders recognise and reward ethical and moral strength. FDR created and held the space for Marshall. General Marshall, in addition to his military success will also be remembered as the driving force behind the Marshall Plan which provided billions of dollars in aid to post-war Europe to restart the economies of the destroyed countries.

If I was putting my dream dinner party guests together, Marshall would certainly make the cut though I probably wouldn't invite James Buchanan, who served as the fifteenth president of the United States from 1857 to 1861 and is considered probably the worst president the US has had. He was the last president before the start of the Civil War, and although he tried to prevent it, many of his policies ended up dividing the Union even further. In Robert Kaplan's book, *Earning the Rockies: How Geography Shapes America's Role in the World,* he notes: *"Buchanan did not have a compass point toward which to navigate in the midst of all the deals he tried to make ... But mostly he was all ambition and technique without direction."*

At the time, Buchanan was probably the most qualified person to become president (the Hillary Clinton of the day), the "most ready" presidential candidate who had been a congressman and senator, US Secretary of State, ambassador to the UK, who went on to simultaneously anger the North and the South culminating in the Civil War, leading to over 500 deaths per day. We can learn a lot from both Marshall and Buchanan. **Qualification and experience are not enough, because without that internal compass, the visceral true north, one is lost and loses others.**

"If you stand for nothing Burr, what'll you fall for?"
– Alexander Hamilton to Aaron Burr, Act 1 "Hamilton"

In my life I have found two things of priceless worth – learning and loving. Nothing else – not fame, not power, not achievement for its own sake – can possible have the same lasting value, for me, anyway. For when your life is over, if you can say "I have learned" and "I have loved," you will also probably be able to say, "I have been happy".

People who speak truth to power elegantly are in high demand.

Piers in Your Pocket: Create a space for thinking

"Every child is an artist.
The problem is how to remain an artist once he grows up."
– Pablo Picasso

I was working with the CPO at a FTSE 100 company recently. We were discussing their effectiveness. I suggested that they needed more thinking time and should set aside and aim for an hour or so per day for thinking. They were shocked – their hope was to get an hour or so a week blocked out. There's a mismatch. If you don't set aside time for thinking, then when will you do it?

Take time now to think about how you are going to share your gifts:

1. Be available – share your knowledge
2. Adopt a worthy cause – become a mentor or take on a NED
3. Stop chasing more material highs – what are you going to do with them all anyway?
4. Start speaking truth to power with confidence – if not now, then when? If not you then who?

It's your call to personal action. Are you at this stage just going to begin the gentle wind down? Or are you, like Dr Who,[7] going to be regenerated? Maybe more interesting, something different, a reinvention, contribution?

7. For my international readers not familiar with Dr Who, the much loved BBC programme, on our screens since 1963, Dr Who is the science fiction story of a "Time Lord" called "The Doctor" traveling through time and space in the Tardis (bigger on the inside than the outside). "The Doctor" has the ability to periodically regenerate themselves into someone completely different!

Chapter 12: Fennel and preserved lemons

"We shall not cease from exploration
And the end of all our exploring
Will be to arrive where we started
And know the place for the first time."
– TS Eliot, Four Quartets

King Lear's fool had the greatest freedom of all – the licence to speak truth to power. By now you will have internalised your own values, you will know deeply who you are and how to move in the world. Additionally, it's time for a little self-indulgence and refinement. It's time for an active surrender, to quieten the perpetual dialogue with the system and the environment. To live in the here and now, to feel exuberant joy, to relish the world you have created.

A better prescription

An advertisement in the *Financial Times* said "Wanted: CEO for a foreign exchange analysis and prediction system start-up in Zurich." Interesting. I jumped in the car, popped the roof down, hot-footed it across Europe and swung through the portcullis into The Dolder Grand, a fairy-tale hotel in the hills above Zurich. Wednesday evening is candlelight dinner night at The Dolder, the place was full of dowager burghers. The trolley came and the chef carved me another slice of *filet de bœuf en croute,* the sommelier offered another glass of delicious Burgundy. By the time I went to bed after drinks I was completely stuffed and feeling quite uncomfortable.

After that trip, and a conversation with my doctor, I became a vegetarian. I spoke to my doctor about this uncomfortable feeling after eating all this fancy food. He told me to cut out red meat. I ignored him. I went back again, hoping for a better "prescription": "Cut out red meats they are absolutely terrible for you." Turns out he was a sixty-two-year-old vegan, who looked about forty. There might be something in what this family doctor was saying. I remember, as a child, he had a sign in his surgery: *Be prepared to leave this surgery empty handed.* He was an early voice warning of the dangers of overprescription of antibiotics. The secret was, of course, if you really needed "white man's medicine" you saw his cousin, Dr Fischthal, who was a more relaxed prescriber.

I decided that I would cut out red meat. But what to eat? I bought some ready cooked chicken. It was oily and disgusting. I didn't eat much fish then. In the space of ten days, I'd gone from eating virtually everything to eating nothing and wondering why I was feeling tired and looking pasty.

Back in Zurich, I went to see the start-up; a spin off from ETH Zurich (Einstein's University). I was given a fantastic presentation of the system. I told him that if what he was showing me was true – the ability to accurately predict foreign exchange rates, commercially it was an enormous opportunity, and we could make an absolute fortune. He looked at me as if I had just crawled out from under a rock and said the real purpose of this project was academic research. I left. After a couple of years his investors agreed with me and now OANDA is one of the world's biggest and most successful retail FX and CFD (contract for differences) trading sites.

Going from the leader's full "diet" of business meetings, decisions, responsibilities etc. to nothing might come as a surprise. You have to eat something. But **right now it's your turn to decide what's on the menu, and more importantly what's in the meal.**

The last chapter of this book is about our complete coming to ourselves, and our absolute appreciation of everything there is. It often tends to come later in life, certainly after the second half. It's the person who's willing to drive twenty miles (or kilometres) to visit the little olive store, because he likes his conversation with the man who sells the olives. And he likes *those* particular olives.

We're talking bigger picture now, not necessarily a long time, but a long visual horizon. You've made it and now you might choose to carry on, you might choose to become chair of a charity, you might choose to colour code your socks, to play endless rounds of golf, or you might just choose to lie down and wiggle your toes. It's time for a little bit of self-indulgence, refinement, **active surrender**, a quiet and perpetual dialogue to live in the here and now.

But, maybe it's not necessarily about the endless rounds of golf nor the everlasting cruises. It's just that maybe – maybe – after you've indulged for a while you might decide to make a new choice.

The great challenge is that maybe you're going to have to give up a significant amount of the trappings of success, as we understand it, to make space to allow some other things to come in. This is a **'second surrender'**.

Are you willing to surrender?

"The Cosmic Dancer, declares Nietzsche, does not rest heavily in a single spot, but gaily, lightly, turns and leaps from one position to another. It is possible to speak from only one point at a time, but that does not invalidate the insights of the rest."
– Joseph Campbell, Hero with a Thousand Faces, The (p. 196)

It hasn't always been that you arrive at a certain age and get to go on cruises. Before Lloyd George followed the example of Otto von Bismarck's Germany which had provided compulsory national insurance against sickness from 1884, most people worked until they died. Lloyd George said in his 1909 Budget speech that Britain should aim to be "putting ourselves in this field on a level with Germany; we should not emulate them only in armaments." This is when the idea of paid sick leave and pensions came to fruition. Of course, Bismarck worked out that he could offer pensions because so few people would actually live long enough to enjoy them. The whole system was designed for the labourer, for people who worked on the land, or shovelled coal, or worked in the steel mills. Their later life expectancy was short.

This fancy generation of mine thought that somehow you could be in college till you're about twenty-five getting their nth degree, work a few years, then retire at fifty-five, with a long forty-year stretch of relax-ing[1]. Forty years of golf might get boring. So most people require an occupation, a passion or hobbies. A friend of mine, he and his wife are hillwalkers. So they sold that big London place and bought a lit-tle flat in the Barbican and a house in the lakes. They plan their year around walking. When they're in London they see their friends, go to the opera and theatre, enjoy a little fine dining. When they're at the lakes they do country things and lots of walking. It's called being rich.

We need to keep active and we need to be stimulated. I don't see this as a passive time. It's not. It's an active time with more choices. For me personally, what I'm doing now – mentoring and coaching execu-tives – brings me joy. **I am revelling in helping my clients find a better version of themselves.** I hope it lasts forever. This has been the most rewarding, successful, fascinating time of my life. Sometimes, as I look back, I can't quite understand now how I blossomed in corporate work.

In 1952 at the age of sixty-five, when most people are looking at slow-ing down and retiring, Harland David Sanders began Kentucky Fried Chicken. Charles Darwin was fifty before he published *On the Origin of the Species* in 1859. Julia Child published Mastering the Art of French Cooking and a year later launched The French Chef on TV at fifty. Ray Kroc began franchising McDonald's at fifty-two.

This stage can be about reinvention. I reinvented myself. It's not about a new miracle time, a certain age. It's about a time in life. **This is a recommitment to being you.**

---

1. Quite how this was going to be funded is a different question.

Maybe time to dig a little deeper in your thinking about who you are and what's really important.

It's as if you've been given a dressing-up box and you can be anybody you want to be. Is that scary? Is it indulgent? Is it defensive? Or is it exciting?

It really isn't about a chronological age. Mozart was a prolific and influential composer leaving us with over 600 compositions.[2] He died at the top of his game when he was just thirty-five. Would his "later" works have been as good? Would he have done something different in his contrapuntal second movement? Orson Welles, one of the greatest and most influential film-makers of all time, headlined early with his first film, Citizen Kane, generally regarded as one of the best films ever made. His list of unfinished works far outweighs the ones you can probably name. What do you do to make sure that your best ideas are still coming when you're older? How do you balance the wisdom and experience of age, with the foolhardiness of youth? In *The Curious Case of Benjamin Button*, the protagonist ages in reverse. It's been a dream of many to have the knowledge and experience we have now, and to be twenty-one again. Are you embracing this time with optimism? Or are you allowing the slightly creaking physical system and the stream of obituaries of childhood heroes to knock you back?

Greg Simidian: *"For me it amounts to planning and executing a structure where I can as effortlessly or easily as possible enjoy the goals I want to achieve. But without all the stress and pain and youthful idiocy, that was a necessary part of growing up, but wasted so much time and effort. I left behind the passion stuff. You've got to enjoy what you do, of course, but the passion thing now feels a bit Disney."*

There was a strange temporal shift occurring for me during Covid Lockdown 1.0, which I think was a comparatively widely shared experi-

2. The Art of Blooming Late – Kevin Evers: https://hbr.org/2019/05/the-art-of-blooming-late

ence, in which the days were almost everlasting but the weeks rushed by: "Oh, it's 'bin day' again". One hundred and fifty years ago, our forefathers, which would probably be now our great-grandfathers, were busy with a plough, drawn by horses. When you think in anthropological terms, the world looked pretty much like it had done for the last couple of thousand years. From then till now, and we're flying in machines faster than the speed of sound, and we've only just come off the savanna. Why on earth do we think we can possibly hold our level of attention on so many things for so long? Hopefully, at this stage, as we reinvent ourselves we will see this madness, and decide to exclude it.

Shakespeare's The Seven Ages of Man from As You Like It, begins:

> *All the world's a stage,*
> *And all the men and women merely players:*
> *They have their exits and their entrances.*
> *And one man in his time plays many parts,*
> *His acts being seven ages.*

The seven ages are the helpless infant, the whining schoolboy, the emotional lover, the devoted soldier, the wise judge, the old man still in control of his faculties, and the extremely aged, returned to a second state of helplessness. So, before you pass into the seventh stage it might be time to take measure of your life.

> *"Truly wealth, which men spend all their lives in acquiring,*
> *is a valueless thing at the last."*
> — H. Rider Haggard, King Solomon's Mines

Steve Reich the American minimalist musician wrote a piece called *Proverb* using a short text from Wittgenstein. "How small a thought it takes to fill a whole life!" This comes from a collection of Wittgenstein's writing entitled *Culture and Value*. Much of Wittgenstein's work is "proverbial" in tone and in its brevity. This particular text was written in 1946. In the same paragraph from which it was taken Wittgenstein continues, **"If you want to go down deep you do not need to travel far."**

Back in Gail Sheehy's *New Passages: Mapping Your Life Across Time*, she promises a Second Adulthood in middle life, and urges: "Stop and recalculate. Imagine the day you turn forty-five as the infancy of another life." Instead of declining, men and women who embrace a Second Adulthood can progress through entirely new passages into lives of deeper meaning, renewed playfulness, and creativity.[3]

Erik Erikson, the German-American developmental psychologist and psychoanalyst, maintained that personality develops in a predeter-mined order through eight stages of psychosocial development, from infancy to adulthood. During each stage, the person experiences a psychosocial crisis which could have a positive or negative outcome for personality development. At this stage in the journey, we're more interested in the final two stages:

Stage 7, 40–65 years: Generativity vs. Stagnation – *care*

Stage 8, 65+: Integrity vs. Despair – *wisdom*

Stage seven: generativity versus stagnation, where the person con-tributes to future generations through raising children and helping others to develop products or come up with creative new ideas. It's about growth and putting unfulfilled dreams aside to find meaning in work and family. If this task is not accomplished, growth is stopped, and the person becomes stagnant and self-centred.

Then stage eight is integrity versus despair, at sixty-five plus. At this stage, people reap the benefits of all that they have done during their lives, accepting that life is temporary. If their task (or ambition) is not accomplished, they may feel sadness, regret, and struggle to find meaning.

3. Looking to the future: https://www.collegesuccess1.com/native%20american/fral-ick10_ch14sample1.pdf

"But we cannot live the afternoon of life according to the program of life's morning; for what was great in the morning will be little at evening..." – Carl Jung

I love how on the Underground in London it tells me how long I will need to wait – if it says eight minutes – it means I can make a decision, I can wait and read my book or maybe, if I'm in a hurry, go and get a cab. You are at that time in your life where the screen is flashing "afternoon", you need to make the decisions.

When clearing out some old papers from my "archives" – a pretentious description of a box of stuff from the year 2000 (remember Y2K when all the computers in the world were due to fail) – I found a "directional" note I had written about my future:

My new career:

The definition and therefore the intent is beginning.

My moving towards desires are (in no specific order):

- Work that I can do (in different amounts) for the next ten to fifteen years.
- Something that the more I do it, the more I will grow as well.
- An occupation that is fulfilling emotionally, intellectually, spiritually and financially.
- Something that will help people grow, fulfil their potential and allow them to truly be themselves.
- Work that is flexible and varied.
- Work that I enjoy so much it is more hobby and passion than work.
- An occupation that will fascinate me, challenge me and that I can excel in.

So how can I achieve all this?

> Well, the process has already started as I'm now defining direc-
> tionality and each action will now be drawn gently, almost
> imperceptibly towards this beacon in the distance. I must start
> to shape and mould all that I do and think to match with my
> intent...with everything going in the same direction all things
> will either support these aims or must be discarded.

Twenty years later and I'm happily working with emotionally and intellectually stimulating people, who I am helping to fulfil their potential. I'm the anti-establishment establishment coach, dismantling the system from the inside. Just as I described when standing outside the chemistry lab all those years ago.

This is a classic example of how to not set "goals" but set "directionality" and surrender to what unfolds. There's a strange paradox of knowing you have less time to do stuff and wanting to do more. A curious reverse situation of folding time and space. The 80/20 principle can come to full fruition.

*"Life is not a problem to be solved but a mystery to be lived.
Follow the path that is no path, follow your bliss."* – Joseph Campbell

The Moravian Muse – What really makes us happy?

"Happiness and moral duty are inseparably connected."
– George Washington

In 2002, Martin Seligman, wrote *Authentic Happiness: Using the new positive psychology to realize your potential for lasting fulfilment,* showing how psychology, when it shifts away from focusing on pathology, victimology, and mental illness to positive emotion, virtue and strength can have huge impact. Seligman developed the Signature Strengths Survey,[4] to measure how much positive emotion people experience and to help determine what their highest strengths are. By identifying the very best in ourselves, we can improve the world around us and achieve new and sustainable levels of authentic contentment, gratification, and meaning.

Seligman's PERMA model of well-being focused on five areas: positive emotion, engagement, relationships, meaning and accomplishments. It's no surprise that an insights article on the McKinsey[5] website on Better Bosses, identified four things you can do to improve workplace happiness: be kind, be thankful, be positive and be healthy.

And while it's claimed a whopping 50% of our "happiness" comes from our parents' genetics,[6] and an additional 10% from the circumstances in which we find ourselves, it looks like we have control over the other 40% – our activities and our outlook. With a positive attitude, practising optimism when imagining the future, learning how best to savour life's pleasures in the here and now, appreciating relationships, an attitude of gratitude, and finding meaning we can create our own authentic happiness.

> *"Life isn't about waiting for the storm to pass.*
> *It's about learning how to dance in the rain."* – Vivian Greene

Dr Michael Kock: "Sometimes I feel lonely, impatient, and angry. But it helps to get older. You learn to accept it."

As you've reached this stage in your career, the afternoon of your life, you probably have an inkling about what makes you happy. What suits

4. You can find out yours here: https://www.viacharacter.org/
5. Better bosses: https://www.mckinsey.com/business-functions/organization/our-insights/five-fifty-better-bosses
6. Lyubomirsky, S. (2007). The how of happiness: A scientific approach to getting the life you want.

you? Do you like a run? Gym? Quiet time? An empty in-box? Gaps between meetings? A walk at lunchtime?

What's your Kryptonite? We all have our own Kryptonite and by now, we should know what it is and avoid it. Whether it's not getting enough sleep, eating too much, chasing the sugar hit, that extra glass of red wine, never getting out of the TV chair … whatever it is, by now we should be avoiding it. One look at the almond croissant and we should know to leave it alone.

I think there are three things you need for happiness:

1. Time
2. Energy and vitality
3. Some money in your back pocket

At different times in your life you've probably got two of them. When you're young, you've got energy and time, and probably no money. Then you're working very hard and you've got energy and money, but no time. There's a sweet spot – the golden period – when you've got all three. You've still got lots of energy. You've got some time. You have some money in your back pocket. Now, what are you going do with this gift?

"Our life is frittered away by detail. Simplify, simplify, simplify! I say, let your affairs be as two or three, and not a hundred or a thousand; instead of a million count half a dozen, and keep your accounts on your thumbnail." – Henry David Thoreau

If you can't find meaning or happiness in your current life, then maybe take yourself a Moravian Muse[7] and create a fantasy. Czech composer Leoš Janáček found his muse when he was sixty-three, and unhappily married. Kamila was twenty-five and also married when Janáček fell madly in love with her, going on to write hundreds of love letters and

---

7. The Moravian Muse Who Inspired Music: http://www.tresbohemes.com/2017/03/moravian-muse-inspired-music/

some of his best work. He loved her until his death eleven years later. Kamila remained a passive inspiration for his compositions. His late flowering was his greatest work.

There is no exact "age" for happiness, achievement, success – nor for the cessation of any activities. Many people believe that late bloomers are happier and more successful – they have overcome difficulties, have demonstrated resilience, fought back. You could call this "grit", an essential ingredient for success at any age, that increases as you get older: *"But grit—a combination of perseverance and determination—rises through middle age and peaks in your 70s, as do a number of other helpful intellectual traits."* says Arianne Cohen in an article *The Psychological Formula for Success After Age 50* for Bloomberg Businessweek.[8]

I think Alain Dromer has a wonderful handle on this phase of life. He started piano lessons at fifteen, which, he says was too late to become a pianist. *"Although I dreamt about it, and it made me physically ill to have to choose something else. I had practised the piano with a Polish teacher, who was 20 years or so older than me, and has accompanied me in my lifelong journey. He is still my professor, at 85 years old. I've reached the ecstatic moment where I can just play the piano only for my pleasure. It's not a career, it's not a money earning thing. It's just pleasure. It's for myself. I've started to play chamber music, and we are comfortable enough to give concerts. This is supervised by my old teacher, Marian Rybicki, who remains an extraordinary man. He's known all over the world, and I'm fortunate enough that he's one of my best friends. The piano gives me total joy and pleasure. **Working towards perfection with other people is my joy, my happiness."***

You have to be able to experience Nirvana in Sainsbury's on a damp November day. If you can only do it at a yoga boot camp in the foothills of the Himalayas, that ain't Nirvana.

---

8. https://www.bloomberg.com/news/articles/2020-12-08/tips-for-finding-career-success-even-as-you-approach-retirement

"Soup of the day: Aperol Spritz"
Sign outside a restaurant in Franschhoek, Western Cape

The US National Youth Poet Laureate, Amanda Gorman, said at President Biden's inauguration: "...you need to be brave enough to see it. But more importantly, you need to be brave enough to be it."

In the war with the roses the buddleia will always win

"I suggest a new strategy, Artoo: Let the Wookiee win." – C-3PO

The law of requisite variety[9] shows that the plant or animal species with the greatest flexibility will take over the system. Roses need particular soil – it can't be too wet nor too dry. They need to face a particular way – south, and a little bit to the west. They are prone to black spot, green fly, white fly, mould, scurfy, powdery mildew, rose rust, and aphids. The amount of work to get a rose to flourish is bonkers. Buddleia, on the other hand need two grammes of soil on the side of a railway bridge and they're off. You'll spot them on motorways, parks, in front of council buildings and from your train carriage. Don't dare cut them back or they'll grow even bigger. Guess which plant is going to take over the planet? The buddleia's incredible flexibility means they will outmanoeuvre, outlive and outperform the roses.

We've looked at flexibility throughout the book. I've probably mentioned it what feels like at least 100 times. It's no surprise to me because **the leaders with the highest amount of flexibility of behaviour will have the most influence on the system.** The more choices you have, the more freedom you will feel, and the better quality of life you can have. Now you have the most freedom of all. You are at

9. W. Ross Ashby was a British cyberneticist and psychologist who, during the 1960s, proposed a law with regards to levels of variety and regulation within biological systems.

your utmost FIFO – fixed on the inside, flexible on the outside. You've decided what you want, set your directionality, you're playing to your strengths. You don't need to worry about being the magician, nor taming the energy of the warrior. You have complete flexibility. And at some deep level, you probably don't care whether you get it or not.

In a wonderful interview in the *FT*,[10] Julian Richer says: "This is my life's work. My dad dropped down dead at the same age as I am today. My greatest fear is that the same happens to me and this gets taken over by venture capitalists, who will mess it up." Richer began his career at nineteen, has a Guinness World Record for the greatest sales in relation to area of store space for his first store, and he personally sent emails – nightly – to stores who made great sales. Now in his seventies, Richer sold a 60% stake of his business to his employees to create an employee owned trust (EOT). He's now an employee of the company he founded.

I was chairman of Greycon from 2005 to 2018, a software house specialising in optimisation products for the paper industry. The CEO, Constantine Goulimis, one of the co-founders did the same where he arranged for more than a third of the business to belong to an EBT (employee benefit trust).

In *The Great Game of Business: The Only Sensible Way to Run a Company*, Jack Stack describes how he took over an old GM diesel engine re-manufacturing plant. He wanted to get all the workforce involved so that when he sold it on, he would make enough money for every employee to be able to pay off the mortgage on their family house in Springfield, Illinois. He thought it would set them free. He told them everything, the profit margins, his salary, what happened last week, and had an incredible impact.

10. FT.com, Jonathan Moules, OCTOBER 20 2019, Julian Richer: Treating people well pays dividends

*"The truly free man is the one who can turn down
an invitation to dinner without giving an excuse."*
– Jules Renard, The Journal of Jules Renard

Perhaps a few stoic reminders of how to live a good life will help here. The leaders of Stoicism crafted four cardinal virtues: justice, wisdom, self-discipline and courage. In *The Little Book of Stoicism: Timeless Wisdom to Gain Resilience, Confidence, and Calmness*, Jonas Salzgeber reminds us to: embrace whatever happens and not fight reality; accept change because nothing is permanent; develop empathy to avoid snap judgements; to be economical with words; to spend more time observing and listening; and to set an example

Your actions are more valuable to others than a lecture.

In, *Essentialism: The Disciplined Pursuit of Less*, Greg McKeown shares a delightful comparison of the nonessentialist and the essentialist. Our nonessentialist comrades think they have to be all things to all people, charge after the undisciplined pursuit of more and live an unsatisfying life. The essentialist thinks "less but better", acts on the disciplined pursuit of less and gets a life that really matters. You get to decide: drive, ditch or delegate.

You also get to decide who you are, because, as Greg says, *"Only once you give yourself permission to stop trying to do it all, to stop saying yes to everyone, you can make your highest contribution towards the things that really matter."* It's your time to make the highest contribution.

*"Things take longer to happen than you think they will and then
they happen faster than you thought they could."*
– Rüdiger Dornbusch, German Economist

Mary McAleese[11], in an interview for Woman's Hour, September 2020 said: *"I am a person of faith, but I'm also a person with a thinking*

---

11. Mary McAleese's autobiography Here's the Story: A Memoir

brain." Mary McAleese was twice president of Ireland, studied canon law when her term ended and, to the surprise of many, as she has a deep personal faith, spoke out against misogyny in the global Catholic Church. "My tiny little voice will permeate."

Louis Armstrong, American trumpeter and vocalist who is among the most influential figures in jazz, was born to the 16-year-old daughter of a slave who took to prostitution to support herself and her child. He spent time in reform school and played jazz in the red-light district of New Orleans.

Louis Armstrong's achievements are remarkable.[12] During his career, he:

- Developed a way of playing jazz, as an instrumentalist and a vocalist, which has had an impact on all musicians who follow.
- Recorded hit songs for five decades, and his music is still heard and enjoyed today
- Wrote two autobiographies, more than ten magazine articles, hundreds of pages of memoirs, and thousands of letters.
- Was the only Black Jazz musician to publicly speak out against school segregation in 1957.

You've got leverage right now. The leverage of networks, of connections, of experience. It might have been a slow process, but you're there. In *Walden; or Life in the Woods,* Henry David Thoreau said: *"If a man does not keep pace with his companions, perhaps it is because he hears a different drummer. Let him step to the music which he hears, however measured or far away."*

Freedom is the acceptance of ourselves and our place in the world. Freedom is moving to our own music or cooking up our own business.

12. The Louis Armstrong Educational Foundation

Sahil Verma: From street performer to accidental accountant to award-winning food industry entrepreneur

When I was young, I wanted to be a theatre artist. I started a street play group, a collective, wearing the same clothes, like a uniform, rocking up in the middle of the road, performing to passers-by, gathering our audience as we sang and danced. I loved it. When I told my dad I had a place to study at the National School of Drama, he told me to get a proper job, or get out of the house. That was the end of my drama career. So I accidentally became an accountant. Firstly with Arthur Andersen then PwC as a consultant. I then joined Regus (now IWG) a large corporate, but very entrepreneurial, and quite chaotic, with a founder led mentality.

But I wasn't really happy. It took me a long time to understand where that unhappiness was coming from: it was because I wasn't creating anything. I was happy when I was creating. But when I was doing deadbeat work, just turning the handle, I was miserable. Unfortunately, the creative vs dead beat ratio was going the wrong way.

Sometimes the universe conspires to make those connections for you. I met Piers, he encouraged me to pursue what makes me happy. It was a moment of reckoning.

Nidhi, my wife, and I had started a cookery school in 2000 because we were both passionate about food. I egged her on, fuelling my own desire and need to do something creative while I was holding a corporate career that paid the bills. When I started working with Piers he asked some very deep questions and the work we did together for six months was invaluable for me, stilling all the noise in my head so I could clearly understand what I had to do. What I have today is the result of the work that we've done together.

Nidhi and I honed in on an idea: *The Cookaway*. Without thinking about anything else, we started doing it, one action after another. Putting one foot after another. No overthinking about what happens if I lose my job, who's going to pay the bills, where's the money going to come from? I removed all of that noise because Piers' support gave me enough confidence to know the path I needed to take, so I did not second guess myself.

We took a very bold approach to become the first non-subscription recipe box company in the UK. We focused on the product, backed by incredible chefs, people connected with the passion that we have for the business and the product that we've developed.

When I look back I realise how much I didn't know about that journey when I started. I've learned and discovered things about myself, about business, about how you do start-ups and raise money. Piers' work led to a very deep belief in myself. It's been one of the most amazing experiences of my life. In the last two years I've focused on family, business, and health. It's been like coming out of a cave. And even if this business is not ultimately a big success, it's been worth doing it just for what I have already gained.

Like every ancient hero, Sahil discovered the gold was already at his feet, or in this case, in his kitchen.

Ghandi said: *"Live as if you were to die tomorrow. Learn as if you were to live forever."* I suggest you plan as if you're going to live forever and live like it's your last day on earth.

This is a time of being orphaned. You will lose your parents, maybe give up familiar roles in your work and the places you go. These are like many small deaths, that unless handled well, may build up and become overwhelming. Tackling difficult but important conversations about death is the subject of a new book from insurer Royal London. In conversation with Barry O'Dwyer, Royal London's inspirational leader, he told me how he and his top team completely buy into the power of being a mutual and their wider connection with the community. They explored how death is one of society's lasting taboos and decided it was their mission to bring experts and leading thinkers together to explore the difficult but crucial conversations around death. *How To Die Well,* is available for free from their website[13] and covers subjects ranging from coping with grief and loss, end-of-life planning, settling estates and arranging a funeral to saying goodbye to loved ones, and coming to terms personally with the final farewell.

Barry says: "Royal London wants to help people be better prepared for death – emotionally, practically and financially – and to encourage society to have more honest conversations about it." In order to have a great life, prepare for a good death. This attitude could also be applied to the "leadership little death" of moving on from work.

"And now 'love' is the name for our pursuit of wholeness."
– Plato from a speech in 387 B.C.

Piers in Your Pocket: I'm loving it

"Plans are worthless, but planning is everything."
– Dwight D. Eisenhower, 1957

Are you living a plentiful, fulfilling, extraordinary life? For many that "extraordinary" has to be meaningful in some way.

Have you discovered your vocation? That something that gives you exuberant joy, and the desire to relish the world you have created?

Have you actively surrendered and quietened the internal dialogue?

How are you going to remain vital?

---

13. How to Die Well: https://www.royallondon.com/mutuality/how-to-die-well/

1. My first recommendation is get an eighteen-year-old mentor.
2. Then take yourself a twenty-five-year-old lover.
3. Finally, buy a mirror that lies to you.

Joking aside, don't necessarily buy the motorbike, throw away your relationships nor play with paramours. Maybe invest in a mentor, practice being more flexible and do things that truly inspire you.

You Were The Future Once

"Only entropy comes easy."
– Anton Chekhov

It was a dark and stormy night ... it wasn't but it should have been ... isn't that how all great journeys begin *and* sometimes end?

After Life, a play written by Jack Thorne (based on a Japanese film of the same name) is a production to stimulate thinking. The concept is that you can bring just one memory from your life with you after you die. That memory will live in your thoughts again and again for all time. The purpose of the play is to prompt you and make you think, if you end up in God's waiting room what memory would you save for eternity?

Naturally, a few ideas popped into my mind straight away but a couple of days after watching the play I found a truly moving memory that somehow fitted both me and the idea like a glove ... It was from a while ago. We'd had a terrible wet and grey spring. We decided to do something we had never done before, go to Europe in the car. An adventure. On went the GB stickers and we were off. We went across the Channel on the car ferry and drove to Annecy, ventured to Grenoble, then up to Switzerland. We arrived in Interlaken at around 10pm in the evening on a late May day, looking for somewhere to stay. We saw a sign by the side of the road: *Zimmer frei*. We were in luck, rooms were available, *"but I don't do breakfast,"* said the matronly owner. We gladly took the room unseen. In the morning we were woken by the sound of clanking bells. We opened the window of this wooden chalet and saw pastures sliding off into the distance. Cows with cow bells, a lake with snow-capped mountains behind.

I love trains. So we went to the little rack railway that runs up to The

Schynige Platte in the Bernese Highlands, connecting the town of Wilderswil, near Interlaken, with the famous wildflower gardens of the Schynige Platte. My senses are already stimulated. High pressure, cool breeze, glorious sunshine. The rack train's cog wheels whirred up the mountain, curving slightly just above the town and there you can see the entire side of a mountain, with a pencil waterfall, and the flowers. Transcendental. This is my memory.

Hold simultaneously, if you can, the vision you'd like to hold forever with the practicalities of the day and what you need to do.

> *"How beautiful it is,*
> *that eye-on-the-object look."*
> – WH Auden "Sext" from Horae Canonicae

This truly "beyond words" feeling can be described as the GDS – Generalised Desired State – which is how the child experiences the world pre language. This incredible sensory overload of experience, linked with appreciation of that which is greater than oneself is a good way to move through the world. **Then it's the tension between doing and being.** Tap into the idea of what memory you would hold forever if you were forced to choose, to find clues as to how you want to move through the world. **In the esoterica there is practicality.**

In this, my last career, I get to sit at top tables, and I'm asked, "What do you think we should do?" I get a chance to encourage tentative chief executives to really step up and get on with making a difference. Maybe thinking more about their wider responsibility, encouraging diversity or perhaps creating a learning culture or winning an award as a great place to work. Simply to become their best and to make a difference.

We've been on a journey together. I hope I was a good leader: strong in face of adversity, but also thoughtful, caring, creative. I hope you can be that too. For us it may seem quite ordinary to be good, wholesome wise leaders. For others it's quite extraordinary – this journey from heart to the head and back again …

David Cameron, when he was first elected leader of the Conservative opposition, taunted Tony Blair, in Parliament: "You were the future once." How are you going to make sure you're also the future now? **It's time for another adventure, but maybe a different one this time?**

If anything in this book has stimulated a thought or two ... get in touch, I'd love to have a conversation.

As Milton Erickson once said: "I have no intention of dying. In fact, that will be the last thing I do!"

The Contributors

I've worked with over 120 C-suite executives in my capacity as a coach and mentor. Many of them anonymously contributed their thoughts to the book. Others have been part of more extended interviews and conversations.

Rachel Grant: Director of Communications and Advocacy at CEPI. In the midst of the pandemic in 2020, Rachel Grant was the Director of Communications and Advocacy at CEPI (The Coalition for Epidemic Preparedness Innovation). She had previously been Director of Communications in the office of Tony Blair, Global Head of Media Relations for McKinsey, has worked in Number 10 and was the head of news at DEFRA and DWP.

Lee McCormack: CEO of Global Home, a technology company focused on the global property development market. Global Home's patented core technology products enable its customers to turn a one-off transaction into a lifetime of recurring revenue opportunity. The company is building the industry's new Platform-as-a-Business model aimed at serving the needs of property developers, investors and consumers interested in sustainable and connected homes. His business is moving from a technology idea into a profit business. He's set up a company with a board, and taken on the title of CEO, instead of his normal "design lead" or founder.

Alain Dromer: Chairman of the board at Arvella Investments. Alain has deep experience in complex strategy settings, proven track record in leading multi-cultural businesses both within Europe and between Europe and Emerging Markets and a particular aptitude to create and develop successful management teams – notably in the area of financial services and asset management. He's had leading roles at Moody's, Santander, HSBC Asset Management, Aviva and Credit Commercial de France.

Robbie McDonnell: former APAC CEO, Trading Technologies. Robbie is a seasoned global technology leader in financial markets with a wealth of international experience in leadership and business development. He was one of the founding members of Trading Technologies London in 1998, led the APAC business expansion opening offices in Hong Kong, Singapore, Tokyo and Sydney. Most recently, Robbie led global operations from head office in Chicago and was a key player in building one of the most successful and pre-eminent brands in trading software for financial futures markets.

Gavin Dalgleish: Group Managing Director at Illovo Sugar Africa. Illovo is Africa's largest sugar producer and has extensive agricultural operations across six southern African countries – Eswatini, Malawi, Mozambique, South Africa, Tanzania and Zambia. Gavin has nearly 30 years producing products from renewable feedstocks. He has over ten years' experience in the agriculture sector within Africa and has worked for Illovo in various roles over the last ten years.

Dr Joseph Riggio: Founder and president of Applied Behavior Technologies, Inc, providing cutting edge, transformational change and performance coaching, consulting, mentoring, and training.

Dr Michael Kock: Michael is Senior VP and innovation catalyst at Inari, who embrace diversity in every aspect of their business to drive innovation and help build a new food system. Their technology matches the complexity of nature to transform seed using predictive design and multiplex gene editing – unlocking the full potential through their SEEDesign™ platform. The result is step-change products that lead to more productive acres and a more sustainable future for the food system.

Raul Vargas: CEO of Zurich Santander Insurance America. CEO and senior insurance industry executive with more than two decades of international leadership experience in global life and non-life insurance markets across Latin America and Europe.

Greg Simidian: Co-founder and CEO at The Ally Venture. Experienced

CEO and fledgling founder. Twenty-five years building, supporting and selling information products to the global investment banking, legal and professional services sectors. Now trying to apply the standards and lessons learned in his past life to supporting the search and recruitment world, by launching Ally.

Alex Bello: Alexander is a Director of Silver Bank, Mauritius. He began his career in the Italian Air Force, and also served under the United Nations and NATO before moving into the business advisory realm, specialising in investment advisory practice. He holds a Bachelor in Aeronautical Engineering, a degree in Political Science with a major in International Relations, and an MBA from HULT International Business School in London and Shanghai.

Anthony Willoughby: Founder of the Nomadic School of Business. Anthony works with a diverse range of elders and nomads to deliver their programmes. Clients include AXA, IBM, EY and London Business School.

Caspar de Bono: After a long and successful career at the *FT*, culminating as Managing Director, B2B, building a "paid for" content business – providing unlimited access to Financial Times journalism for corporate, government and education customers via forty media platforms. In August 2021, Caspar formed Edward de Bono Ltd to develop, promote, licence and protect the work of Dr Edward de Bono in teaching thinking as a skill.

Sahil Verma: Founder and CEO at The Cookaway. A non-linear thinker who likes the idea of multiple possible outcomes to any problem, like looking through a telescope from both ends. Passionate about creativity and innovation in business and currently enjoying dealing with the (organised) chaos of a fast-growing start-up!

Who Is Piers Fallowfield-Cooper?

I've been described by a Number 10 insider as the **anti-establishment establishment coach.** That might be all you need to know, but if you want a little more read on.

I was just like all the other babies, fed on Cow & Gate baby milk, bounced on the knees of aproned aunts. Undiagnosed dyslexia meant that I was something of a late starter. However, making up for lost time, I now have over thirty years' experience as a senior executive having held various MD, President, CEO and Chairman roles in finance, FinTech and e-publishing.

I've always felt that I had a book in me and for the last 15 years I've been collecting cuttings, notes, and ideas – virtually none of which, unfortunately, have found their way into this book. Greg, a favourite client, started me on my lunacy of attempting to codify what I do and how I do it when he told me he needed, *"Piers in your pocket"*. While this book is my noble attempt, it's a pale shadow of what I actually do with young leaders who want to be inspired, and mature leaders who appreciate a thoughtful dialogue and a reminder to be inspiring.

I've always been a bit of an outsider but it never ruled me out. I've tended to find fertile ground. I've always done the best I could do. I'm lucky that in my career I've experienced the gung-ho 80s through the Jack Welch cookie cutter "dominate your market" years, and now on to something more consensual and thoughtful. I've enjoyed the journey. I can see the pressures on business people rising, and I'm honestly not sure I'd want to be a CEO right now.

A former colleague, Gareth Chick, quipped: *"It's as if Piers has found the trick of being able to handle the highs and lows of business and of life, and – as Rudyard Kipling might have said – of treating them both the same; as experiences to be savoured, celebrated and welcomed."*

A great believer in the use of all the human "talents", I was interviewed by the *FT* on the use of intuition in business and featured as an example of an inspiring holistic leader. Whether you are in a minority group, have come from much hardship, or have what some would consider extreme interests, bring 'em on. They are as much a part of you as your academic credentials, and are assets that you can uniquely exploit. It truly is OK to be your true self, bringing everything to your work, to be authentic.

Beginning my career in the financial markets in the City, rapid promotion took me to Chicago, learning about the futures and commodity markets. Later, after working with a major US bond house, I moved into general management with a focus on the development of global sales and marketing strategies working on projects in Europe, the Middle-East and Asia-Pacific – developing, in the process, a significant insight into geographical cultural differences.

I then became president, and later chairman, of the International Division of Oster Communications Inc. best known for its FutureSource real-time market data service and the Oster-Dow Jones News services. Responsible for expanding the business internationally, I was a key member and then leader of the team that increased the enterprise value of the business by a factor of five during an eleven-year period, while also taking the company from bottom quartile to top quartile in areas of service reliability, customer satisfaction and client retention. Later, while Chairman of Itsmobile, a Dublin-based pioneer in the mobile payment arena, remarkably we managed to raise VC funding for a high-tech start-up in the weeks following the dot-com fall-out.

I am a passionate believer in the power of people, and I have a keen interest in travel, music and a lifelong love of learning. In 2003, I decided to follow what had by then become my real passion: the development of senior executive talent. I now work full-time as a business coach, mentor and facilitator specialising in leadership skills and the development of executives and their teams, travelling the world, breaking bread.

With a Master's degree in Coaching, a Certificate in Applied Neuro-science and my business experience, I find I am well equipped to deal with the many and varied client situations I encounter. Working with my client's "personal mythology", I seek to discover their unique strengths and internal compass to act as a guide and anchor for all the work that we subsequently do together.

Over the last two decades, I am privileged to have coached and men-tored over 120 C-suite executives from all over the world, worked with a dozen entrepreneurs and many "leaders of tomorrow". **I am always their strongest supporter and sometimes their toughest critic.** I'm very fortunate that I've been given the opportunity to, as Joseph Campbell would say, "follow my bliss". I know in my heart that coach-ing and mentoring is the work I was born to do.

You can contact me at: AreYouStillTheFuture.com – I'm looking for-ward to hearing from you.

Printed in Great Britain
by Amazon

20589956R00169